SUSTAINABLE DEVELOPMENT

Volume 5

Caring for the Earth
A strategy for sustainable living

Full list of titles in the set
SUSTAINABLE DEVELOPMENT

Caring for the Earth
A strategy for sustainable living

IUCN, UNEP and WWF

earthscan
from Routledge

First published in 1991

This edition first published in 2009 by Earthscan

ISBN 978-1-84407-936-0 (hbk)
ISBN 978-0-415-84636-3 (pbk)
ISBN 978-1-84407-931-5 (Sustainable Development set)
ISBN 978-1-84407-930-8 (Earthscan Library Collection)

For a full list of publications please contact:

Earthscan
2 Park Square, Milton Park, Abingdon, Oxon OX14 4RN
Simultaneously published in the USA and Canada by Earthscan
711 Third Avenue, New York, NY 10017
Earthscan is an imprint of the Taylor & Francis Group, an informa business

First issued in paperback 2013

Earthscan publishes in association with the International Institute for Environment and Development

A catalogue record for this book is available from the British Library

Library of Congress Cataloging-in-Publication Data has been applied for

Publisher's note
The publisher has made every effort to ensure the quality of this reprint, but points out that some imperfections in the original copies may be apparent.

Caring for the Earth

A Strategy for
Sustainable Living

Published in partnership by

IUCN-The World Conservation Union
UNEP-United Nations Environment Programme
WWF-World Wide Fund For Nature

Gland, Switzerland, October 1991

Sponsors

CIDA — Canadian International Development Agency
Canadian Wildlife Federation
DANIDA — Danish International Development Assistance
FINNIDA — Finnish International Development Agency
International Centre for Ocean Development
Ministère de l'Environnement du Québec, Ministry of Environment of Quebec
The Johnson Foundation Inc.
Ministero degli Affari Esteri, Direzione Generale per la
Cooperazione allo Sviluppo, Italy
Netherlands Minister for Development Cooperation
NORAD — Royal Ministry of Foreign Affairs, Norway
SIDA — Swedish International Development Authority

Collaborators

Asian Development Bank
FAO-Food and Agriculture Organization of the United Nations
IIED-International Institute for Environment and Development
ILO-International Labour Office
ICHM-Istituto Superiore di Sanità
OAS-Secretariat: Organization of American States
United Nations Centre for Human Settlements — Habitat
UNDP-United Nations Development Programme
UNESCO-United Nations Educational, Scientific and Cultural Organization
UNFPA-United Nations Population Fund
The World Bank
WHO-World Health Organization
WMO-World Meteorological Organization
WRI-World Resources Institute

Second World Conservation Strategy Project

Project Director: David A. Munro
Senior Consultant and Writer: Robert Prescott-Allen
Production: Peter Hulm and Nikki Meith
Secretary: Margrith Kemp
Cover and graphics: Kurt Brunner/Art Center College of Design (Europe)

Final text edited by David A. Munro and Martin W. Holdgate
English ISBN 2-8317-0074-4; French ISBN 2-8317-0075-2;
Spanish ISBN 2-8317-0076-0; Earthscan edition 1-85383-126-3

Citation: IUCN/UNEP/WWF. (1991). *Caring for the Earth. A Strategy for Sustainable Living.*
Gland, Switzerland.

Contents

Foreword

This strategy is founded on the conviction that people can alter their behaviour when they see that it will make things better, and can work together when they need to. It is aimed at change because values, economies and societies different from most that prevail today are needed if we are to care for the Earth and build a better quality of life for all.

Over a decade ago our organizations published the *World Conservation Strategy*. It stated a new message: that conservation is *not* the opposite of development. It emphasized that conservation includes both protection and the rational use of natural resources, and is essential if people are to achieve a life of dignity and if the welfare of present and future generations is to be assured. It drew attention to the almost limitless capacity of people both to build and destroy. It called for globally coordinated efforts to increase human well-being and halt the destruction of Earth's capacity to support life.

The World Conservation Strategy and its successors

The *World Conservation Strategy* was published in 1980. It emphasized that humanity, which exists as a part of nature, has no future unless nature and natural resources are conserved. It asserted that conservation cannot be achieved without development to alleviate the poverty and misery of hundreds of millions of people. Stressing the interdependence of conservation and development, the WCS first gave currency to the term "sustainable development".

Sustainable development depends on caring for the Earth. Unless the fertility and productivity of the planet are safeguarded, the human future is at risk. The *World Conservation Strategy* therefore emphasized three objectives:

- essential ecological processes and life-support systems must be maintained;
- genetic diversity must be preserved;
- any use of species or ecosystems must be sustainable.

Since 1980, the *World Conservation Strategy* has been tested by the preparation of national and subnational conservation strategies in over 50 countries. In 1987, in its report *Our Common Future*, the World Commission on Environment and Development advanced our understanding of global interdependence and the relationship between economics and the environment. It contributed significantly to the growing recognition of the need for sustainable development and international equity. Also in 1987, governments adopted an Environmental Perspective to the Year 2000 and Beyond, which defined a broad framework to guide national action and international cooperation for environmentally sound development. In June 1992 they will meet in Rio de Janeiro to agree an agenda for environment and development in the 21st Century.

In the decade since 1980 the complexity of the problems we face has become clearer, and the need to act has become more pressing. In this new document we set out the broad principles, and an array of consequent actions, upon which we believe the future of our societies depends.

We accept that the actions called for in this Strategy will not be taken easily. Inertia is strong within human societies. Governments have to balance the gains of change against the inevitable costs of upheaval, and tend to develop policies through a succession of cautious steps. People cling to what they have, especially if they perceive that change threatens their personal power and wealth. It will be difficult for many communities to switch resources from war to peace, national to global advantage, or immediate gain to future welfare. But the conflicts, famine and strife that persist in an over-stressed world show how essential it is to seek a new approach. This reinforces our conviction that this Strategy must go ahead.

Caring for the Earth has been prepared through a wider process of consultation than was possible when we wrote the *World Conservation Strategy* a decade ago. It is intended to re-state current thinking about conservation and development in a way that will inform and encourage those who believe that people and nature are worth caring about and that their futures are intertwined. It is also intended to persuade people at all levels that they can do something, or help cause something to be done, that will lead to better care for the Earth.

The actions of our organizations and others will have to be reshaped if we are to ensure speedy and efficient implementation of this Strategy. We urge all governments, intergovernmental organizations, non-governmental groups, and individuals to help achieve that essential goal.

Martin W. Holdgate
Director General
IUCN - The World
Conservation Union

Mostafa K. Tolba
Executive Director
UNEP - United Nations
Environment Programme

Charles de Haes
Director General
WWF - World Wide Fund
For Nature

User's guide to Caring for the Earth

The aim of *Caring for the Earth* is to help improve the condition of the world's people, by defining two requirements. One is to secure a widespread and deeply-held commitment to a new ethic, the ethic for sustainable living, and to translate its principles into practice. The other is to integrate conservation and development: conservation to keep our actions within the Earth's capacity, and development to enable people everywhere to enjoy long, healthy and fulfilling lives. It extends and emphasizes the message of the World Conservation Strategy, published by the same organizations in 1980.

Caring for the Earth is intended to be used by those who shape policy and make decisions that affect the course of development and the condition of our environment. This is a much larger group than might at first appear. While it must include politicians, and executives in the public and private sectors at the national and international levels, it also includes leaders, business people and other citizens in communities and settlements everywhere. Caring for the Earth is everyone's business.

Structure of the text

The text has three parts. Part I, The Principles for Sustainable Living, begins with a chapter that defines principles to guide the way toward sustainable societies. The principles are: respect and care for the community of life, improve the quality of human life, conserve the Earth's vitality and diversity, minimize the depletion of non-renewable resources, keep within the Earth's carrying capacity, change personal attitudes and practices, enable communities to care for their own environments, provide a national framework for integrating development and conservation, and forge a global alliance. The following eight chapters recommend activities that will give substance to the principles.

Part II, Additional Actions for Sustainable Living, describes corresponding actions that are required in relation to the main areas of human activity and some of the major components of the biosphere. These chapters deal with energy; business, industry and commerce; human settlements; farm and range lands; forest lands; fresh waters; and oceans and coastal areas.

Each chapter begins with a brief survey of the issues with which it deals. This is followed by a series of recommended priority actions.

Part III, Implementation and Follow-up, consists of one chapter which proposes guidelines to help users adapt the strategy to their needs and capabilities and implement it, and sets out how the sponsors propose to follow up the Strategy and involve the community of users in its follow-up. It also contains a listing of all the recommended priority actions and suggested targets.

While the text has three parts and comprises 17 chapters, this should not obscure the reality that environmental, social and economic issues are joined in a network of sobering complexity. Thus no single chapter really stands alone, and while linkages are indicated by a system of cross references, it is an imperfect system and it would be useful to read at least Part I in full and preferably the whole text.

Gambling with survival or living sustainably?

This strategy is based on three points.

The first is simple and obvious. It is that we, the world's people, want to survive; but more than that, we want a satisfactory life for all of us and for our descendants. To achieve that goal we need a new kind of development, and we must learn to live differently.

The second is that we depend on the resources of the Earth to meet our basic and vital needs; if they are diminished or deteriorate we risk that our needs and those of our descendants will go unmet. Because we have been failing to care for the Earth properly and living unsustainably, that risk has become dangerously high. We are now gambling with the survival of civilization.

The third point is that we need not lose. We can eliminate the risk by ensuring that the benefits of development are distributed equitably, and by learning to care for the Earth and live sustainably.

Gambling with survival

Our civilizations are at risk because we are misusing natural resources and disturbing natural systems. We are pressing the Earth to the limits of its capacity. Since the industrial revolution, human numbers have grown eight-fold. Industrial production has risen by more than 100 times in the past 100 years.

This unprecedented increase in human numbers and activity has had major impacts on the environment.

The capacity of the Earth to support human and other life has been significantly diminished. In less than 200 years the planet has lost six million square kilometres of forest; the sediment load from soil erosion has risen three-fold in major river basins and by eight times in smaller, more intensively used ones; water withdrawals have grown from 100 to 3600 cubic metres a year.

Atmospheric systems have been disturbed, threatening the climate regime to which we and other forms of life have long been adapted. Since the mid-eighteenth century, human activities have more than doubled the methane in the atmosphere; increased the concentration of carbon dioxide by 27%; and significantly damaged the stratospheric ozone layer.

Pollution of air, soil, fresh waters and the oceans has become a serious and continuing threat to the health of humans and other species. Humanity is causing emissions of arsenic, mercury, nickel, and vanadium that are now double those from natural sources; zinc emissions are triple and those from cadmium and lead are respectively five and eighteen times higher than natural rates.

Most astonishing of all, the 5.3 billion people now on Earth are already using 40% of our most elemental resource — the energy from the sun made available by green plants on land.

Yet despite this vast takeover of nature, hundreds of millions of people struggle in poverty, lacking a tolerable quality of life. One person in five cannot get enough food properly to support an active working life. One quarter of the world's people are without safe drinking water. Every year millions of children die from malnutrition and preventable disease. Such conditions are grossly unjust. They also threaten the peace and stability of many countries now, and of the whole world eventually.

The resources of the Earth are overtaxed now, but without calamitous loss of life the

continued . . .

global human population cannot stabilize at less than 10 billion. It may reach 12 billion. How can this vast increase in human numbers be supported without doing irreversible damage to the Earth? Clearly not by going on living as we are now. Clearly not by a policy of business as usual.

Living sustainably

The change to living sustainably and caring for the Earth will be a major one for most people.

For a start we will need to understand and accept the consequences of being part of the great community of life and to become more conscious of the effects of our decisions on other societies, future generations and other species. We will need to perfect and promote an ethic for living sustainably.

Living sustainably must be a guiding principle for all the world's people, but it never will be while hundreds of millions live without enough of even the basic essentials of life. To make it possible for us all to think of the welfare of later generations and other species, we need a new kind of development that rapidly improves the quality of life for the disadvantaged.

The Earth has its limits; with the best technology imaginable, they are not infinitely expandable. To live within those limits and see that those who now have least can soon get more, two things will need to be done: population growth must stop everywhere, and the rich must stabilize, and in some cases, reduce, their consumption of resources. Ways exist to do this without reducing the real quality of life.

Sustainable living must be the new pattern for all levels: individuals, communities, nations and the world. To adopt the new pattern will require a significant change in the attitudes and practices of many people. We will need to ensure that education programmes reflect the importance of an ethic for living sustainably and that information campaigns are mounted to disseminate it.

Local communities are the focus for much that needs to be done in making the change to living sustainably, but there is little they can do if they lack the power to act. Subject to vital interests of the larger community, they must be enabled to manage the resources on which they depend and to have an effective voice in the decisions that affect them.

Progress towards sustainability has been slow because of the belief that conservation and development are opposite. Legal, social, economic and technical measures aimed at sustainability must be integrated in planning and action at all levels, particularly in national governments which have the main levers for strategic action.

Much of what needs to be done if we are properly to care for the Earth is of global significance and requires a global response. The framework exists for the cooperation, monitoring and management that are necessary, but programmes are poorly coordinated and rarely integrated. Funding is far from equal to the task. A new alliance of all the countries of the world is needed to effect needed reforms and improve the quality of life in the less developed areas of the world.

Part I

The Principles of
a Sustainable Society

1. *Building a sustainable society*

This is a strategy for a kind of development that provides real improvements in the quality of human life and at the same time conserves the vitality and diversity of the Earth. The goal is development that meets these needs in a sustainable way. Today it may seem visionary, but it is attainable. To more and more people it also appears our only rational option.

Most current development fails because it meets human needs incompletely and often destroys or degrades its resource base (see pp. 4-5: Gambling with survival or living sustainably). We need development that is both people-centred, concentrating on improving the human condition, and conservation-based, maintaining the variety and productivity of nature. We have to stop talking about conservation and development as if they were in opposition, and recognize that they are essential parts of one indispensable process.

Caring for the Earth sets out a broad and explicit world strategy for the changes needed to build a sustainable society. We need such a strategy because:

- the most important issues we face are strongly interlinked, and therefore our actions must be mutually supportive and aimed at a common goal;
- the changes we must make in the ways in which we live and develop will be fundamental and far-reaching: they will demand our full dedication. The task will be easier if we work together;
- no single group can succeed by acting alone.

Any strategy has to be a guide rather than a prescription. It cannot be followed slavishly. Human societies differ greatly in culture, history, religion, politics, institutions and traditions. They also differ importantly in wealth, quality of life and environmental conditions, and in their awareness of the significance of these differences. Nor are these features fixed in time: change is continual. For these reasons, the principles and actions in this Strategy are described in broad terms. They are meant to be interpreted and adapted by each community. The world needs a variety of sustainable societies, achieved by many different paths.

Principles of a sustainable society

Living sustainably depends on accepting a duty to seek harmony with other people and with nature. The guiding rules are that people must share with each other and care for the Earth. Humanity must take no more from nature than nature can replenish. This in turn means adopting life-styles and development paths that respect and work within nature's limits. It can be done without rejecting the many benefits that modern technology has brought, provided that technology also works within those limits. This Strategy is about a new approach to the future, not a return to the past.

The principles of a sustainable society are interrelated and mutually supporting. Of those listed below, the first is the founding principle providing the ethical base for the others. The next four define the criteria that should be met, and the last four directions to be taken in working towards a sustainable society at the individual, local, national and international levels.

The principles are:

Respect and care for the community of life.

This principle reflects the duty of care for other people and other forms of life, now and in the future. It is an ethical principle. It means that development should not be at the expense of other groups or later generations. We should aim to share fairly the benefits and costs of resource use and environmental conservation among different communities and interest groups, among people who are poor and those who are affluent, and between our generation and those who will come after us.

All life on earth is part of one great interdependent system, which influences and depends on the non-living components of the planet — rocks, soils, waters and air. Disturbing one part of this biosphere can affect the whole. Just as human societies are interdependent and future generations are affected by our present actions, so the world of nature is increasingly dominated by our behaviour. It is a matter of ethics as well as practicality to manage development so that it does not threaten the survival of other species or eliminate their habitats. While our survival depends on the use of other species, we need not and should not use them cruelly or wastefully.

Improve the quality of human life.

The real aim of development is to improve the quality of human life. It is a process that enables human beings to realize their potential, build self-confidence and lead lives of dignity and fulfilment. Economic growth is an important component of development, but it cannot be a goal in itself, nor can it go on indefinitely. Although people differ in the goals that they would set for development, some are virtually universal. These include a long and healthy life, education, access to the resources needed for a decent standard of living, political freedom, guaranteed human rights, and freedom from violence. Development is real only if it makes our lives better in all these respects.

Conserve the Earth's vitality and diversity.

Conservation-based development needs to include deliberate action to protect the structure, functions and diversity of the world's natural systems, on which our species utterly depends. This requires us to:

Conserve life-support systems. These are the ecological processes that keep the planet fit for life. They shape climate, cleanse air and water, regulate water flow, recycle essential elements, create and regenerate soil, and enable ecosystems to renew themselves;

Conserve biodiversity. This includes not only all species of plants, animals and other organisms, but also the range of genetic stocks within each species, and the variety of ecosystems;

Ensure that uses of renewable resources are sustainable. Renewable resources include soil, wild and domesticated organisms, forests, rangelands, cultivated land, and the marine and freshwater ecosystems that support fisheries. A use is sustainable if it is within the resource's capacity for renewal.

Box 1. Sustainability: a question of definition

Caring for the Earth uses the word "sustainable" in several combinations, such as "sustainable development", "sustainable economy", "sustainable society", and "sustainable use". It is important for an understanding of the Strategy to know what we mean by these terms.

If an activity is sustainable, for all practical purposes it can continue forever.

When people define an activity as sustainable, however, it is on the basis of what they know at the time. There can be no long-term guarantee of sustainability, because many factors remain unknown or unpredictable. The moral we draw from this is: be conservative in actions that could affect the environment, study the effects of such actions carefully, and learn from your mistakes quickly.

The World Commission on Environment and Development (WCED) defined "sustainable development" as "development that meets the needs of the present without compromising the ability of future generations to meet their own needs".

The term has been criticized as ambiguous and open to a wide range of interpretations, many of which are contradictory. The confusion has been caused because "sustainable development", "sustainable growth" and "sustainable use" have been used interchangeably, as if their meanings were the same. They are not. "Sustainable growth" is a contradiction in terms: nothing physical can grow indefinitely. "Sustainable use" is applicable only to renewable resources: it means using them at rates within their capacity for renewal.

"Sustainable development" is used in this Strategy to mean: improving the quality of human life while living within the carrying capacity of supporting ecosystems.

A "sustainable economy" is the product of sustainable development. It maintains its natural resource base. It can continue to develop by adapting, and through improvements in knowledge, organization, technical efficiency, and wisdom.

A "sustainable society" lives by the nine principles outlined in this chapter.

Minimize the depletion of non-renewable resources.

Minerals, oil, gas and coal are effectively non-renewable. Unlike plants, fish or soil, they cannot be used sustainably. However, their "life" can be extended, for example, by recycling, by using less of a resource to make a particular product, or by switching to renewable substitutes where possible. Widespread adoption of such practices is essential if the Earth is to sustain billions more people in future, and give everyone a life of decent quality.

Keep within the Earth's carrying capacity.

Precise definition is difficult, but there are finite limits to the "carrying capacity" of the Earth's ecosystems — to the impacts that they and the biosphere as a whole can withstand without dangerous deterioration. The limits vary from region to region, and the impacts depend on how many people there are and how much food, water, energy and raw materials each uses and wastes. A few people consuming a lot can cause as much damage as a lot of people consuming a little. Policies that bring human numbers and life-styles into balance with nature's capacity must be developed alongside technologies that enhance that capacity by careful management.

Change personal attitudes and practices.

To adopt the ethic for living sustainably, people must re-examine their values and alter their behaviour. Society must promote values that support the new ethic and discourage those that are incompatible with a sustainable way of life. Information must be disseminated through formal and informal educational systems so that the policies and actions needed for the survival and well-being of the world's societies can be explained and understood.

Enable communities to care for their own environments.

Most of the creative and productive activities of individuals or groups take place in communities. Communities and citizens' groups provide the most readily accessible means for people to take socially valuable action as well as to express their concerns. Properly mandated, empowered and informed, communities can contribute to decisions that affect them and play an indispensable part in creating a securely-based sustainable society.

Provide a national framework for integrating development and conservation.

All societies need a foundation of information and knowledge, a framework of law and institutions, and consistent economic and social policies if they are to advance in a rational way. A national programme for achieving sustainability should involve all interests, and seek to identify and prevent problems before they arise. It must be adaptive, continually re-directing its course in response to experience and to new needs. National measures should:
- treat each region as an integrated system, taking account of the interactions among land, air, water, organisms and human activities;
- recognize that each system influences and is influenced by larger and smaller systems — whether ecological, economic, social or political;
- consider people as the central element in the system, evaluating the social, economic, technical and political factors that affect how they use natural resources;
- relate economic policy to environmental carrying capacity;
- increase the benefits obtained from each stock of resources;
- promote technologies that use resources more efficiently;
- ensure that resource users pay the full social costs of the benefits they enjoy.

Create a global alliance.

No nation today is self-sufficient. If we are to achieve global sustainability a firm alliance must be established among all countries. The levels of development in the world are unequal, and the lower-income* countries must be helped to develop sustainably and protect their environments. Global and shared resources, especially the atmosphere, oceans and shared

---

* With the adoption of broader concepts of development, reflecting social and ecological as well as economic conditions, conventional classifications of countries as "developed" or "developing" have become less useful. Throughout this document, therefore, countries are grouped by income (lower-income, upper-income, etc.) following a classification set out in Annex 2.

ecosystems, can be managed only on the basis of common purpose and resolve. The ethic of care applies at the international as well as the national and individual levels. All nations stand to gain from worldwide sustainability — and are threatened if we fail to attain it.

| Action 1.1. | Develop new strategies for sustainable living, based on the nine principles |

The nine principles outlined in this chapter are far from new. They reflect values and duties — especially the duty of care for other people, and of respect and care for nature — that many of the world's cultures and religions have recognized for centuries. The principles also reflect statements that have appeared in many reports about the need for equity, for sustainable development, and for conservation of nature in its own right and as the essential support for human life.

The need now is to build practical strategies for sustainable living around these principles. Governments should review and adjust their national development plans and conservation strategies in the light of the imperative for sustainability. They should cooperate, directly and within international organizations, to ensure that sustainability is achieved at the global level. (See Actions 8.2, 9.2, 9.4, 17.7 and 17.8).

2. Respecting and caring for the community of life

This Strategy proposes that the respect and care we owe each other and the Earth be expressed in an ethic for living sustainably. A framework for this ethic — a set of consistent and morally-compelling principles to guide human conduct — is set out in Box 2.

The ethic is founded on a belief in people as a creative force, and in the value of every human individual and each human society. It recognizes the interdependence of human communities, and the duty each person has to care for other people and for future generations. It asserts our responsibility towards the other forms of life with which we share this planet. It also recognizes that nature has to be cared for in its own right, and not just as a means of satisfying human needs.

An ethic is important because what people do depends on what they believe. Widely shared beliefs are often more powerful than government edicts. The transition to sustainable societies will require changes in how people perceive each other, other life and the Earth; how they evaluate their needs and priorities; and how they behave. For example, individual security is important, but people need to understand that it will not be attained solely (or even largely) through indefinite growth in their personal level of consumption.

We need to re-state and win support for the ethic of living sustainably because:

- it is morally right;
- without it the human future is in jeopardy; poverty, strife and tragedy will increase;
- individual actions are, perhaps for the first time, combining to have global effects; and since these worldwide problems arise from today's conflicting aspirations and competition for scarce resources, the ethical principles enabling us to resolve them must also be agreed globally;
- no major society yet lives according to a value system that cares properly for the future of human communities and other life on earth.

Establishment of the ethic needs the support of the world's religions because they have spoken for centuries about the individual's duty of care for fellow humans and of reverence for divine creation. It also needs the backing of secular groups concerned with the principles that should govern relationships among people, and with nature. Such alliances will be timely and right even if the first purposes of religions and humanist groups are not the same as those of this Strategy.

An ethic defines both rights and responsibilities. Thus each human individual has a responsibility to respect the rights of others. Statements of human rights, and especially the Universal Declaration of Human Rights, have played an important part in defending the individual from subjugation in the name of some "common good". The need to defend individual rights is a great as ever. At the same time, concerted action is required to protect and preserve common needs and shared resources. The obligations of individuals must be emphasized just as much as their rights.

People in many societies need to change their attitudes towards nature, because it can no longer meet their demands or withstand their impacts. We have a right to the benefits of nature but these will not be available unless we care for the systems that provide them. Moreover, all the species and systems of nature deserve respect regardless of their usefulness to humanity. This is the central message of the World Charter for Nature and the Declaration of Fontainebleau. This belief also links many religions and non-religious groups.

Respect for other forms of life is easiest in those cultures and societies that emphasize that humanity is both apart from and a part of nature. It is most evident in those communities whose lives are lived in close contact with nature, and whose traditions of care for it endure. This is the basis of the special contribution that indigenous peoples can make to the rediscovery of sustainable living by the world community.

Priority actions

Winning support for the ethic for living sustainably will require action on a broad front. It is not enough to publicize and teach the new approach, because well-informed people do not necessarily take the right decisions. Since value systems determine how people pursue political, legal, economic or technological goals, values associated with the ethic must pervade all spheres of human action if it is to succeed.

Box 2. Elements of a world ethic for living sustainably

Every human being is a part of the community of life, made up of all living creatures. This community links all human societies, present and future generations, and humanity and the rest of nature. It embraces both cultural and natural diversity.

Every human being has the same fundamental and equal rights, including: the right to life, liberty and security of person; to the freedoms of thought, conscience, and religion; to enquiry and expression; to peaceful assembly and association; to participation in government; to education; and, within the limits of the Earth, to the resources needed for a decent standard of living. No individual, community or nation has the right to deprive another of its means of subsistence.

Each person and each society is entitled to respect of these rights; and is responsible for the protection of these rights for all others.

Every life form warrants respect independently of its worth to people. Human development should not threaten the integrity of nature or the survival of other species. People should treat all creatures decently, and protect them from cruelty, avoidable suffering, and unnecessary killing.

Everyone should take responsibility for his or her impacts on nature. People should conserve ecological processes and the diversity of nature, and use any resource frugally and efficiently, ensuring that their uses of renewable resources are sustainable.

Everyone should aim to share fairly the benefits and costs of resource use, among different communities and interest groups, among regions that are poor and those that are affluent, and between present and future generations. Each generation should leave to the future a world that is at least as diverse and productive as the one it inherited. Development of one society or generation should not limit the opportunities of other societies or generations.

The protection of human rights and those of the rest of nature is a worldwide responsibility that transcends all cultural, ideological and geographical boundaries. The responsibility is both individual and collective.

Action 2.1.   Develop the world ethic for living sustainably.

While the broad philosophy of the world ethic for living sustainably is clear, much still needs to be done to develop it to the point where it can be promoted and applied. Action is therefore needed to:

- establish purposeful communication among religious leaders and thinkers, moral philosophers, leaders of organizations concerned with conservation and development, and politicians and writers concerned with the principles of human conduct;
- continue the process by which major religions have begun to identify and emphasize the elements of their faiths and teachings that establish a duty of care for nature;
- involve people in development of the world ethic through existing religious and citizens' groups and through environmental and humanitarian non-governmental organizations;
- establish new coalitions of groups concerned with respecting and caring for the community of life, and with the consequent personal and social obligations. These coalitions should be formed nationally, and linked in a simple and inexpensive international network through which each can learn how the others are progressing. Existing partnerships such as WWF's Network on Conservation and Religion and IUCN's Ethics Working Group should be brought within this framework.

Box 3. Two potential conflicts between human well-being and the world ethic for living sustainably

The obligation to respect every species independently of its worth to people may conflict with human interests, if a species endangers human health or survival. Many people feel that it is morally justified to eradicate a human pathogen that is not present in any other host and is responsible for considerable loss of human lives, poor health and disability. Such species include human immunodeficiency viruses (HIV-I, HIV-II), smallpox virus, poliomyelitis virus, *Plasmodium falciparum* (the cause of malignant malaria), and guineaworm.

Many people also feel that it is ethically justified to eradicate other harmful species — such as carriers of an animal disease communicable to people — if this is the only way to save human lives. Some would go further and extend this proposition to pathogens that attack livestock.

But it can also be argued that while control of harmful species may be justified, in no case is it right to seek the extinction of a species. Perhaps we should keep the last surviving pathogens in internationally controlled laboratories, as happened with the smallpox virus.

The obligation to protect all creatures from cruelty, avoidable suffering and unnecessary killing can also conflict with the requirement that no people should be deprived of its means of subsistence. The campaign against the fur trade has deprived indigenous peoples in Greenland and northern Canada of a major source (and for some communities, the only source) of income, even though they were harvesting those resources sustainably. Elephant conservation may have been made more difficult in several southern African countries because they can no longer obtain a financial return from the animals they have to cull. The ban under CITES of trade in elephant products could thus reduce the perceived value of elephants to communities that are well aware of the damage that this species can cause.

Perhaps there is no other issue over which human rights and animal rights have collided with such emotional force. Such conflicts reveal radically different cultural interpretations of the ethic for living sustainably.

Ethical principles need to be developed to resolve these dilemmas.

One result of this action should be the further development of the principles in Box 2, clarifying the relationships between human obligations, human rights and the rights of nature, and helping to resolve any conflicts among them (see Box 3). The statements of principle should go beyond the Universal Declaration of Human Rights and the World Charter for Nature, emphasizing individual and social obligations towards future generations and defining the ethical treatment of other species. They should lead to codes of practical conduct that implement the world ethic within the cultural context of each society.

Action 2.2.	Promote the world ethic for living sustainably at national level.

Governments should:
- adopt a Declaration and Covenant that commits States to the world ethic for living sustainably and defines their rights and responsibilities accordingly (see Action 9.4);
- incorporate the principles of the world ethic, and the obligations incurred under this Covenant into their national legislation, or where appropriate, their Constitution (see Action 8.4).

Action 2.3.	Implement the world ethic for living sustainably through action in all sectors of society.

The effective implementation of the world ethic will only be possible if it is taken up by all sections of the community. The range of actions that could be taken is very large, but should include:
- parents teaching their children to act with respect for other people and other species;
- educators incorporating the world ethic into their teaching;
- children helping their parents to become aware and change their behaviour by explaining at home the new ideas they have learned at school;
- artists in all media using their creative skills to inspire people with a new understanding and respect for nature, and a wish to conserve it;
- scientists improving understanding of ecosystems, their sensitivity to human impact, and their capacity to meet human needs, and at the same time ensuring that findings are communicated accurately and applied responsibly;
- lawyers evaluating the legal implications of the world ethic, and drafting the laws required to support it;
- technologists, economists and industrialists entering into dialogue with the coalitions and groups created under Action 2.1, and establishing new technologies and business approaches to implement the world ethic;
- politicians, other policy makers and public administrators working similarly to evaluate the changes needed in public policy, and then to put them into effect.

Action 2.4. Establish a world organization to monitor implementation of the world ethic for living sustainably and to prevent and combat serious breaches in its observation.

Promoting the world ethic will inevitably be slow and uphill work. Many people will not see the need for change, and others will resist it because they think it threatens their personal interests. Hence, some special machinery is needed to confront the most stubborn obstacles. This could be provided by a world organization with a role analogous to that of Amnesty International in defending human rights.

The goal would be to secure observance of the world ethic in every country. The world organization would explain the links between human rights and the rights of nature, and emphasize human responsibilities, including those towards future generations. It would be an independent people's movement, whose members would be committed to observing the ethic in their own lives, and doing what they could — through letter-writing and other campaigns — to publicize, prevent, and reverse serious breaches of it. A first task would be to define serious breaches of the ethic and decide which ones the organization would concentrate on. The members would be linked by national organizations, working closely with the coalitions and international networks established under Action 2.1.

3. Improving the quality of human life

The purpose of development is to enable people to enjoy long, healthy and fulfilling lives. As Chapter 1 emphasized, development has to be both people-centred and conservation-based. Otherwise it will not achieve this purpose and investment will be wasted. This chapter focuses on the people-centred aspects of development, while Chapter 4 examines the actions needed to conserve the environmental resources on which it must be based.

Indicators of development range from explicit statistics, such as those relating to life expectancy, literacy and the availability of basic necessities, through measures of the enjoyment of goods and services that enable escape from drudgery, to less measurable evidence of environmental quality and cultural and spiritual fulfilment.

Most lower-income countries have achieved improvements in some indicators over the past decades. Life expectancy has risen from 46 to 62 years, although there are still 19 countries where it is less than 50 years (see Annex 3). There has been a rise in the provision of water and sanitation. By 1987, 80% of the urban population in the lower-income countries (and 55% of people overall) had access to safe drinking water and 59% had sanitation services. Food production per head had kept pace with or outstripped population growth in all continents except Africa, where it fell by 8% between 1978 and 1988.

Such figures should not lead to complacency. The world's basic needs for food, shelter and health are still not being met. The number of people living in absolute poverty is likely to increase from 1 billion to 1.5 billion by the end of the century. The biggest increase is expected in Africa, from about 270 million to 400 million. Although global food production has increased, the surpluses are accumulating where they are not needed, while starvation brings suffering and death elsewhere.

Quality of life also depends on the opportunity and capacity to play a meaningful part in the community. Illiteracy and unemployment lock the poor into poverty. Although there has been some progress (the adult literacy rate in lower-income countries rose from 43% in 1970 to 60% in 1985), a quarter of the adult men and half the adult women in those countries (900 million people in all) still cannot read and write. Unemployment and under-employment remain serious problems in many countries, wasting human resources, provoking social unrest and preventing personal fulfilment.

The international economic situation weighs heavily on the poor. The purchasing power of lower-income country exports has declined in recent decades, as a result of both the way world markets work and the burden of debt (see Chapter 9). Between 1970 and 1988 the commodity price index fell from around 120 to under 80 while the indebtedness of the developing world soared from around 200 to over 1000 billion dollars.

The poorest and most debt-ridden countries have the greatest difficulty in securing the resources for human development — and the greatest need. Many of them have above-average rates of human population growth, yet government revenues and average incomes are declining. In many of these countries, living conditions are becoming intolerable. As a consequence of human desperation, pressures on natural resources are increasing, and too many countries are suffering from a vicious spiral of degradation which will further undermine their long-term prospects.

Many countries cannot (or do not) invest as much in social or environmental programmes as is needed. There are many causes of this shortfall. Some of them, including failure to institute an equitable taxation system, corruption, capital flight, inefficiency and deliberate choice to invest in other sectors, could be dealt with by the countries themselves. Other causes such as lack of export earnings, high interest payments on loans, and insufficient development assistance, can only be dealt with by changes in global economic relationships. Greater international financial assistance is needed for social purposes and to support the conservation and rehabilitation of nature and essential natural resources. Aid for social purposes is more important than that for major capital development. Debt cancellation and improving conditions of trade offer other ways forward (see Actions 9.5 and 9.6).

All governments need to review their budgetary priorities, and many should redistribute the wealth they have so as to finance essential human development and environmental care. Military expenditures, which in 1986 totalled some $825 billion, create no lasting benefits and are widely regarded as an obvious source of savings for redeployment (Box 4). The scope for redeploying resources from military to civil uses is considered further in Box 29 (Chapter 17).

Good social policies can redistribute resources, and thereby compensate to some degree for poor income distribution (Box 5). But they cannot substitute for the economic activity needed to finance these policies over the long run. Policies to sustain or restore the economy are thus critical for all lower-income countries. Since all economies are ultimately based on natural resources and life support systems, economic and social policies and measures must be complemented by policies and measures to conserve the environment and prevent the waste of natural resources.

Box 4. Reducing military expenditure

There are two key elements to reducing military expenditure. The first is to satisfy governments that the security of their frontiers and internal order can be maintained with less investment — and that their own economic health will benefit from the change. At the same time, those countries whose economies gain from the vigorous export of arms need to be persuaded that their interests will be served better by the transfer of workers and investment to other sectors. None of this will be easy, but it is certainly in the interests of the world's people. Such structural adjustments would make a major contribution to global sustainability. Actions that can be taken include:

- accelerating agreements on weapons and military personnel limitations between States;
- development of international agreements on the regulation of the arms trade;
- development of codes of conduct that constrain international financial assistance for military activities;
- development of international legal instruments that outlaw certain types of military action. Existing Conventions and agreements excluding chemical and biological warfare should be extended to cover nuclear weapons and to exclude deliberate damage to the environment as a military practice;
- collaborative action to redeploy military personnel, vehicles and equipment for conservation and development projects, and to use military skills especially in disaster relief;
- reduction of military expenditures and effort to the minimum needed for security.

Box 5. Ways of ensuring that economic development helps those who need it most

---

This usually requires a mixture of:
- basic health services and education for everyone (see Actions 3.3 and 3.4);
- targeted schemes for the poorest. These include income support, food subsidies, special nutrition programmes, conservation programmes and affordable credits.

Countries where incomes are already distributed fairly across the population may need only to step up health and education services.

Income support schemes. Sensitively planned and managed public works have provided income through employment to the poor in Chile and India (Maharashtra drought relief scheme). Direct cash payments can help households in extreme poverty and are common in richer countries. They are less suited for lower-income countries where many more families are in need and the administrative machinery is weaker. However, some lower-income countries (such as Chile) have successfully used cash support programmes for needy households.

Food subsidies. These need to be carefully managed. They should not reduce the incentive to food production, they should reach only those in need (perhaps by subsidizing foods mainly consumed by low-income households) and they should not impose too great a national cost burden. They can do much to stabilize food prices, transfer incomes to the poor, and maintain social and political stability. At their peak they accounted for 16% of the purchasing power of low-income families in Sri Lanka. Food subsidies increased consumption of the poorest 15% of the urban population of Bangladesh by 15% to 25% in 1973-74. They contributed about half the income of low-income families in Kerala, India, in the late 1970s. They can provide an essential social safety net in many poor societies at reasonable cost (1% to 2% of Gross National Product). In high-income countries food subsidies have often compensated for inadequate social security schemes.

Special nutrition programmes. These can be designed for particular groups, such as free school lunches in primary schools (which also encourage attendance and improve concentration at school). Chile and Botswana have used such programmes to combat extreme malnutrition.

Increasing Gross National Product can provide the means to meet basic needs and improve living conditions but it does not guarantee quality of life for all citizens and should not be the main focus of development. Affluence has not protected high-income countries or the wealthy minority in poor countries from drugs, alcoholism, AIDS, street violence and family breakdown. Many fast-growing lower-income countries are discovering that high GNP growth does not automatically reduce social and economic deprivation. For that, more positively directed social policies are needed. By contrast, some lower-income countries have shown that relatively poor nations can reach high levels of human development if they use skilfully the human abilities and resources available to them. Examples are Costa Rica and Sri Lanka.

Clearly, strategies for improving the quality of life will vary from country to country. For lower-income countries improving the economy will remain a high priority for some time. They will need both to increase incomes and to devote a greater proportion to social spending and environmental protection.

Upper-income countries will have a different agenda, since virtually all of them have already achieved high levels of human development (exceptions are the United Arab Emirates, Saudi Arabia, Oman, Libya and South Africa). The principal challenge to upper-income countries is to extend a high quality of life to all their citizens while reducing energy and resource consumption. They also need to curb excessive per capita generation of greenhouse gases and other global pollutants. They face a difficult task in making those changes and at the same time maintaining employment and industrial activity.

No country has achieved development of the kind we are advocating in this Strategy. No nation has a system of resource use and social policy that is likely to be sustainable, without major adjustments. Those adjustments should begin with the steps needed to enhance the quality of human life.

Priority actions

Improving the quality of human life requires a strategy to redirect development priorities to give people:

- access to the resources needed for a decent standard of living on a sustainable basis;
- levels of health and nutrition that permit a long and healthy life;
- education that allows each person to realize his or her intellectual potential, and become equipped to contribute to society;
- opportunities for rewarding employment.

Improving the quality of life also depends upon maintaining and enhancing the productivity and quality of the environment (see Chapter 4) and stabilizing human populations and resource consumption (see Chapter 5).

Action 3.1. In lower-income countries, increase economic growth to advance human development.

In lower-income countries faster economic growth is needed, for long enough to secure satisfactory standards of living and to finance investment in both human development and environmental conservation. The policies needed will vary according to national environmental, cultural and political circumstances. They include:

- an overall strategy for sustainability (see Actions 8.2 and 17.7);
- the opening of national markets. Economic performance is likely to improve if market systems are enabled to work efficiently, but measures need to be taken to prevent damage to the environment and to cushion the social impact of sudden change. Appropriate laws, taxes and charges need to be adopted, and liability, process and product standards applied;
- the opening of international markets. Ensuring that the poorer countries can sell their produce at prices that give a reasonable rate of return is likely to be more effective than much development aid, and will contribute directly to internal stability and the development of other measures essential for sustainability;
- investment in future skills. As an aid to further sustainable development, 15% to 20% of Gross Domestic Product should go into investment, with special emphasis on science, technology, education and training;
- more equitable access to land and resources. In many countries, land is not distributed in ways that promote the best economic, social or environmental returns. Lower-income groups often depend on access to common resources, and this must be safeguarded (see Action 7.1);
- allocation of more resources to rural areas to reduce rural-urban disparities;

- encouragement of greater use of health and educational facilities by lower-income groups, for example through nutritional support programmes in health clinics;
- action to ensure that economic development helps those who need it most (see Box 5);
- action to ensure that decisions about priorities and resource allocations are made locally, and that special consideration is given to indigenous communities (see Action 7.3);
- action and investment to improve the institutional and regulatory framework for environmental management (see Actions 8.5 and 8.6);
- action to reduce gender disparities, and ensure that women are enabled to play a full part in the process of national development (see Box 6);
- provision of greater opportunities for productive employment to raise incomes and spread the benefits throughout the population. Industrialization is urgently needed in many lower-income countries, but must be done in ways that safeguard the environment (see Chapter 11);
- action to promote private initiative, for example by legislation and regulations that encourage the growth of the private sector, and the development of small and medium-sized enterprises through such mechanisms as small-scale credit schemes, volunteer executive programmes and provision of venture capital;
- action to promote foreign investment, for example for the transfer of technology that will allow environmentally sound industrialization (see Chapter 11);
- action to help people to undertake their own development, for example by increasing their control over management of local resources and their participation in other development decisions, providing vocational training and other types of skill formation, and granting credit, particularly to the poor. Citizens' groups can promote participatory development very effectively;
- monitoring the state of the environment and public health and well-being, to provide a basis for continuing adaptation of policy (see Action 8.10).

Action 3.2.   In upper-income countries, adjust national development policies and strategies to ensure sustainability.

Most people in upper-income countries enjoy a high material standard of living, but this is not sustainable in global terms, because of their excessive consumption of natural resources.

These countries face as severe a challenge as the lower-income countries, but of a different kind. They need to find ways of maintaining their quality of life, while reducing resource consumption, energy use and environmental impact (see Chapters 5, 8 and 10). They also have an obligation to help the lower-income countries achieve the development they need (see Action 3.1).

The requirements are likely to include development of a truly cross-sectoral approach in government, making care of the environment a responsibility of all departments, and incorporating environmental values and criteria as key factors in all national and business decision processes (see Actions 8.1 and 11.3).

Using regulation and economic measures as appropriates governments should give high priority to:

- improvements in the living standards of the poorest;
- major reductions in water and air pollution, and especially curbs on the "greenhouse gases" contributing to climate change (see Action 4.3);

Box 6. Recognizing and extending women's role in the community

Women are important managers of natural resources: they can restore, sustain and create liveable and productive environments. Their skills, experience and perspectives are essential for sustainability. Yet in most countries, women have limited access to and control over income, credit, land, education, training, health care and information; and they suffer the worst effects of poverty and environmental degradation.

As a consequence, many lack the opportunity for self-fulfilment, and potential contributions to the community are lost. Steps that can help women to improve their status include:

- extensive consultation with women (not just educated women) to find out what their present role is, what they believe their role should be and what support they need;
- ratifying and upholding the Convention on the Elimination of All Forms of Discrimination Against Women. Legislation should ensure equal pay for equal work, equal representation of women in on-the-job training programmes, maternity leave benefits, and provisions for day care of the elderly, sick, disabled and children;
- correcting traditional biases in the household against the young, especially girls;
- providing education for women, giving priority to extending mandatory primary schooling to females in rural areas and assuring more equal representation of females in secondary schooling and vocational training;
- recognition of the important role of women in the care and management of the environment;
- increasing economic opportunities for women, for example, by helping women to set up their own businesses, providing training in business management, and fostering savings clubs and loan facilities for women;
- reviewing laws that have an impact on family size. For example, raising the minimum legal age for marriage to 18 tends to reduce the birth rate because it shortens the reproductive span of married couples;
- ensuring that health and nutrition programmes cater for the special needs of mothers, particularly during pregnancy and following birth;
- giving women access to the means of controlling their own fertility and the size of their families;
- providing education to change attitudes towards women's roles and especially concerning family size. In many parts of the world, the oppression of women is *caused by* traditions; and in some societies there are strong cultural pressures on males to have large families;
- instituting reforms to give women a full voice in political, bureaucratic, and economic decision making at every level;
- providing universal suffrage.

- conservation of landscape, cultural heritage and biological diversity (see Action 4.9);
- public information and education campaigns that help people understand their own role in solving environmental problems and attaining sustainability (see Actions 6.1 and Box 9);

- new approaches to international economic, trading and political relationships that will help the lower-income countries achieve their essential development, and reduce the risk of social stress and upheaval in those countries, and of consequent mass migration and international tension (see Chapter 9);
- massive improvements in energy conservation and efficiency and a switch to renewable or non-polluting energy sources (see Chapter 10);
- increased recycling and much less waste of materials in the production of consumer goods;
- development of "closed" industrial processes, i.e. those that release only simple and non-polluting materials to the biosphere (see Chapter 11);
- writing, phoning, faxing and other means of communication instead of business travel (see Box 21, Chapter 12).

Action 3.3.　　Provide the services that will promote a long and healthy life.

One of the major benefits of economic development in the lower-income countries should be improved health care. At present common and preventable infectious diseases kill millions of children each year, and parasitic infections such as malaria kill or weaken many adults and impose a heavy burden on society. Simple remedies (such as rehydration in cases of acute diarrhoea) could save many lives yet are not sufficiently available, while expensive and less effective drugs are being promoted. Primary health care needs to be strengthened in many countries as part of wider social policies, including the provision of family planning services (see Action 5.7) to bring human populations into a sustainable balance with environmental resources.

The following targets for the year 2000, set by the United Nations and other international bodies, should be pursued:

- **Complete immunization of all children.** If lower-income countries maintain past progress, most could immunize all their children against the worst childhood diseases by the year 2000.
- **Reduction of under-five mortality by half or to 70 per 1,000 babies born alive, whichever is lower.** Most countries are now unable to meet this target, particularly in Africa. At present rates, 23 countries will not reach this goal until after 2050. Malnutrition, increasing poverty resulting from economic stagnation, and the spread of AIDS all increase child mortality. Higher female literacy, cleaner water, better sanitation, availability of rehydration therapy and broader immunization are all linked to higher rates of child survival, and in turn to population stabilization.
- **Elimination of severe malnutrition, and a 50% reduction in moderate malnutrition.** Most countries will need to reduce malnutrition by around 5-7% a year to meet this target. This is within reach of properly targeted nutrition policies and programmes, which usually cost little and have a large payoff.
- **Universal access to safe water.** Most lower-income countries can reach this target if they maintain past progress. Provision of safe water requires careful attention to land use practices in watersheds and thoughtful planning of human settlements development. Major capital investment must be balanced with provision for recurring expenditures for training and for maintenance of the equipment required for water supply and sanitation. User fees or community financing can cover all or some of these costs, but must be designed to avoid depriving the poor.

Action 3.4. Provide universal primary education for all children, and reduce illiteracy.

Education that fits people for living sustainably is essential in both upper- and lower-income countries. Basic needs in education are outlined below and elaborated in Chapter 6. The targets for the year 2000 include:

- **Universal primary schooling for all children.** This is the most important human development target, because it can unleash the potential of so many people. The cost of providing primary schooling for those children that at present receive no education is estimated at $48 billion over a 10-year period, or just under $5 billion a year. This means annual increases in expenditure well over double the rates of previous years. In some circumstances, informal education can be particularly effective, and should be supported.

- **Ensure that enrolment in primary schools leads on to attendance.** Action to end the current high dropout rates in primary schools, which sometimes climb above 70%, is crucial. Girls are particularly likely to be withdrawn from school for social reasons. Investments to keep children in schools can have a high payoff. Often the key is high quality and relevant teaching.

- **Halve the 1990 level of adult illiteracy, and bring female and male literacy to the same level.** The target for male literacy is attainable by many countries if they maintain or somewhat accelerate current progress. The biggest problem is in populous countries with very low literacy rates. The effort required for female literacy is even greater and is hampered by male-female disparities that are deeply rooted in tradition. The target might be approachable if citizens' groups and governments collaborated to expand literacy programmes.

Carrying out Actions 3.3 and 3.4 will require increased investment. But many lower-income countries put only half as much of their budgets into health and education in 1990 as in the 1970s. Budget priorities should be reordered among sectors and more international assistance should be made available for social programmes to help achieve sustainability.

Action 3.5. Develop more meaningful indicators of quality of life and monitor the extent to which they are achieved.

National and international statistics record some of the parameters of quality of life (e.g. health care provision, life expectancy, disease incidence, water and sanitation provision, settlement conditions, food availability, levels of environmental pollution and degradation, employment and education). But there is no established overall Quality of Life Index that compares with GNP in the economic field and provides a better measure of the success of development. Governments, international organizations, and the academic community should:

- develop and integrate economic and environmental accounting systems to create sustainable income accounts (see Action 8.7);
- review the parameters (including environmental quality measures) that might be combined to measure the quality of life;
- support the improvement of the Human Development Index prepared by the United Nations Development Programme;
- undertake surveys to determine where and how far policies are succeeding in enhancing the quality of life, and what the obstacles are to better performance;

- improve systems of social statistics (coverage; reliability; breakdown of data by sex, income group and area; accessibility).

Action 3.6.   **Enhance security against natural disasters and social strife.**

As populations increase, more and more people are living in flood plains, coastal zones and areas vulnerable to earthquakes and volcanic eruptions. Climate change may increase these risks in future. A high-quality life is impossible if there is constant fear of disaster. While it is impossible to prevent settlement in vulnerable areas, much can be done to reduce risk (see also Action 15.8). Governments, local authorities and citizens' groups should:

- assess the vulnerability of settlements in various regions to natural disaster;
- as far as possible, discourage settlement in the areas of highest risk;
- pay particular attention to the vulnerability of low-lying coastal areas to climate change and sea-level rise;
- avoid increasing the risk by inappropriate development such as deforestation of upland catchments, destruction of mangroves, coral reefs and other natural sea defences, and canalization of rivers;
- provide early warning, shelter and adequate relief facilities, training members of citizens' groups to play their part in an emergency.

War and oppression bring other, no less terrible, threats. Both are exacerbated by weaknesses in the organization of human society. Governments, international organizations and non-governmental organizations should:

- work constructively to resolve frontier disputes peacefully;
- respect and protect the rights of ethnic minorities and other sub-groups within their national communities;
- reduce military expenditures and effort to the minimum needed for security (see Box 4).

4. Conserving the Earth's vitality and diversity

Chapter 1 emphasized that development must be conservation-based as well as people-centred. Development will only succeed if it maintains the productivity, resilience and variety of the biosphere. On the other hand, conservation will provide lasting benefits only when it is integrated with the right kinds of development.

Because the Earth is continually changing, conservation must maintain the capacity of ecosystems and the human communities that depend on them to adapt. In practical terms, this is a matter of:

- conserving the life-support systems that nature provides;
- conserving the diversity of life on Earth;
- ensuring that all uses of renewable resources are sustainable.

Life-support systems are the ecological processes that shape climate, cleanse air and water, regulate water flow, recycle essential elements, create and regenerate soil, and keep the planet fit for life.

Human activities are radically altering these processes through global pollution and the destruction or modification of ecosystems. "Greenhouse" gases, mainly produced by burning fossil fuels, clearing forests, and raising crops and livestock, are accumulating in the atmosphere, intensifying its heat-trapping properties. If present trends continue, and if current models of Earth's climate are correct, the average temperature of the planet is expected to increase by 1°C between 1990 and 2025 and by 3°C before the end of the next century.

This may not sound much, but it is a faster change than has occurred over the past 10,000 years. If it continues, climatic regions will shift; precipitation patterns will change; sea-levels will rise; and crippling droughts and storms could increase in frequency and intensity.

The shield of stratospheric ozone is being depleted, mainly by chlorofluorocarbons (CFCs), which are also greenhouse gases, and which are produced exclusively by human action. The ozone layer filters out ultra-violet rays from the sun that would otherwise reduce the productivity of the seas, suppress human immunity to disease, and cause eye damage and skin cancer.

Climate change and ozone depletion are new global threats. At the same time, old pollution problems that once were local in scale now affect large regions. Over much of Europe and North America acid rain pollutes water, kills aquatic life, acidifies soils, kills trees and corrodes buildings and materials. Photochemical oxidants cause severe damage to crops, forests and natural vegetation. Many soils and groundwaters have been so contaminated by heavy metals and persistent organic compounds that they have become unusable. The productivity and diversity of surface waters are threatened by pollution, clearance of forests in upper catchments and on flood plains, the damming and channelling of streams, drainage of wetlands, and introduction of non-native species.

Coastal ecosystems are rapidly deteriorating in many areas due to intense and mounting human pressure, including poorly controlled urban, industrial, commercial, tourist and agricultural development, and uncontrolled waste disposal. Human inputs of nutrients into some coastal waters already equal those from natural sources. Within 20-30 years they are likely to be several times greater, causing excessive growth of marine plants, and, in particular, more frequent "red tides" of poisonous micro-organisms.

Biological diversity is the total variety of genetic strains, species and ecosystems. It is continually changing as evolution gives rise to new species, while new ecological conditions cause others to disappear. Human activities are now accelerating the depletion and extinction of species and changing the conditions for evolution and this is a matter of considerable concern. Biological diversity should be conserved as a matter of principle, because all species deserve respect regardless of their use to humanity (see Chapter 2) and because they are all components of our life support system. Biological diversity also provides us with economic benefits and adds greatly to the quality of our lives.

Plants and animals, evolving over hundreds of millions of years, have made the planet fit for the forms of life we know today. They help maintain the chemical balance of the Earth, and stabilize climate. They protect watersheds and renew soil. We are only beginning to understand these roles, and know too little about the relative importance of different ecosystems or of the species that compose them. All societies, urban and rural, industrial and non-industrial, continue to draw on a wide array of ecosystems, species and genetic variants to meet their ever-changing needs. The diversity of nature is a source of beauty, enjoyment, understanding, and knowledge — a foundation for human creativity and a subject for study. It is the source of all biological wealth — supplying all of our food, much of our raw materials, a wide range of goods and services, and genetic materials for agriculture, medicine and industry worth many billions of dollars per year. People spend additional billions of dollars to appreciate nature through recreation and tourism.

Prudence dictates that we keep as much variety as possible. But natural diversity is more threatened now than since the extinction of the dinosaurs 65 million years ago. The trend is steadily downward, as more habitats are converted to human uses. While we are still uncertain about how many species now exist, some experts calculate that if present trends continue, up to 25% of the world's species could become extinct, or be reduced to tiny remnants, by the middle of the next century. Many more species are losing a considerable part of their genetic variation.

The most threatened ecosystems — those with the smallest proportion remaining in a nearly natural condition — are those of fresh waters, wetlands, coral reefs, oceanic islands, Mediterranean-climate areas, temperate rain forests, temperate grasslands, tropical dry forests, and tropical moist forests. Since tropical moist forests contain the greatest proportion of the world's species, their continuing destruction will cause the biggest losses (see Chapter 14).

Renewable resources are the base of all economies: people cannot live without them. They include soil; water; products we harvest from the wild such as timber, nuts, medicinal plants, fish, and the meat and skins of wild animals; domesticated species raised by agriculture, aquaculture and silviculture; and ecosystems such as those of rangelands, forests and waters. If used sustainably, such resources will perpetually renew themselves. But because much present-day fishing, exploitation of forests and use of grazing lands are not sustainable, the future of many human communities is threatened.

An estimated 60-70,000 sq km of agricultural land is made unproductive each year by erosion — more than twice the rate in the past three centuries. Badly managed irrigation schemes, leading to waterlogging, salinization and alkalinization, have ruined large areas of formerly fertile soils and are still reducing the productivity of an additional 15,000 sq km each year (see Chapter 13).

Global water withdrawals are believed to have grown more than 35-fold during the past three centuries, and are still rapidly increasing. Many arid and semi-arid areas already suffer serious water shortage. Growing competition among water users is threatening the sustainability of established development, and taxing the management skills of institutions. Waterborne pathogens are the biggest cause of death and illness in lower-income countries (see Chapter 3).

Every year, an average of 180,000 sq km of tropical forests and woodlands is cleared. Some of this is for shifting cultivation (in which case the land may later revert to forest), and some for more permanent agriculture. Logging, much of it unsustainable, is reducing the diversity of another 44,000 sq km a year. Much woodland in dry regions is cut for fuelwood. Temperate and boreal forests are stable in extent, but air pollution, logging and urbanization are degrading and fragmenting these resources (see Chapter 14).

Overfishing combined with natural fluctuations has caused the decline of some fisheries and greater instability in others. Most fisheries are exploited beyond levels that are likely to be sustainable in the long term.

Priority actions

To conserve the Earth's vitality and diversity, in its own right and as an essential foundation for human development, action is needed to:

* prevent pollution;
* restore and maintain the integrity of the Earth's ecosystems;
* conserve biological diversity;
* ensure that renewable resources are used sustainably.

A number of the following actions will contribute to more than one of these objectives.

Preventing pollution

Pollution is the process of overloading the Earth's ecosystems with damaging materials or waste energy. It has grown from a local nuisance to a global menace. Action now has to be taken by governments, municipalities, and industries in both upper- and lower-income countries. Both regulatory and economic instruments should be used. High priority should be given to the protection of river systems (especially international ones), and to preventing the pollution of the sea from land-based sources. Special attention should also be given to sewage treatment, to minimizing the run-off of fertilizers and livestock wastes from farmland, and to curbing the discharge of persistent organic substances and heavy metals. Many actions are needed, but the following are the most vital.

Action 4.1.   Adopt a precautionary approach to pollution.

All governments should adopt the precautionary principle of minimizing, and wherever possible preventing, discharges of substances that could be harmful and of ensuring that products and processes are non-polluting. Upper-income countries should intensify their efforts to clean up existing emissions. Lower-income countries should ensure that they do not create problems for themselves by accepting new industrial development that emits pollution that will be intolerable in future (see Chapter 11). Action should be taken in four key areas:

* Governments in all countries should adopt an integrated approach to pollution prevention, employing a mix of economic and regulatory measures. Discharges to air, rivers and the sea, and the disposal of solid wastes, should be controlled by a single agency, with adequate powers and resources to enforce high standards. Integrated pollution control avoids the risk that polluting materials will simply be transferred from one medium to another. The same agency should have the power to control the use of

chemicals in agriculture, and potentially polluting household products such as sprays and detergents. It should set standards for vehicles, and ensure that the environmental impact of all new development is assessed. Governments in lower-income countries have a great opportunity to create an effective integrated control system before they proceed with new industrialization.

- Municipalities and public utilities should be given powers, resources and direction to maintain air quality in their areas, and to bring sewage treatment works up to modern standards. This is particularly important in many cities in lower-income countries, where air quality is deteriorating and waterborne diseases, many of them linked to inadequate sanitation, are a major problem (see Action 12.2).

- Industries can do much to prevent pollution by good design. They should always use the best available technology (it being understood that availability has to be assessed in economic as well as technical terms). Industries should continue to develop new processes that do not release pollutants, better methods of reclaiming useful or hazardous materials from wastes, and non-polluting consumer goods (see Action 11.3).

- Farmers should use agricultural chemicals sparingly, and should where possible adopt integrated pest control methods (they need advice and help to this end). Run-off of fertilizers and livestock wastes from agricultural land should be minimized (see Actions 13.7 and 13.8).

Action 4.2. Cut emissions of sulphur dioxide, nitrogen oxides, carbon monoxide, and hydrocarbons.

Europe and North America account for 80% of the world's emissions of these pollutants, which are the causes of acid rain and oxidant smog. Some lower-income countries are also at risk from acid rain. As these countries industrialize, the problems will get worse, threatening the sustainability of their development. China is particularly vulnerable: already it is the third largest emitter of sulphur dioxide, after the Soviet Union and the United States. Other East Asian countries are in the path of the prevailing northwesterly winds that carry pollutants from major sources such as Beijing.

Motor vehicles are major sources of carbon monoxide, hydrocarbons and nitrogen oxides. Badly tuned or maintained engines (including diesels and two-strokes) are especially polluting. This pollution, and the oxidant smog it creates under still, sunny conditions, is increasingly prevalent in the cities of both high-income and low-income countries. It is a hazard to human health, and damages forests and crops.

Action is necessary in four particular areas:

- Governments in Europe and North America should commit themselves under the ECE Convention on Long-range Transboundary Air Pollution to at least a 90% reduction of sulphur dioxide (based on 1980 levels) and a 75% reduction in emissions of nitrogen oxides (based on 1985 levels) by the year 2000. Eastern European countries will need help to meet these targets.

- The same governments should strengthen the protocol on nitrogen oxides by agreeing reduction targets; develop a second phase of the sulphur protocol to further reduce emissions; and finalize and adopt the draft protocol on volatile organic compounds (hydrocarbons). They should continue work to define the tolerance of ecosystems to acid deposition and develop new standards and controls that ensure that these "critical loads" are not exceeded. All parties should report annually on national action to reduce emissions.

- Governments in other regions threatened by air pollution should consider adopting regional conventions on the prevention of trans-boundary air pollution. Higher-income countries should help with the transfer of the technology that will be needed.
- All Governments should impose the highest standards practicable under their national circumstances to curb pollution from motor vehicles. Catalytic converters are the best present technology, but industry should intensify efforts to produce less polluting ("lean burn") engines, and improve fuel efficiency. Governments should use both economic and regulatory measures to encourage fuel economy (see Actions 10.4 and 12.3).

Action 4.3.   Reduce greenhouse gas emissions.

Climate change, induced by the addition of greenhouse gases to the atmosphere, is one of the greatest threats to sustainability. Action to limit it must focus on the phasing out of chlorofluorocarbons and the curbing of emissions of carbon dioxide. Responsibility for reducing carbon dioxide emissions must fall especially on the industrialized countries, since they are the source of some three-quarters of total carbon dioxide emissions to date, and also have the economic resources and technical skills for corrective action. The governments of all high- and medium-energy countries (see Annex 5) should commit themselves to reduce their carbon dioxide emissions by at least 20% (from 1990 levels) by 2005, and by 70% by 2030. Ultimately, permissible emissions should be defined in per capita terms rather than as reductions from an arbitrary base.

Technically feasible and cost-effective ways of reducing emissions already exist.

- Governments should use publicity campaigns, regulations and economic incentives to promote more efficient energy use in homes, offices, industry and transport (see Actions 10.4 and 12.3). Incentives should be provided in this way to industry to develop more energy-efficient processes and vehicles.
- Industry and public utilities should, where practicable, substitute natural gas for coal. The petroleum industry should as far as possible eliminate the wasteful burning ("flaring") of gas during oil extraction. Government and industry should accelerate the development and adoption of solar and other low-impact renewable energy systems, and more efficient energy storage devices (batteries) (see Action 10.2).
- Governments should ensure that the impact of new greenhouse gas sources — such as new power plants — is offset by conservation that cuts current carbon dioxide emissions by the amount that the new source will emit; by closing older and more polluting facilities; or by establishing tree plantations to fix an equivalent amount of carbon. Forests should be maintained, or where possible expanded because they are both major absorbers of carbon dioxide from the atmosphere and important reservoirs of biological diversity (see Action 4.8).
- All governments should implement the Montreal Protocol on Substances that Deplete the Ozone Layer, as revised in London in June 1990, and eliminate chlorofluorocarbon production and use. This will protect the stratospheric ozone layer and eliminate one of the most powerful and long-lived groups of greenhouse gases. As agreed at the London meeting, governments of high-income countries should assist lower-income countries to introduce substitutes for the chemicals to be eliminated.
- Governments and research institutions should cooperate to develop ways of reducing methane emissions, and governments should prepare and implement action plans. Actions could include recovery and use of methane from coal mining and fossil fuel storage; better maintenance of oil and natural gas production systems to reduce methane leakage; recycling or incinerating wastes; better maintenance of landfills; and better management

of livestock wastes. Higher-income countries should develop and use systems to recover methane from landfills and wastewater treatment plants.
- Governments should also develop and implement national plans to reduce greenhouse gas emissions from agriculture. Actions could include reducing nitrous oxide emissions by using improved fertilizers, animal manures and compost, and better technologies and practices for applying fertilizers. Cultivated areas that are marginally suitable for annual cropping could be converted to perennial cover crops or forests (thereby increasing carbon uptake) (see also Actions 4.7 and 4.8).

Action 4.4. Prepare for climate change.

There is a broad scientific consensus that even if action is taken at once to curb emissions of greenhouse gases, some warming of the Earth's climate is inevitable. Adaptive measures therefore require urgent consideration.

Governments should:
- review their development and conservation plans in light of the most plausible scenarios of climate change and sea-level rise;
- adjust their criteria for long-term investments and zoning, and other aspects of land use planning, in the light of these reviews;
- prepare for likely changes in agriculture, by assembling stocks of crop plants likely to be more suited to future conditions, reviewing irrigation schemes, and developing guidance to farmers and village communities whose cropping or livestock husbandry systems may have to change;
- adopt stringent measures to protect vulnerable low-lying coastal areas, for example by prohibiting the destruction of offshore coral reefs, safeguarding mangrove vegetation and sand dunes, and other action to maintain natural defences for which no engineered substitutes are possible at acceptable cost (see Action 16.2);
- review their plans for dealing with emergencies and disasters, especially those related to climate (see Actions 3.6 and 15.8).

International agencies should offer help in the preparation of such reviews, plans and actions, as well as in disaster relief and rehabilitation (see Action 3.6).

Restoring and maintaining the integrity of the Earth's ecosystems

The following actions need to be taken within development plans and processes aimed at increasing the sustainable production of natural and modified systems (see Fig. 1).

Action 4.5. Adopt an integrated approach to land and water management, using the drainage basin as the unit of management.

Water links the activities of human communities to each other and to communities of animals and plants. All uses of land and water within a drainage basin may affect water quality and flow, and hence have an impact on other uses downstream and in coastal zones.

Governments and their agencies, especially integrated pollution control agencies, and water, agriculture and forestry authorities, should as far as possible use drainage basins as the natural units for land and water management. They should evaluate the full economic value of each basin's ecosystems, taking into account their role in regulating water quality and quantity, and in controlling productivity of agriculture and coastal and floodplain fisheries.

Water policy should be based on evaluation of drainage basin carrying capacity. It should provide for the full range of appropriate uses. Development of water resources should be integrated with maintenance of ecosystems that play a key role in the water cycle, such as watershed forests and wetlands (see Actions 15.5 and 15.6).

Action 4.6. **Maintain as much as possible of each country's natural and modified ecosystems.**

There are virtually no ecosystems in the world that are "natural" in the sense of having escaped human influence. Natural ecosystems as defined in Fig. 1 have largely disappeared from most upper-income countries and densely populated lower-income countries, and are under pressure wherever they remain. Forests, wetlands, scrublands and grasslands are all being converted to agriculture, and much high-quality farmland is being built on (Chapter 12). This is being done to meet compelling human needs, or to satisfy what are perceived as human interests. It will be very difficult to halt such activity, when human populations and needs are increasing so greatly. But many of these conversions are reducing diversity and productivity and are unsustainable.

Striking the right balance between alternative uses of the environment is the most difficult task for conservation today. Sustainability depends on converting to intensive human use only the areas able to support such use, while retaining natural systems where they provide the greatest benefits or are essential to maintain diversity and ecological functions. Care is needed because once land has been converted to cultivation, restoration to a diverse natural system like a mature forest can take centuries, while urbanization may take even longer to reverse.

Governments should therefore:

- protect remaining natural ecosystems, unless there are overwhelming reasons for change;
- work out ways of using such ecosystems sustainably, thereby improving their economic and social value;
- maintain as large an area as possible of modified ecosystems to support a diversity of sustainable uses and species;
- take the full social costs and benefits into account when considering converting land to agriculture and urban systems. Local communities and land owners and occupiers should be encouraged to maintain as much diversity as possible in these systems, for example by preserving areas of wetland, woodland and species-rich meadow within blocks of intensively-used farmland or even in urban zones; and by raising diverse crop and livestock mixes. Urban gardens and trees should be encouraged both for their role in conservation and as an important contribution to quality of life;
- restore or rehabilitate degraded ecosystems.

Action 4.7. **Take the pressure off natural and modified ecosystems by protecting the best farmland and managing it in ecologically sound ways.**

The Earth may have to support more than twice as many people a hundred years hence. There are no great unused resources of cultivable land that can safely be taken from nature. Consequently, the land now used for agriculture will need to be cropped more intensively.

Fig. 1. Classification of ecosystem conditions

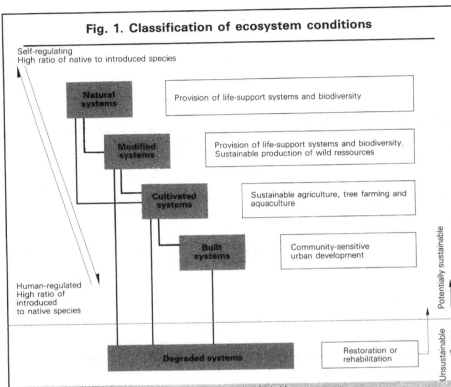

Self-regulating
High ratio of native to introduced species

Natural systems — Provision of life-support systems and biodiversity

Modified systems — Provision of life-support systems and biodiversity. Sustainable production of wild ressources

Cultivated systems — Sustainable agriculture, tree farming and aquaculture

Built systems — Community-sensitive urban development

Human-regulated
High ratio of introduced to native species

Potentially sustainable

Unsustainable

Degraded systems — Restoration or rehabilitation

1. The main conditions of ecosystems are shown in the shaded boxes:

Natural systems. Ecosystems where since the industrial revolution (1750) human impact (a) has been no greater than that of any other native species, and (b) has not affected the ecosystem's structure. Climate change is excluded from the definition, because human-caused climate change is likely to affect all ecosystems and eliminate all natural ecosystems as defined here.

Modified systems. Ecosystems where human impact is greater than that of any other species, but whose structural components are not cultivated. Most of the planet is now modified, including land and sea areas usually considered "natural". For example, naturally regenerating forest used for timber production; naturally regenerating range land used for livestock production.

Cultivated systems. Ecosystems where human impact is greater than that of any other species, and most of whose structural components are cultivated: e.g. farmland, sown pasture, plantations, aquaculture ponds.

Built systems. Ecosystems dominated by buildings, roads, railways, airports, docks, dams, mines, and other human structures.

Degraded systems. Ecosystems whose diversity, productivity and habitability have been substantially reduced. Degraded land ecosystems are characterized by loss of vegetation and soil. Degraded aquatic ecosystems are often characterized by polluted water that can be tolerated by few species.

2. The arrows on the left indicate that the slope from natural systems to built systems represents a change from self-regulation toward regulation by humans, a decline in the diversity of native species, and a rise in the diversity of introduced species.

3. Main steps today in the conversion of natural ecosystems to other conditions are shown by the heavy lines; other significant steps by the light lines.

4. Potentially sustainable ecosystem conditions are above the dotted horizontal line. Potentially sustainable uses of each ecosystem condition are summarized to the right of the shaded boxes. Uses of an ecosystem are sustainable if they are compatible with maintenance of the ecosystem in that condition. Unsustainable uses lead to conversion of the ecosystem to some other condition.

5. Living sustainably calls for protection of natural systems + sustainable production of wild renewable resources from modified systems + sustainable production of crops and livestock from cultivated systems + development of built systems in ways that are sensitive to human and ecological communities + restoration or rehabilitation of degraded systems.

By Robert Prescott Allen

Today's losses of soil and productivity through erosion, salinization, desertification and misuse are intolerable in such a context. The development of techniques for more intensive, more sustainable agriculture applicable at the local level in the lower-income countries has highest priority.

Governments should map and monitor the more productive areas of farmland. They should ensure that the best farmland is not lost to other uses. Market forces cannot be relied on to achieve this.

Management of cultivated lands should aim to:

- improve the soil conditions for root growth and crop production in ways that also conserve water and soil, and avoid salt accumulation (see Action 13.3);
- keep pests and weeds down in an economically efficient and ecologically sound manner; pesticides and herbicides should be specific, non-persistent, and used selectively in support of other means of control (see Action 13.7);
- conserve the habitats of crop pollinators and the natural enemies of pests (see Action 13.7);
- encourage integrated plant nutrition systems, raise the efficiency of synthetic fertilizer use, and promote effective low-input systems (see Action 13.5).

Action 4.8.   **Halt net deforestation, protect large areas of old-growth forest, and maintain a permanent estate of modified forest.**

Governments should establish explicit long-term goals for national forest policy, and prepare, publish and implement national forest plans (see Chapter 14). These should:

- be based on inventories of their old growth woodlands, and assessment of how much remains in each ecological region and habitat-type;
- define criteria for protection and how much should be protected, but in any event include provision for safeguarding large areas of old-growth forest in reserves. These should represent the full range of variation among the forests (see Actions 14.1 and 14.2);
- give priority to the establishment of reserves in regions or ecological systems where less than 20% of the original forest remains, or where old-growth forest is most at risk;
- ensure that, wherever practicable, the strict forest reserves are surrounded by large tracts of modified forest or of modified plus planted forest, used sustainably;
- review national policy, and existing concessions for logging in each region, considering explicitly whether logging should be halted, slowed, or directed elsewhere;
- review other uses of the national forest estate.

Local communities should be involved in forest policy, and enabled to earn sustainable livelihoods without damaging old-growth forest that should be protected (see Action 14.6).

Governments and forest management authorities should use regulations and economic incentives to:

- encourage industries based on multiple-use forestry, in areas assigned for this purpose in the national plan;
- eliminate excessive or destructive harvesting;
- encourage management to ensure sustainability of yields.

Governments should press ahead with the negotiation of an international legal instrument that will support concerted action to conserve the world's forests. This is important because of the value of forests as a resource; their importance in maintaining biological diversity; and their role as a major carbon store. The aim of global action should be to:

- maintain a total global forest area no smaller than in 1990;
- ensure that where essential conversion takes place, it is compensated for by the extension of forests in other regions;
- conserve the diversity of the world's forests (see Action 14.2);
- ensure that human exploitation is made more concentrated and efficient by the establishment of long-rotation plantations to store more carbon, and short-rotation plantations to provide fuelwood. Plantations should be managed to high standards of land, water and soil conservation so that they maintain vegetation cover, use nutrients efficiently, and support a high biomass (see Action 14.4).

Conserving biological diversity

Biological diversity should be conserved by a combination of measures to safeguard species and genetic stocks, the establishment and maintenance of protected areas, and wider strategies that combine economic activities and conservation over entire regions. In addition to the actions described below, governments should consider designating areas of special importance for their biological diversity as Biodiversity Conservation Regions (BCRs). In these regions an overall strategy would be developed by local communities, government agencies and corporate and other interests, to provide for human development in ways that conserve biological diversity.

More detailed action to conserve biodiversity is set out in the IUCN, UNEP and WRI Biodiversity Strategy and Action Plan.

Action 4.9.   **Complete and maintain a comprehensive system of protected areas.**

Protected areas are established to safeguard outstanding examples of the natural or cultural heritage, for their own sake, for the conservation of life-support systems and biological diversity, and for human enjoyment. There are many kinds of protected area (see Annex 4), each providing distinctive benefits (Box 7). Every country should establish a comprehensive national system of protected areas, which will include examples in many categories.

Governments should establish or maintain professional agencies to provide leadership, a management infrastructure, trained staff, and the funds for them to plan, designate and care for the national network of protected areas. Without adequate resources, the protected areas system will be little more than a list on paper, and will eventually be destroyed. Already, protected areas have been degraded in many countries, and priority should be given to their restoration.

Every national system also requires:

- a sound legal and administrative base, which allows flexibility in design and management. Managers must be able to respond to advances in scientific understanding, and to protect the system from arbitrary changes and pressures;
- an overall plan setting out the objectives of the national system, its coverage of ecological regions and habitat types, and a timetable for filling gaps.

National systems of protected areas should be governed by an explicit policy that:

- ensures that each protected area has an up-to-date and adequate management plan, which is effectively implemented;
- ensures citizen involvement in establishing and reviewing national protected areas policy;

- ensures the effective participation of local communities in the design, management and operation of protected areas;
- maintains a sustainable economic return from protected areas but makes sure that much of this goes to manage the area and returns to local communities;
- encourages local communities, including especially communities of indigenous peoples, and private organizations to establish and manage protected areas within the national system;
- ensures that protected areas safeguard the full range of national ecosystem and species diversity;
- provides for use of the protected area system to establish comprehensive *in situ* (on the spot) protection of populations of the main genetic variants of the wild relatives of plant and animal domesticates and other important wild genetic resources (see Action 4.12 and 13.11);
- ensures that the protected areas do not become oases of diversity in a desert of uniformity, by providing for their integration within policies for the management of surrounding lands and waters.

Box 7. Functions and benefits of a protected area system

A system of protected areas is the core of any programme that seeks to maintain the diversity of ecosystems, species, and wild genetic resources; and to protect the world's great natural areas for their intrinsic, inspirational and recreational values.

A protected area system provides safeguards for:

- natural and modified ecosystems that are essential to maintain life-support systems, conserve wild species and areas of particularly high species diversity, protect intrinsic and inspirational values, and support scientific research;
- culturally important landscapes (including places that demonstrate harmonious relationships between people and nature), historic monuments and other heritage sites in built-up areas;
- sustainable use of wild resources in modified ecosystems;
- traditional, sustainable uses of ecosystems in sacred places or traditional sites of harvesting by indigenous peoples;
- recreational and educational uses of natural, modified and cultivated ecosystems.

Protected areas can be especially important for development when they:

- conserve soil and water in zones that are highly erodible if the original vegetation is removed, notably the steep slopes of upper catchments and river banks;
- regulate and purify water flow, notably by protecting wetlands and forests;
- shield people from natural disasters, such as floods and storm surges, notably by protecting watershed forests, riverine wetlands, coral reefs, mangroves and coastal wetlands;
- maintain important natural vegetation on soils of inherently low productivity that would, if transformed, yield little of value to human communities;
- maintain wild genetic resources or species important in medicine;
- protect species and populations that are highly sensitive to human disturbance;
- provide habitat that is critical to harvested, migratory or threatened species for breeding, feeding, or resting;
- provide income and employment, notably from tourism.

All governments and national conservation agencies should evaluate, and if necessary extend, their protected area systems to ensure that they are adequate to maintain species diversity under likely future climatic conditions. To do this, the systems must allow for changes in species' distribution. They will be most likely to achieve this, if the systems:

- protect the diversity of physical environments;
- include as wide a topographic diversity and altitude range as possible in each protected area;
- ensure that protected areas are linked to other areas by corridors of suitable habitat along which species can disperse.

Action 4.10.   Improve conservation of wild plants and animals.

Each country should do all it can to prevent the extinction of any species, accepting particular responsibility for endemic species confined to its territory. Threatened species should be restored to safe levels. Non-threatened stocks should not be allowed to decline significantly.

Many species can be conserved through management of their habitats in protected areas, providing these are large enough to hold populations that are viable in the long term. However, others, especially the larger and commercially more valuable ones, often require more intensive management techniques. Many countries lack the expertise for such management, or have it in short supply.

Important actions for governments, to which NGOs can contribute, include:

- development and implementation of national recovery plans for threatened species, with quantifiable targets. International plans should be agreed by countries that share threatened populations;
- adoption and enforcement of strict measures to prevent the release into the wild of non-native species of animals, plants and pathogens. Invasive introduced species are a major cause of loss of biodiversity, and they can be very difficult, if not impossible, to control. In preventing invasions by exotics, countries should give particular attention to monitoring and developing codes of conduct for aquaculture facilities and to enforcing import, export and quarantine regulations;
- development of techniques to manage small populations of plant and animal species, taking into account the need to prevent inbreeding and to prevent local extirpation resulting from accidents, ecological catastrophes and climate change;
- special training in important wildlife management techniques, including animal capture and translocation, management of crop-raiding animals, veterinary diagnosis and management of diseases (including enforcement of quarantine regulations), operation of culling programmes, development and management of village-level use of wild species, management of sport-hunting and associated industries, including taxidermy (see Action 4.13), implementation of re-introduction programmes for both plants and animals, and programmes to exterminate damaging introduced and invasive species (in particular plants, rodents and predators);
- adherence to the Convention on International Trade in Endangered Species (CITES), and strong action to improve its effectiveness;
- development of strong national and local conservation authorities, with well-trained staff and adequate resources;

- improvement of management techniques to eliminate the illegal and unsustainable taking of animals and plants, especially from protected areas — such anti-poaching schemes always involving local people and providing them with an incentive for maintaining their wild resources;

- special action to protect species along migration routes when these cannot be included in protected areas. This can involve the control of hunting, pollution regulation, and thorough environmental impact assessment of proposed developments.

Action 4.11. **Improve knowledge and understanding of species and ecosystems.**

Knowledge of the status and distribution of many animal and plant species, especially in tropical countries, is still very poor. So long as it remains so, conservation measures will be less than adequate. Similarly, the impacts of human actions on ecosystems remain poorly understood. The amount and quality of biological monitoring and research should be increased, so that each country can make the best possible decisions when seeking to conserve its biological diversity.

The world is suffering from a decline in taxonomic and systematic expertise at the very moment that it is most needed. There are also a number of new and improved survey and census techniques that are not being widely applied. This further reduces the effectiveness of conservation.

Important actions include:

- giving strong support to taxonomic and systematic research and relevant training throughout the world;

- establishing national surveys and inventories of species and ecosystems, making full use of indigenous expertise from national universities, museums and conservation authorities;

- developing linkages between universities and museums in upper-income countries and their counterparts in lower-income countries to support and develop survey and inventory programmes, and to provide training in taxonomic skills;

- developing and implementing mechanisms for the rapid assessment of biological diversity in key areas, through censuses of some highly visible environmental indicator species;

- developing regional cooperation for sharing expertise, especially in the taxonomy of plants and invertebrates, as well as sharing between countries all data that might assist them in conserving shared species and ecosystems;

- developing expertise in aerial and ground census techniques, and in interpretation of their results, for key groups of animal species;

- including in surveys an assessment of actual and potential contributions of species and ecosystems to national economies;

- documenting, as a matter of urgency, all traditional uses of wild resources, giving highest priority to retrieving knowledge that seems likely to be rapidly lost;

- incorporating the results of all surveys in national conservation databases on natural resources, to be used for setting priorities and making conservation-related decisions;

- designing all national conservation databases so that they can be linked with each other and the World Conservation Monitoring Centre, which should become the global repository for all data relating to biological diversity; this should permit the sharing of information on biological diversity among all countries and conservation organizations;

- undertaking research on the effects on biological diversity of habitat fragmentation, logging and firewood collection in forests, and different fire regimes. The nature of sustainable use for selected important species and ecosystems, and the extent to which such uses can contribute to increasing species diversity in a variety of habitats, should also be studied. Results should be used to assess conservation priorities for species and ecosystems on a regional and global, as well as a national basis.

Action 4.12.   **Use a combination of *in situ* and *ex situ* conservation to maintain species and genetic resources.**

The highest priority for the conservation of biological diversity is *in situ* conservation of species in their natural habitats. However, in certain circumstances, habitats have become so degraded or population sizes have fallen so low that is is not possible to guarantee the survival of certain species in the wild. Under these circumstances, a comprehensive genetic conservation programme for such species should include both *in situ* and *ex situ* elements, the latter being established before populations become critically low. Management considerations should include:

- close integration between *ex situ* and *in situ* programmes, with captive breeding and propagation programmes designed to support programmes aimed at conserving the species in the wild, and providing specimens for reintroduction where appropriate;
- management of captive populations to ensure that they are genetically and demographically viable and do not require continuous addition of wild specimens;
- management of captive populations collaboratively by a number of institutions so as to maximize demographic security and genetic diversity;
- in captive breeding programmes of threatened species, emphasis on the benefit to the species, and avoidance of commercial transactions.

Zoological and botanical gardens have a key role in maintaining *ex situ* populations of animals and plants respectively. All botanic gardens should contribute to the implementation of the Botanic Gardens Conservation Strategy and join the Botanic Gardens Conservation Secretariat. All zoos should join the network established by the IUCN/SSC Captive Breeding Specialist Group (CBSG) and should work with the CBSG in developing and implementing a Zoological Gardens Conservation Strategy.

For a number of groups of species, in particular birds, fish, reptiles and certain plants, important populations of globally threatened species are held in private collections. These should take full part in the regional and international agreements. Countries should adopt legislation that prevents private individuals from keeping internationally threatened species, unless the collections are attested, after inspection, as meeting high professional standards, are properly integrated in national and international breeding schemes, or it can be demonstrated that their specimens are surplus to the overall requirements for captive breeding programmes and reintroductions to the wild.

Both *ex situ* and *in situ* conservation are also important for wild relatives of domesticated animals and crop plants, and for races of domesticated species that are in danger of being lost. Crop and livestock breeders continually draw on these resources for the development of new strains, and these will be even more important in future. Appropriate measures are dealt with in detail in Actions 13.10 and 13.11 but the main needs are for:

- national plant genetic resources systems and regional cooperation among them;

- national monitoring and evaluation of indigenous and threatened livestock breeds;
- a World Watch system on indigenous livestock breeds; strengthening of the Animal Genetic Resources Data Bank; and completion of the system of Regional Animal Gene Banks (FAO);
- use of protected area systems to maintain important need genetic resources;
- support for grassroots associations of farmers and gardeners for conservation of traditional and local varieties and breeds;
- exchange of information and germplasm among grassroots, national and international agencies.

Using biological resources sustainably

Biological resources are renewable if used sustainably and destructible if not.

Action 4.13.   Harvest wild resources sustainably.

In most countries wild species and uncultivated ecosystems are an important resource. Harvests need to be regulated if they are to be sustainable. Local needs should have priority over external commercial and recreational uses.

Management of wild resources for sustainable use requires:
- an ability to assess stocks and productive capacities of exploited populations and ecosystems, and keep use within those capacities;
- establishment of harvest levels that allow for ignorance and uncertainty about the biology of harvested species, the condition of the ecosystems on which they depend, and other uses of (and impacts on) the species and ecosystems;
- ensuring that where many species are harvested at once (as in some fisheries) harvest rates are sustainable for the species most vulnerable to overexploitation;
- ensuring that harvest of a resource does not exceed its capacity to sustain exploitation. This can be done by regulating access (for example, by limiting the number and size of fishing boats and the duration of the "open season") or by catch quotas (rights to catch a specific quantity of fish, the sum of individual quotas being no more than the sustainable yield of the stock);
- conservation of the habitats and ecological processes supporting the resource.

In assessing whether use is sustainable, governments need to take four sets of factors into account:
- the status of the resource itself;
- the status of the ecological processes and biological diversity that support the resource;
- the impacts of harvesting and processing on other renewable resources, human health, life-support systems, and biological diversity;
- the main socioeconomic influences on the sustainability of the resource sector concerned.

Many of these factors may not be known today, and it is important that research and monitoring, as an aid to sound management, are given due priority by governments and supported by international aid agencies. Emphasis should be on species that are important economically, play a central role in ecosystems, or are severely depleted. Social and economic influences on resource use can generally be evaluated as part of a national or subnational strategy for sustainability (see Action 17.7).

Action 4.14. Support management of wild renewable resources by local communities; and increase incentives to conserve biological diversity.

Incentives to use natural resources sustainably depend on the property rights of users. People with an exclusive right to a fishery have an incentive to limit their harvests to conserve the resource, whereas those in a competitive open-access fishery do not. Someone whose rights to graze livestock extend far into the future has an incentive to manage the rangeland for continued productivity, whereas a grazier whose rights are limited to one season does not. Thus the exclusivity, duration and other characteristics of property rights profoundly influence the incentives of users to conserve resources.

Governments and local communities should jointly develop policy for renewable resource management. Local communities should be granted secure land tenure and property rights, and encouraged to develop strong community institutions. These are particularly important for indigenous peoples and other groups with a long attachment to a particular area.

Economic return to local communities is important. Those that successfully conserve wildlife stocks should be enabled to export the sustainable surplus and to receive the revenues earned.

Combinations of incentives can promote conservation by local communities. They can include shares of entrance fees to a protected area, the proceeds of fines for illegal use of wild resources, and compensation for wildlife damage. Indirect incentives include exemptions from taxes, food security, and assistance for community development. Social incentives include measures to maintain strong communal organizations for resource management (see Chapter 7).

Governments, development aid agencies, and conservation organizations should support projects that combine rural development and the conservation and sustainable use of wild species and ecosystems. To succeed, the projects should:

- provide a direct, immediate, legally guaranteed and sustainable economic return to the communities concerned (see Action 7.6);
- make use of native species of plants or animals, applying the knowledge of local communities to select the species;
- provide increased revenue for local government. This increases commitment and management capacity;
- recognize and integrate existing land rights and uses with conservation activities (see Action 7.1);
- establish a locally-adapted system of indicators and monitoring to ensure that populations of the species being used are maintained or enhanced.

5. Keeping within the Earth's carrying capacity

Human impact on the Earth depends both on the number of people and on how much energy and other resources each person uses or wastes. The maximum impact that the planet or any particular ecosystem can sustain is its carrying capacity. Carrying capacity for people can be expanded by technology, but usually at the cost of reducing biological diversity or ecological services. In any case, it is not infinitely expandable. It is limited ultimately by the system's capacity to renew itself or safely to absorb wastes.

Sustainability will be impossible unless human population and resource demand level off within the carrying capacity of the Earth. If we apply to our lives the rules we seek to apply when managing other species, we should try to leave a substantial safety margin between our total impact and our estimate of what the planetary environment can withstand. This is the more essential because while we know that the ultimate limits exist we are uncertain at exactly what point we may reach them. It is important to remember that we are seeking not just survival but a sustainable improvement in the quality of life of several billion people.

The actions needed to keep within the Earth's carrying capacity will vary greatly from nation to nation — and even among communities within nations — because of the wide variations in population size, population growth rates, human needs, resource consumption patterns, and the availability of resources. Five major features of today's human situation must be taken into account when development strategies are planned:

- A minority of people, mostly but not all in upper-income countries, enjoy a high standard of living, consume a disproportionate share of available energy, food, water, minerals and other resources, and suffer from the diseases of affluence (mostly linked to excessive consumption).

- That minority may accept a reduction in its resource consumption through gains in efficiency, and a stabilization of its standard of living, but it is unrealistic to expect people willingly to reduce that standard.

- The majority of people today, mostly but not all living in lower-income countries, have a standard of living ranging from the miserable to the barely tolerable, use far less than their arithmetical share of the Earth's resources, and in many cases suffer from the diseases of poverty (linked to malnutrition and compounded by inadequate health care).

- The poor are locked into poverty largely because the rich control the world's markets, resource flows, prices, and finance. But they are aware of one another. Modern communications and tourism bring the luxury of the rich before the eyes of the poor, and the latter no longer accept these disparities with patience or as a part of some natural historical order.

- Population growth rates are highest where poverty is most intense. Lack of health care, education and social infrastructure, and of facilities to allow those who want to limit their fertility to do so, are among the factors conspiring with tradition to keep birth rates high in the countries least able to give each new citizen the prospect of a life of dignity. Box 8 gives some facts and figures that illustrate these disparities.

The situation is clearly unstable and inequitable. Gross disparities in resource consumption and rates of population growth have to be overcome. Otherwise we can expect some communities to become defensively isolationist and others to slide into insecurity and conflict.

A concerted effort is needed to reduce energy and resource consumption by upper-income countries. Between 1970 and 1986, several high consumption countries significantly reduced their per capita energy consumption: USA (down by 12%); Luxembourg (down by 33%); UK (down by 10%) and Denmark (down by 15%). But most of the other big consumers increased it.

Trends that favour more widespread and rapid reductions include the increasing productivity of modern economies in terms of energy and materials (OECD countries as a whole significantly reduced energy consumption per unit of GNP) (see Fig. 2); the development of technologies that produce and use energy and materials more efficiently, including recycling; and public demand for products with lower environmental impacts.

World population doubled from 2.5 to 5 billion people between 1950 and 1987. The growth rate is declining but the population will continue to increase rapidly because of the population structure of countries with high total fertility rates. The United Nations' medium projection is for world population to grow by a billion people per decade, reaching 6.4 billion by the year

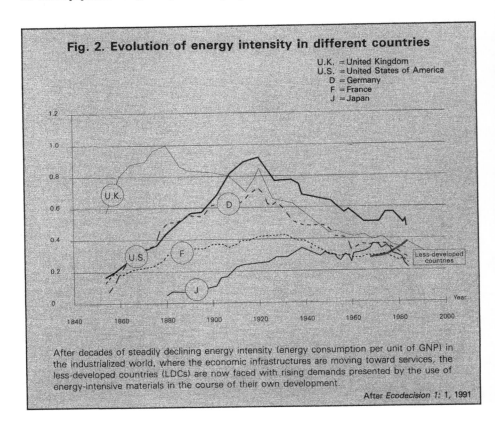

Fig. 2. Evolution of energy intensity in different countries

U.K. = United Kingdom
U.S. = United States of America
D = Germany
F = France
J = Japan

After decades of steadily declining energy intensity (energy consumption per unit of GNP) in the industrialized world, where the economic infrastructures are moving toward services, the less-developed countries (LDCs) are now faced with rising demands presented by the use of energy-intensive materials in the course of their own development.

After *Ecodecision 1: 1*, 1991

2000, 8.5 billion by 2025, 10 billion by 2050, and an ultimate size of between 11 and 12 billion.

This assumes that fertility rates will fall to 3.3 births per woman by the year 2000. However, family planning programmes in the 1980s failed to keep pace with the demand for fertility control in lower-income countries. Regular contraceptive use must grow from 51% to 59% of couples in lower-income countries by 2000, requiring a doubling of annual expenditures on family planning — from $4.5 billion to $9 billion — by that year. If fertility rates decline more slowly, the population could be even bigger than the UN's medium projection, unless environmental degradation leads to a substantial increase in death rates.

By contrast, a successful effort to achieve the UN's low projection could enable the world population to stabilize at an ultimate size of around 10 billion. The task is enormous but feasible: in the past 20 years, Suriname has halved and China, Cuba, Singapore, and Thailand have more than halved, their total fertility rates (and another 15 countries cut their TFRs by 40-48%).

Box 8. Some facts and figures about human population and resource consumption

Commercial energy consumption per person is a useful measure of environmental impact. This is because it is energy that enables people to take renewable and nonrenewable resources from ecosystems, to transform them into products and consume them, and eventually to return them to ecosystems as waste. The more polluting the energy source, the bigger the impact.

The 42 countries with high and medium-high levels of energy consumption per person contain a quarter of the world's population but account for four-fifths of its use of commercial energy (see Annex 5).

The 128 countries with low and medium-low levels of energy consumption per person contain three-quarters of the world's population but account for only a fifth of commercial energy consumption.

On average, someone in a "high consumption" country consumes 18 times the commercial energy used by a person in a "low consumption" country, and causes much more pollution: a North American causes the emission of twice as much carbon dioxide as a South American, and ten times as much as someone living in South Asia or East Asia (excluding Japan).

A citizen of the lower-income countries consumes on average 2,380 calories per day, mostly from plants. A citizen of the upper-income countries consumes 3,380 calories, a considerable amount from meat.

Most high-income countries have near-stable populations. But their resource consumption continues to rise.

Most of the low-consumption countries have high and medium-high total fertility rates, and their populations are expanding fast. Most already have great difficulty meeting their needs for food, water, health care, sanitation, housing, jobs, energy, and productive land. Rapid population growth adds to these difficulties and undermines prospects for sustainable development, because governments must draw on scarce financial reserves or add to their foreign debt to meet basic needs. This in turn often prompts them to increase demands on their shrinking stocks of timber, fish, petroleum, or other resources.

For each 1% of population growth, at least 3% of GNP is needed as "demographic investment" to expand the stock of buildings and machines for the new workers.

Stabilizing human populations and putting resource consumption on a more equitable and sustainable footing are the greatest challenges of our time, and they touch human sensitivity deeply. All of us — but particularly those who live in upper-income countries — need to alter our life-styles now, for the sake of a decent standard of living for our contemporaries and a dignified future for our descendants.

Priority actions

To stay within the Earth's carrying capacity — and well enough clear of its limits to allow real improvement in human quality of life (as emphasized in Chapter 3), communities throughout the world will need to:

- manage their environmental resources sustainably (as described in Chapter 4);
- address the issues of population growth and resource consumption in an integrated way;
- reduce excessive consumption and waste;
- provide better information, health care and family planning services.

A combined approach to resource and population issues

Actions to reduce resource consumption in the high-income countries, make more resources available to citizens in the lower-income countries, and to stabilize populations everywhere, have to be taken together.

| **Action 5.1.** | **Increase awareness about the need to stabilize resource consumption and population.** |

Governments, educational bodies and non-governmental groups in all countries should support and undertake formal and informal education to make people aware that:

- the carrying capacity of the Earth is not unlimited;
- excessive and wasteful use of resources, particularly in upper-income countries, is a major threat to the Earth's carrying capacity;.
- people in high-consumption countries can eliminate wasteful consumption without reducing their quality of life, and often with financial savings (for example, through energy conservation);.
- consumption patterns, family health and size, and social welfare are closely interrelated;.
- population stabilization is essential, and men and women must accept their shared responsibility for achieving it;.
- enhanced, but sustainable, production of agricultural and other renewable resources is essential to meet the inevitable rise in human needs.

The campaigns and programmes will be more effective if guided by the ethic for living sustainably (see Chapter 2) and by the results of research on cultural attitudes to these issues.

Action 5.2. Integrate resource consumption and population issues in national development policies and planning.

Governments should adopt explicit policies to limit resource consumption and population, and build these into national development planning. High-income and high-consumption countries should give priority to curbing wasteful overconsumption and pollution. Countries with high rates of population growth should give priority to achieving stability. The policies and plans should:

- monitor trends in resource consumption and population and assess their implications for sustainability;
- set goals for reducing consumption of energy (see Chapter 10) and other resources to a sustainable level (high-consumption countries);
- set goals for higher, but sustainable, agricultural production (low-consumption countries) (see Action 13.1);
- set goals for the stabilization of population at a sustainable level;
- integrate resource consumption and demographic goals with other social and economic objectives (see Action 17.7 and Annex 8);
- encourage the private sector and non-governmental groups to carry out programmes that support family planning and reduced resource consumption;
- involve the public fully in the establishment of policies and goals and the taking of action.

Action to reduce excessive consumption and waste of resources

If resources are to be conserved while quality of life is improved, three main kinds of action must be taken in an interlinked way. First, new and more efficient technologies must be developed. Second, national economic and regulatory policies must vigorously promote the switch to a less wasteful society. Third, individuals must be informed about how they can gain from changes in their own activities and consumption patterns.

Action 5.3. Develop, test and adopt resource-efficient methods and technologies.

Governments in high-income countries should use economic instruments and regulations to encourage industries and public utilities to adopt resource-efficient technologies and methods. Governments and development aid agencies in those countries should support the transfer of such technologies to lower-income countries. Actions that should be considered include:

- establishing awards for environmentally sound processes and products. In the United Kingdom a Better Environmental Awards for Industry (BEAFI) scheme has been in operation for some years, as a partnership between government, industry and a national non-governmental organization which runs the scheme. Such arrangements can be linked directly to "green consumer" movements, and to the development of national standards for products and processes (Actions 5.5, 10.4 and 11.2);

- providing capital aid and technical assistance to lower-income countries, including training in designing energy-efficient systems for use in homes, offices, agriculture and industry. The aim would be the speedy replacement of present energy-wasting practices in energy production and transmission and in industry; these practices impose an unnecessary burden on the countries concerned (see Action 9.7);
- providing more efficient domestic stoves and other devices and more energy to improve household light, cooling and refrigeration in lower-income countries. These would replace the present wasteful and inefficient wood-burning stoves (which add to the work of those who gather fuelwood or the economic burden if an urban household has to buy charcoal).

The scope for gain in these sectors is very large. It has been estimated that the energy needs of lower-income countries for a combination of domestic and industrial uses could be met with an increase of only 20% in per capita energy use if efficient methods were used, whereas without them the increase would have to be 100% or more. If China were to achieve the energy efficiency of an average high-income country, it could double its GNP without building any more power stations.

Action 5.4.   Tax energy and other resources in high-consumption countries.

Governments in high-consumption countries should:

- first remove any subsidies and other factors that distort resource prices, except for subsidies that have been introduced to promote sustainability;
- then, if necessary, introduce taxes so that the prices of resources match their real costs to society. Higher prices should induce more efficient technology and patterns of consumption, even though energy price increases do not always reduce demand.

Governments in other countries, while seeking the same goal, should introduce such measures more gradually and specifically, applying them first to industrial sectors and urban areas where energy consumption is high and wasteful.

Each government will obviously need to work out for itself how such changes can be brought about without increasing poverty. It is not difficult to do this while keeping the overall tax burden unchanged, for example by reducing income tax — particularly on lower incomes. Electricity and fuel credits could be given to pensioners. Making resources cost relatively more, and labour less, might also help employment.

This approach would get round the present political objection that resource taxes (including a carbon tax) are additional to existing taxes and so are politically unacceptable. Here it is proposed that energy and other resource taxes wholly or partly replace existing taxes. Energy and resource taxes are consistent with the principle of "the user pays" — the more you consume, the more you pay.

Well-designed taxes on energy should encourage more efficient technologies and a switch to energy sources that emit less carbon dioxide and other pollutants. The cleanest source of energy should be taxed only enough to achieve efficiency, while other sources are taxed at progressively higher rates to deter pollution. Taxes on fossil fuels would, for this reason, be high for coal, moderate for oil, and low for natural gas (see Actions 10.1 and 10.2).

Taxes on raw materials could be set similarly to encourage more efficient technologies, more use of renewable resources, and more durable products.

Action 5.5.   Encourage "green consumer" movements.

Consumers in upper-income countries can use their buying power to strengthen the market for goods that do the least possible harm to the environment. They can switch from one brand to another; or they can stop buying a particular product. As a "green" consumer, the individual can do something positive, however serious the problem, and whatever the government of the day is doing. The cumulative effect of "green" actions by millions of consumers can significantly change patterns of resource consumption.

If they are to do this, consumers need reliable information. At present, lack of standards and of reliable labelling hampers informed choice. Governments should work with consumer groups, environmental groups and industry to develop national standards and a "green consumer" label for products.

Developing such a scheme is not without difficulties. Decisions about environmental acceptability are matters of judgement. We often do not know all the environmental effects of the products we use. And there may be difficult choices. For example, is cotton clothing better than polyester because synthetic fibres use up nonrenewable resources? Or is polyester better because cotton growers use a lot of pesticides and fertilizers? Despite such problems, the government of Germany has set up a national scheme to identify and promote environment-friendly products, and this is now being broadened to cover the whole European Community.

Individuals should help move the market forward by:

- becoming informed consumers of products and services;
- asking for environmentally friendly products;
- telling manufacturers and retailers the reasons for choosing certain products or brands and avoiding others;
- informing others about the issues: writing to local and national media, to utilities, and to legislators;
- joining campaigning and lobbying organizations;
- encouraging family, friends, neighbours, and co-workers to do the same.

Action to stabilize population

Many factors act together to determine family size. They include access to (and information on) family planning services for both women and men; family income and security; maternal and child health care; women's status in society; education for women and men; and religious and cultural factors, including the attitudes of men. The factors reinforce each other. Population stability can be achieved only if action is taken on them all.

People limit family size when it makes sense to them socially and economically — that is, when women's education and role in society improve, when men are prepared to accept changes in the roles of women and men, when families can survive without relying on the income from children, and when maternal and child mortality drop.

The status of women needs to be improved (see Chapter 3, Box 6). Women who have completed primary school have fewer children than those with no schooling, and families become smaller as the education level of mothers rises. In Brazil, "uneducated" women have an average of 6.5 children each, whereas those with secondary education have only 2.5. And in Liberia, women who have been to secondary school are ten times more likely to be using family planning services than those who have never been to school at all. In four Latin American countries, education was found to be responsible for between 40% and 60% of the decline in fertility registered over the past decade.

Action 5.6.   Improve maternal and child health care.

Dramatic results can come from inexpensive health services that provide:

- prenatal and postnatal care at the local level, especially giving food supplements to undernourished pregnant and lactating women, and promoting breast feeding;
- education to women, men and children on the importance of simple hygiene such as sanitary treatment of food and drinking water, washing hands before meals, and safe disposal of excreta;
- family planning services (see Action 5.7).

Health support to poor households in rural and marginal communities should be improved. It is necessary to:

- create facilities in villages and urban neighbourhoods using paramedical personnel, with referral to, and supervision from, district or subdistrict medical centres;
- expand outreach to the household, using workers recruited from the local community;
- work with and through such local organizations as mothers' clubs;
- integrate services at the local level and decentralize many aspects of programme management.

Both health and population stabilization will benefit from measures that encourage traditional methods of child spacing. More births are averted in sub-Saharan Africa by ovulation suppression during breast feeding than by the use of modern methods of contraception. Although bottle feeding may be necessary when mothers work away from home, the use of milk formula under unhygienic conditions by families who neither need nor can afford it kills babies and increases fertility.

Governments and employers should make breast feeding easier for working mothers. This can be done by providing creches at work, making working times flexible so that mothers can give feeds, and encouraging work at home. Commercial pressures to promote unnecessary bottle feeding are unethical and should be condemned. The International Code of Marketing of Breast Milk Substitutes should be enforced.

Action 5.7.   Double family planning services.

In 1990 some 381 million couples (51%) in lower-income countries used a family planning method. To achieve fertility rates consistent with the UN medium population projection of 6.4 billion by the year 2000, an additional 186 million couples (a total of 567 million or 59%) must be using contraception by the end of the century.

Despite traditional opposition and the fact that for some a large family is seen as a living pension and a source of prestige, family planning is widely desired. Health and demographic surveys conducted in a large number of lower-income countries show that 50-80% of married women wish to space or limit their childbearing.

This need is not being met. In Africa less than a quarter of women not wanting any more births are practising contraception; in Asia the figure is 43%, and in Latin America 57%. Perhaps a quarter of all pregnancies in lower-income countries end in abortion, often because contraception is not available. If all women who said they wanted no more children were able to stop childbearing, the number of births would be reduced by 27% in Africa, 33% in Asia, and 35% in Latin America. Maternal mortality could be halved. It has been estimated that family planning alone would save the lives of 200,000 women and 5 million children by helping couples to space their children and avoid high-risk pregnancies.

Governments and international aid agencies should increase their support to family planning services. Currently, $4.5 billion per year are spent on family planning services in the lower-income countries, $3.5 billion coming from the countries themselves and $0.7 billion from OECD countries. Many services cannot expand because their supply of contraceptives is not assured. Some actually run out of contraceptives. The OECD contribution represents only 1.3% of development assistance by OECD countries. The total should be increased to $9 billion per year by 2000, with $4.5 billion coming from development assistance. These are not impossible sums. Much of the cost is current rather than capital and may be financed largely in local currency; and the money saved by lower expenditure on maternal and child health can be greater than the initial costs of family planning. Another benefit of more investment in family planning is better educational opportunities for children.

Wherever realistic family planning facilities have been made available, fertility has declined. Experience from 83 countries shows that a 15% increase in contraceptive availability decreases fertility by nearly one child per woman. Birth rates have fallen two to seven times faster in lower-income countries with effective family planning programmes than they did in Europe and North America during a similar transition from high to low fertility.

Governments, local administrations and development aid agencies should ensure that family planning is a part of all rural and urban development programmes and is funded as a part of their budgets. People should be advised about the alternative methods available (traditional or natural; barrier; hormonal and surgical) and helped in their choice. Contraceptive pills should not be distributed without professional supervision. At present only 15% of people in lower-income countries use natural and barrier methods, as against 50% in upper-income countries, yet these are the methods that do not need a medical input. Surgical and hormonal methods have been promoted disproportionately in countries with poor health services, and this needs to change. Effective and safe birth control can be achieved only if it is linked to improvement in the provision of health services to poor people (see Action 3.3).

6. Changing personal attitudes and practices

There are many reasons why people live unsustainably. Poverty can force them to do things that will help them to survive for the present, even though they know that they are creating problems for the future. Changing economic factors can make it difficult for people to improve their circumstances, and their efforts to escape from poverty can actually make their impact on the environment worse. In many lower-income countries the first priority is therefore to increase per capita income and build the infrastructure — the health care, social services, housing and other support — that will give people more secure livelihoods. These issues are discussed in Chapter 3. More affluent groups and countries live unsustainably because of ignorance, lack of concern, or incentives to wasteful consumption. For them particularly, the need is to change attitudes and practices, not only so that communities use resources more sustainably but also to bring about alterations in international economic, trade and aid policies.

People in different countries need to be persuaded and helped to change their life-styles in different ways. But despite these differences, there is a widespread need to prepare people for changes that are likely to conflict with the values they have grown up with. Education will be important in bringing these changes about.

There is a base to build on. Various opinion polls suggest that concern about environmental deterioration is widespread in all countries. Many people are voicing demands to protect nature and show responsibility for future generations. However, other surveys show that people quickly tire of messages of doom, and that the links between individual lifestyles, the alleviation of poverty, the use of resources and world economic and trading patterns are not widely understood. Many people simply do not see how changing their behaviour would help others.

Even those who accept the need to live differently often fail to follow their ideals. Not enough people in high-income countries adopt a driving style that conserves energy, recycle their garbage, or place "environmental friendliness" above "convenience" when shopping. Faced with recession or rising unemployment, even environmentally aware governments are tempted to slacken standards if their application might reduce the profitability of an existing industry or prevent a new one from starting up.

People will adopt the ethic for sustainable living (see Chapter 2) when they are persuaded that it is right and necessary to do so, when they have sufficient incentives, and when they are enabled to obtain the required knowledge and skills. Most formal education does not now give them the knowledge and understanding they need. With a few notable exceptions, the most powerful influences on popular attitudes in upper-income countries — advertising and entertainment — promote over-consumption and waste.

There are two lessons from this. First, a new approach is essential to build understanding of human relations with the natural world into formal education. Second, the power of non-formal education and communication must also be harnessed, through parental influence, newspapers and magazines, television and radio, advertising and entertainment and places like zoos and botanical gardens. The second, non-formal, element is just as important as the first.

Environmental groups have been successful in creating public concern about issues such as deforestation, the loss of biological diversity, local pollution and inappropriate development projects. Humanitarian groups have helped raise concern about poverty, famine and lack of development. They should now join in campaigns aimed at wider social change, based on the acceptance of the ethic for living sustainably. IUCN and WWF, which together link a significant proportion of the world's major environmental NGOs, should give a lead.

The need for universal education has been mentioned in Chapter 3. Formal education should not only be provided more widely but changed in content. Children and adults should be schooled in the knowledge and values that will allow them to live sustainably. This requires environmental education, linked to social education. The former helps people to understand the natural world, and to live in harmony with it. The latter imparts an understanding of human behaviour and an appreciation of cultural diversity. To date, this blend of environmental and social education has not been widely applied. It needs to be — at all levels.

Priority actions

Transforming people's attitudes and practices requires a concerted public information campaign, encouraged by governments and led by the non-governmental movement. Formal environmental education for children and adults needs to be extended and more support should be given to training for sustainable development. The success of all these actions will depend on how far it has been possible to improve people's quality of life in the ways advocated in Chapter 3.

Action 6.1.   **Ensure that national strategies for sustainability include action to motivate, educate and equip individuals to lead sustainable lives.**

Plans for action should be joint initiatives of governments, citizens' groups, educational institutions, the media, and businesses. UNESCO and UNEP can extend useful support in preparing such plans. The goals of action plans should be to explain why a sustainable society is essential and to provide all citizens with the values, knowledge, skills and incentives to help them achieve and flourish in it. The plans should promote both the principles of sustainability and the actions that flow from them. They should be implemented through both the educational system and public campaigns (see Box 9).

Any action plan needs to be guided by knowledge of what is needed and how well the needs are being met. Systematic surveys should find out how well the principles of sustainability are understood, what people are willing to do (and pay for), and how satisfied they are with the progress being made. Periodic reviews of the influence of school curricula, advertising campaigns, widely followed television and radio programmes, and other expressions of popular culture would also be useful.

Every society is likely to have special symbols, stories, sacred places, and other cultural features that can support the world ethic for living sustainably as well as its own cultural needs. These should be identified, so that educational programmes can be tailored to the culture and environment of the society that they serve.

Children may be taught one thing in school, and influenced to do quite the opposite by what they see and hear outside. Adults also may take television programmes, popular songs, and the behaviour of role models to represent the values in which society really believes. To

---

Box 9. Elements in a campaign for a sustainable society

Everyone is a participant in the quest for a sustainable society. There is no "audience" or campaign "target". Therefore, the campaign should encourage a two-way flow of information, enabling people to contribute as well as receive ideas and information.

The methods used will inevitably vary with country, cultural tradition, religion and stage of development. But the following "toolbox" of guidelines and methods covers the spectrum.

- Involve everyone and encourage their ideas. Use local languages.
- Use all available media (print, radio, television, film, videotapes, theatre, street theatre, dance, song, traditional storytelling) according to audience. Face-to-face and audio-visual means of communication should be used in areas of low literacy. Traditional methods can work very well. Poster campaigns and environmental literacy programmes can give useful backing.
- Relate national and global issues to local situations, using familiar examples and experiences.
- Get people to interact and discuss their vision for their areas. Explain how that future may be threatened by current global and local trends and what the solutions are.
- Give people summaries and syntheses of the facts, in appropriate form. Encourage development of syntheses for teachers, labour unions, business groups, government officials and politicians. Include case studies of what has and has not worked in the past.
- Make sure people have access to clear, comprehensible information. Show people how to change their practices. Help them with advice and practical support to implement schemes they devise for themselves. Training in techniques and access to credit, land or other resources may be needed (see Chapter 7). People get frustrated by, and eventually ignore, proposals that they cannot turn into action.
- Involve volunteers, especially children, in projects in their areas, for example to restore degraded land, create " green belts", and plant trees.
- Use information centres and exhibits, both within local communities close to home and in places people visit like museums, zoos, botanic gardens and national parks. These are especially effective because people choose to go to them and expect to learn.

---

ensure that informal education, formal education, and training reinforce each other, the action plan has to cover them all, unifying the other actions called for in this chapter.

The media should be enlisted as allies in promoting social change. They should build up a corps of journalists and editors who are environmentally educated. Citizens' groups concerned with ecologically sustainable development should encourage their members to enter journalism. This has been done successfully in New Zealand, and in Pakistan where a Journalists' Resource Centre has been established as a source of information about the environment.

Action 6.2.   **Review the status of environmental education and make it an integral part of formal education at all levels.**

Governments, through central and local education authorities, should review the present state of environmental education (including social education) and should make it a part of all courses at primary and secondary, and many at tertiary level. This is one of the major objectives of UNESCO and UNEP's International Environmental Education Programme (IEEP). Actions already taken in Australia provide one model of how this might be done. In doing this the following points should be considered:

- While some special environmental courses will be needed, notably at tertiary level, it is usually most effective to incorporate environmental themes in other courses. Teachers can work together to do this, helped by colleagues with environmental training. In the longer term, environmental education should be a standard part of teacher training. Under IEEP, model curricula are being developed for every region, covering primary, secondary, primary teacher, and secondary teacher levels. WWF prepares and distributes teacher's kits and other practical materials.

- Environmental education is easily included in literacy programmes. By focussing on the daily lives of families and the resources they depend on, it can increase the immediate relevance and attractiveness of education, and so enhance efforts to improve enrollment.

- Traditional methods of education will remain powerful in many parts of the world. Formal education should not try to supplant, but to work with, traditional educators.

- Teaching in schools should be practical as well as theoretical, and linked to field projects. Audits of the use of energy, paper, and other resources in school can point to ways of reducing consumption without harming school activities (and with financial benefits). The lesson that sustainability pays will be taken home.

- Teachers trained in the social sciences need to work closely with environmental educators, using their methods to build social awareness of the need for sustainability into their courses. Secondary and tertiary level courses should provide training in the technical and managerial skills required for people to support themselves in a sustainable economy.

Environmental education deals with values. Many school systems regard this as dangerous ground, and many teachers (particularly in the natural sciences) are not trained to teach values. The "whole school" approach, in which the school tries to behave consistently with what is taught, may also be dauntingly novel. Yet no lifestyle or educational system is value-free. It is vital that schools teach the right skills for sustainable living. It is equally important that what the school does reinforces what it teaches.

Development assistance agencies need to give more support to environmental education. It is the key to sustainability. A country that is environmentally literate is most likely to make a success of its development. Where the significance of the environment is not understood, development will fail.

UNESCO, UNEP and IUCN should establish an international clearing house for information on environmental education. All countries would benefit from the exchanges of information and experience which this would permit.

Action 6.3.   Determine the training needs for a sustainable society and plan to meet them.

Governments, in partnership with the teaching profession, should evaluate the new combinations of professional and technical skills a sustainable society will require. At the professional level, there will be great need for specialists in ecology, the various sectors of resource management, environmental economics, and environmental law. All professionals will need a broad understanding of how ecosystems and societies work, and of the principles of a sustainable society.

At the technical level, the main need is for more extension workers who are trained to understand ecological relationships and can help resource users to develop better practices. They should have a broad approach, and be able to give cross-sectoral advice rather than focus, as many now do, on a single sector, such as agriculture or fisheries.

The urban poor, and many farmers, fisherfolk, forest workers, artisans and other land and water users would be helped by opportunities to learn how to use resources sustainably and profitably. They should also be encouraged to share knowledge they already have. They would benefit from advice that combines information about income development, farming methods, soil and water conservation, self-help water supply, sustainable production of fuelwood, timber and forage, sustainable management of wild resources, cottage industries, sanitation, nutrition, family health, and cheap, environmentally sound technologies for housing, cooking, heating and other needs. Training can be provided by course work, extension services and demonstrations, all of which are most likely to be effective if they are delivered through a community-based organization.

People could increasingly train each other. In middle- and low-income countries, they particularly need to exchange information on conservation and development projects, planning methods, training workshops, distribution of training materials, local networks for sustainable development, and effective communication. These exchanges should lead to the transfer of technology directly between lower-income countries ("south-south transfers") (see Action 7.2).

Development assistance agencies should give high priority to supporting action plans to meet these needs; and to travel and other means for grassroots groups to exchange personnel and information.

7. Enabling communities to care for their own environments

Care for the Earth and sustainable living may depend upon the beliefs and commitment of individuals, but it is through their communities that most people can best express their commitment. People who organize themselves to work for sustainability in their own communities can be a powerful and effective force, whether their community is rich, poor, urban, suburban or rural.

A sustainable community cares for its own environment and does not damage those of others. It uses resources frugally and sustainably, recycles materials, minimizes wastes and disposes of them safely. It conserves life-support systems and the diversity of local ecosystems. It meets its own needs so far as it can, but recognizes the need to work in partnership with other communities.

> Community is used here to mean the people of a local administrative unit, such as a municipality; of a cultural or ethnic group, such as a band or tribe; or of a local urban or rural area, such as the people of a particular neighbourhood or valley.

People can do this if they make it a priority, and if they are given the necessary powers to make full use of their own intelligence and experience. The process by which communities organize themselves, strengthen their capabilities for environmental care, and apply them in ways that also satisfy their social and economic needs has been termed Primary Environmental Care (PEC).

The objective is to sustain productive local environments, managing soil, water and biological diversity for the benefit of local people. Conservation action, pollution control, rehabilitation of degraded ecosystems and the improvement of urban environments are all essential elements in a community plan.

Communities must be guided in these tasks by the ethic of living sustainably. They must have secure access to the resources required to meet their needs, and an equitable share in managing them. Community environmental action will not work unless all citizens have a right to participate in decisions that affect them. Education, training and access to information will be needed. Programmes of action may require initial outside financial support, but many should become increasingly self-supporting.

Communities vary in their ability to care for their environment. Lack of consensus, organization, knowledge, skills, suitable technologies and practices, funds or other resources can all undermine their capacity. So can adverse local, national and international policies, laws, institutions, and economic conditions. Many community problems are caused by external factors and cannot be solved by community action alone; the external factors must be addressed as well.

Problems also arise because of conflicts within a community. Individual needs, perspectives and roles differ. There are wide variations in cohesion, sense of identity, consciousness of problems, and access to resources. Some communities exclude women and ethnic or religious minorities from major decisions. In some cases a lengthy process of community-building may be necessary before any common environmental action can be undertaken. Every interest group should be identified and enabled to participate.

Priority actions

Three overlapping types of action are needed:

- actions that give communities greater control over their own lives, including secure access to resources and an equitable share in managing them; the right to participate in decisions; and education and training;
- actions that enable communities to meet their needs in sustainable ways;
- actions that enable communities to conserve their environment.

Action 7.1.	**Provide communities and individuals with secure access to resources and an equitable share in managing them.**

Communities and individuals need secure access to the land and other natural resources necessary for livelihood. Without this, people will not be motivated to use resources sustainably.

In many countries, land tenure reforms are essential. Hunters and nomadic herders need legally guaranteed access to hunting grounds (and supporting habitats) and to grazing areas. Farmers, including shifting cultivators, require clear title to their land. Cases in the Philippines, Thailand, and India show that sustainable use is most likely when farmers have the right to occupy or harvest land for a long enough period to make it rational for them to manage resources for the long term.

In urban areas, a legal right to house sites is essential. Self-built and self-managed housing should be supported. Community organizations of owner-builders generally use resources efficiently and also generate a diversity of activities and demands for local employment (see Chapter 12 and Box 20).

Allocation systems that are acceptable to the majority of users are most likely to be developed if communities manage their own resources. Shared resources need to be managed with the agreement of all interested parties. Local communities that depend on a resource take a longer view of management requirements than outside commercial interests that come and go. If effective communal property rights and resource management systems exist they should be recognized in legislation. If they are declining but are potentially effective, they should be restored, or incorporated in a modified system (see Action 4.14).

Government agencies should support community resource management, rather than simply police the use of resources. If local rules are insufficient to assure sustainability, central governments may need to intervene, for example to establish cooperative management arrangements. This may be especially important where a resource is migratory or shared by different user-groups.

Land management authorities should support property rights in each community by undertaking surveys to define landholdings, legalizing land tenure, improving the system of property transfer and registration, and keeping survey and registry records up to date.

Action 7.2.   **Improve exchange of information, skills, and technologies.**

Communities require information in their own languages and idioms, and need to be involved in the assembly and analysis of environmental data. The provision of information and advice should be based on a consultation with the community. Using local knowledge and integrating it with the results of scientific studies is essential. But this is likely to occur only when the communities see the research as useful, and are fully involved in setting priorities and testing the methods and technologies that research recommends. In addition, more information about local perceptions, experiences, needs and capacities needs to go from the local to the national and international levels.

Especially in lower-income countries, there is great need for exchange of information and technical assistance among communities. Grass-roots and national citizens' groups are increasingly providing the links for this exchange. They need support so that they can extend their contacts to other lower-income countries. Access to sources of information, training, research and long-term institutional support is essential. Training programmes should be designed to improve local capacities to solve problems using local knowledge and skills (see Action 6.3).

Environmentally sound technologies are best developed through participatory research so that they meet the needs perceived by the community, are suited to local conditions, take proper account of the roles of men and women, and are efficient, affordable, usable and repairable by local people (see Action 8.10).

Action 7.3.   **Enhance participation in conservation and development.**

Local governments, communities, business and other interest groups should help set the agenda for human development. They should be full partners with central governments in decisions on policies, programmes and projects that directly affect them, their environments and the resources on which they depend. Where possible, and especially for projects that do not significantly affect the national interest, communities and organizations should make the decisions themselves. Procedures are needed to make sure one community does not override the interests of another. Undertaking a local strategy for sustainability, which would take account of the environmental impact of proposed projects, is a means of doing this (see Action 17.5 and Annex 8). Information about proposed actions, including the results of environmental impact assessments, must be provided to other communities with an interest and to national governments.

Full participation is essential. Communities are invariably more diverse than their local governments, which may not represent disadvantaged groups well. Central governments should ensure that all groups can express and defend their interest. All community members need to play a role in decisions that affect their livelihoods, and particularly decisions on the use and management of common resources. Women must be able to participate in these processes and contribute their often unrecognized expertise as environmental managers. Schools, businesses, youth organizations, and community groups including environmental NGOs, should be involved. The building of awareness could lead to the emergence of new groups, acting for interests that were previously unexpressed. Ways to facilitate community participation are shown in Box 10.

Action 7.4.   Develop more effective local governments.

Local governments are key units for environmental care. Their responsibilities vary greatly from country to country, but can include land use planning, development control, water supply, waste water treatment, waste disposal, health care, public transport and education. They collect taxes, and enact laws. They are the units of government that should be best able to understand the day to day needs of their citizens, that represent them most directly, and with which citizens have most contact. They should be enabled to:

- respond to citizen demands for infrastructure and services; and ensure there is a legislative and regulatory system that will protect citizens from exploitation by landlords, entrepreneurs and employers;
- enforce land use planning and pollution prevention laws, in accordance with national standards, or with more stringent standards where local interests so demand;
- ensure safe and efficient water supplies, sewage treatment and waste disposal;
- regulate transport and local industry, again in accordance with national standards or higher;
- strengthen sustainable economic activities in the region;
- invest in and promote environmental improvement.

Action 12.2 gives additional detail on local governments.

Box 10. Community participation

Community participation helps ensure that decisions are sound and all parties will support them. It is facilitated by:

- conducting consultations where the people are;
- working with traditional leaders, and the full range of community groups and organizations;
- ensuring that the scope of consultation is appropriate to the decision being made;
- limiting the number of management and consultative bodies to which communities have to relate;
- giving communities and other interested parties adequate, readily intelligible information and enough time to consider it, contribute to proposals themselves and respond to invitations to consult;
- ensuring that consultations are in a culturally acceptable form. For example, indigenous people with a tradition of decision making by communal discussion should not be expected to respond with a written submission from one representative. If indigenous consultation mechanisms exist, they should be used;
- ensuring that the timing of consultations is right. Consultation must not take place so early that no useful information is available, or so late that all people can do is react or object to detailed proposals.

Action 7.5. Care for the local environment in every community.

All communities should take action to care for their environment. They should be encouraged by the governments to debate their environmental priorities and to develop local strategies (for example, through workshops involving invited experts). Governments should then help the communities to convert their strategies into action (see Action 17.5).

In upper-income communities the aim should be to reduce resource consumption, waste production and harmful impacts on the environment, and to restore local habitat and species diversity. It is also important to form citizens' groups, including green consumer groups, and for businesses to ensure their activities are sustainable. Other actions could include the clean-up of degraded urban and rural environments and the creation of local nature areas. Information campaigns should stress that everyone's behaviour affects the environment and that everyone needs to take action to protect it.

Actions in lower-income communities should focus on communal projects in agroecology, agroforestry, soil and water conservation, and restoration of degraded land. They could also

---

Box 11. Indigenous peoples

Some 200 million indigenous people (4% of the world's population) live in environments ranging from polar ice to tropical deserts and rain forests. The lands where they still live are usually marginal for sustainable high-energy agriculture or industrial resource production, but they are distinct cultural communities with land and other rights based on historical use and occupancy. Their cultures, economies and identities are inextricably tied to their traditional lands and resources.

The subsistence component of indigenous economies remains at least as important as the cash component. Hunting, fishing, trapping, gathering or herding continue to be major sources of food, raw materials and income. Moreover, they provide native communities with a perception of themselves as distinct, confirming continuity with their past and unity with the natural world. Such activities reinforce spiritual values, an ethic of sharing, and a commitment to stewardship of the land, based on a perspective of many generations.

It is often assumed that indigenous peoples have only two options for the future: to return to their ancient way of life; or to abandon subsistence and become assimilated into the dominant society. They should also have a third option: to modify their subsistence way of life, combining the old and the new in ways that maintain and enhance their identity while allowing their society and economy to evolve.

The main needs are to:

* Recognize the aboriginal rights of indigenous peoples to their lands and resources, including the rights to harvest the animals and plants on which their ways of life depend, to obtain water for their stock, to manage their resources, and to participate effectively in decisions affecting their lands and resources.

* Ensure that the timing, pace and manner of development minimizes harmful environmental, social and cultural impacts on indigenous peoples; and that indigenous peoples have an equitable share of the proceeds.

* Ensure that policy makers, development planners, conservation scientists and managers cooperate with indigenous peoples in a common approach to resource management and economic development.

involve low-cost water and sanitation projects and communally-built housing and infrastructure in villages and neighbourhoods. In many cases, environmental action programmes should be combined with business development and help for people, particularly women, to obtain access to resources and services, including adequate education, training, primary health care and family planning.

Communities should initiate and be involved in all stages of environmental action, from setting objectives and designing activities to doing the work and evaluating the results. Participation should be as broad as possible, involving all segments of the community, and emphasizing that individual actions can make a difference. The participatory approach aims for fair consideration of all viewpoints in reaching reasoned and informed decisions. It takes all factors into account, including people's feelings and values. It draws on all relevant knowledge and skills, and uses "expert" assistance with care and sensitivity.

Evaluation should be continual; objectives should be re-examined and (if necessary) redefined. Plans should be subject to modification in light of experience. Information should be exchanged among the participants and, if possible, with others engaged in similar activities. Assessment, monitoring and evaluation are essential, preferably using participatory methods. Monitoring helps to inform people of progress, since they sometimes forget how far they have come. Independent evaluation is useful so that people can develop a body of experience from which everyone may learn.

The experiences of individual communities should be evaluated centrally so that handbooks of effective practice can be prepared and distributed. Machinery set up to monitor and evaluate national and local strategies for sustainability could be used for this (see Annex 8).

Action 7.6. Provide financial and technical support to community environmental action.

Governments and development assistance agencies should enhance the conditions for, and support, community environmental actions. Other potential partners of local communities include universities, banks, religious groups, local and non-local environment and development NGOs and national and international institutions. Supporters should recognize that like all paths to sustainability community environmental action is based on changing attitudes and practices. It may not require a lot of money but it will almost certainly need a lot of time.

Governments can help communities obtain financing by guaranteeing low interest loans for urban and rural community organizations, small businesses and individuals. Extension of credit should not be totally dependent upon the availability of collateral. Experience has shown that small loans provided to poor people for concrete, clearly specified, business purposes are most often honoured, and useful records of repayment are thus built up. Another powerful incentive is the matching of funds raised by the community by national or subnational government.

Economic and regulatory instruments such as tax concessions, subsidies and product standards can all encourage environmental improvement. Communities and governments should jointly design economic incentives for communities to develop their resources sustainably and ensure that they earn a reasonable return from them. Governments should review the effects of taxes, subsidies, external trade and payments, and government expenditures on local economies and environments.

The price of products made from, or with the use of, natural resources, should reflect the full value of those resources, and provide a reasonable return to communities. Economic incentives can motivate communities to use their resources sustainably and ensure that they earn a fair return. The communities should be involved in the design of the incentives.

Central government tax, trade and expenditure policies can place communities, particularly in rural areas, at a disadvantage. For example, policies often favour export agriculture instead of production for local needs because the former yields revenue. This is particularly important in countries which need to service external debt. Effects on local economies and environments should be evaluated before such policies are decided.

All parties, including management and funding agencies, must learn as they go along. This means that projects should be managed with more than usual flexibility, as long as this is consistent with sustainability.

8. Providing a national framework for integrating development and conservation

Human development and environmental conservation must be integrated if a society is to be sustainable. It is essential to build a public consensus around an ethic for living sustainably, and to enable individuals and communities to act, as discussed in Chapters 2, 6 and 7. But it is equally important to ensure an effective national approach, and for this purpose governments must provide a national framework (and, in federal countries, provincial or state frameworks as well) of institutions, economic policies, national laws and regulations, and an information base.

During the past two decades, many countries have established administrative departments and other institutions concerned with the environment. Over 100 have established special agencies for environmental protection. However, many of these units have been added to existing bureaucracies, or set up as sectoral bodies with limited mandates and inadequate budgets. Environmental policy has generally been reactive, responding to problems after they have developed and when they are more expensive to treat than if they had been tackled early on. Links with resource management agencies are often weak, and environmental policy has seldom been coordinated with the economic development decisions that commonly shape the environment. This sectoralism obscures potential compatibilities among competing interests, and increases the difficulty of resolving conflicts.

Environmental laws — provided that they are enacted with sufficient regard for cultural differences and social and economic realities — are important tools giving effect to policies needed for sustainability. They protect and encourage the law-abiding, and guide citizens on the actions they should take. An important function of the law is the application of sanctions to those who break it. No less important is its role in defining anti-social behaviour and discouraging people from acting in anti-social ways. The law sets standards, often forcing technological advances in the process, and moulds public and administrative attitudes. Indeed, it strengthens the hand of environmental administrators by empowering or obliging them to perform their functions, and providing them with a clear mandate and authority for their work. The law can also require changes that vested interests would otherwise resist.

Economic policy can be an effective instrument for sustaining ecosystems and natural resources. Policies and regulations that aim to protect the environment and conserve resources without adequate economic incentives are fighting an up-hill battle.

Every economy depends on the environment as a source of life-support services and raw materials. But neither market nor planned economies take account of the full value of these goods and services, or of the costs borne by society if the supply of environmental resources is reduced or the services are impaired, now or in the future. Instead, conventional systems of valuation treat the environment and its functions as limitless or free of charge, so providing an incentive for people to deplete resources and degrade ecosystems. New models that incorporate ethical, human and ecological factors as well as economic considerations are being developed. They are badly needed as we face the challenges of sustainable human development.

To take advantage of the efficiency of markets while protecting people and the Earth from their inadequacies, markets must work within laws that uphold human rights, protect the disadvantaged and the interests of future generations, and conserve ecosystems and natural resources. Here economics and law must work together. The law sets the rules and standards. The market ensures that society works within the rules and standards as efficiently as possible.

Policies and programmes for sustainability must be based on scientific knowledge of the factors that they will affect, and be affected by. Because knowledge is incomplete, uncertainty is unavoidable. Meanwhile, governments and communities have to act on the best information they have. At the same time research that will improve understanding of the environment, and reduce uncertainty, must continue. So must monitoring of changes in the environment, since this is the most useful direct measure of the effectiveness of the actions that governments and communities are taking.

Priority actions

Integrating human development and environmental conservation requires:

- institutions capable of an integrated, forward-looking, cross-sectoral approach to making decisions;
- effective policies and comprehensive legal frameworks that safeguard human rights, the interests of future generations, and the productivity and diversity of the Earth;
- economic policy and improved technology that increases the benefits from a given stock of resources and maintains, or even enhances, natural wealth;
- sound knowledge, based on research and monitoring.

Institutions for integrated decision making

The environment is the fundamental resource on which human societies are built. It affects all sectors of social activity, and any action that alters the environment is likely to have wide repercussions. The current fragmented and sectoral approach to policy must therefore be replaced (or buttressed) by new structures that ensure integration.

Action 8.1.   **Adopt an integrated approach to environmental policy, with sustainability as the overall goal.**

Governments should set the creation of a sustainable society as an overall policy goal. To achieve it, they will need to ensure that all sectors and components of government give due consideration to the environmental impact of their activities. This is likely in turn to require them to:

- incorporate the objective of sustainability in the terms of reference of cabinet and legislative committees dealing with national economic policy and planning, as well as those dealing with key sectoral and international policies;
- form a powerful interdepartmental conservation and development coordinating unit, probably attached to the cabinet office or finance ministry, with a mandate to examine departmental policy and investment proposals before they go to cabinet (or equivalent);
- as a first step, incorporate sustainability in the mandates and policies of sectoral agencies. As a second step, change their mandates so that they become cross-sectoral, for example combining responsibility for natural resource utilization, human development and

resource conservation as equal objectives, and at the same time requiring that resource production does not exceed the capacities set by resource conservation;

- establish or upgrade the capacity to assess the environmental impacts of proposed programmes and projects, analyze the environmental implications of policy and public investments, and formulate policies that incorporate sustainability;

- adopt the precautionary principle in decisions on development and environment, and progressively strengthen standards and controls in the light of knowledge and technological capability (see also Action 8.5);

- promote common approaches by establishing collaborative policy forums which bring together representatives of government, environmental groups, business and industry, indigenous people and other interests on an equal footing and in a non-adversarial setting. They can be permanent consultative bodies with a broad continuing mandate, or task forces set up to deal with a particular issue.

Action 8.2.   **Develop strategies for sustainability, and implement them directly and through regional and local planning.**

Governments should develop national and subnational strategies for sustainability that integrate conservation and development (see Action 17.7). They should broaden the scope of planning to include decisions on long-term ideals and desired futures, international interactions, institutional structures, allocation of resources and priorities. Development strategies for sustainability should replace national development plans. If this is not possible, complementary and conservation strategies should be prepared together.

National plans should be extended by regional and local land-use plans enabling a society to translate the goal of sustainability into specific objectives and to integrate a wide range of decisions (see Action 4.5). Each plan should be a joint project of government and the people who live in the region (see Action 7.3). The plans should integrate urban and rural policies. Urban centres and rural areas are tightly linked, the former providing economic services, the latter natural resources and life-support services. Urban policies need to be assessed for their impact on rural areas (see Action 12.1). Policies on agriculture, forestry, and other rural activities need to be assessed for their assumptions about urban change.

Action 8.3.   **Subject proposed development projects, programmes and policies to environmental impact assessment and to economic appraisal.**

Environmental impact assessment (EIA) is used to predict and address the likely environmental consequences of a proposed activity. EIA might better be called "development impact assessment", since social and economic consequences should be examined as well. EIA is an important means of identifying and preventing problems, and an essential step in planning. One of its great benefits is its capacity to bring together a wide range of environmental, social and economic considerations before investments are committed.

EIA should:

- be applied to development projects that are shown by a preliminary screening as likely to have significant environmental, social or economic impacts;

- go beyond assessing the physical impacts of projects, and include social and economic benefits and costs;
- also go beyond assessing and mitigating the impacts of projects to assessing alternatives — including that of not proceeding with the project.
- always be undertaken early in the project cycle, beginning at the pre-feasibility and feasibility stages;
- provide for full public participation, involving all groups that might be affected (see Action 7.3);
- be applied to new technologies, policies and laws that are likely to have significant impacts on the environment;
- also be applied to regional and sectoral programmes;
- include an environmental management programme for all projects that go ahead, providing for monitoring to compare reality with prediction, and allowing for adjustment of the development if necessary;
- be subject to independent review.

In some cases full economic appraisal of the environmental impact of investment programmes and projects will be necessary. Economic appraisal of the costs and benefits of development proposals has been extended in recent years to the assessment of environmental impacts. Such appraisals are important tools for assessing the sustainability of these investments, provided that environmental factors are taken properly into account.

Impacts beyond the borders of the jurisdiction should also be considered. Other countries that might be affected should have an input into decision-making. The public in areas likely to be affected on both sides of a border should be given the opportunity to make comments and objections during the EIA process (the Economic Commission for Europe's Convention on EIA in a Transboundary Context is an example of this.)

Development aid agencies should give priority to assisting countries to develop their capacity to undertake and evaluate EIAs.

The legal framework

Environmental law, in its broadest sense, is an essential tool for achieving sustainability. It requires standards of social behaviour and gives a measure of permanency to policies. Environmental law, based in turn on scientific understanding and a clear analysis of social goals, should set out rules for human conduct which, if followed, should lead to communities living within the capacity of the Earth.

Action 8.4.   **Establish a commitment to the principles of a sustainable society in constitutional or other fundamental statements of national policy.**

Governments should incorporate a commitment to the principles of a sustainable society in the constitution or other fundamental definition of a nation's governance and policy. The commitment should lay down the obligation of the state to safeguard the human rights of its citizens, protect the interests of future generations, conserve the country's life-support systems and biological diversity, ensure that all uses of renewable resources are sustainable, and provide for effective participation of communities and interest groups in the decisions that most affect them. It should grant individuals and citizens' groups enforceable rights corresponding to these obligations.

Action 8.5.   Establish a comprehensive system of environmental law and provide for its implementation and enforcement.

Governments should ensure that their nations are provided with comprehensive systems of environmental law, covering as a minimum:

- land use planning and development control;
- sustainable use of renewable resources, and non-wasteful use of non-renewable resources;
- prevention of pollution, through imposition of emission, environmental quality, process and product standards designed to safeguard human health and ecosystems;
- efficient use of energy, through the establishment of energy efficiency standards for processes, buildings, vehicles and other energy-consuming products;
- control of hazardous substances, including measures to prevent accidents during transportation;
- waste disposal, including standards for minimization of waste and measures to promote recycling;
- conservation of species and ecosystems, through land-use management, specific measures to safeguard vulnerable species and the establishment of a comprehensive network of protected areas.

The national legal system should provide for:

- the application of the precautionary principle and the use of best available technology, when standards for pollution prevention are set;
- use of economic incentives and disincentives, based on appropriate taxes, charges and other instruments;
- the requirement that all proposed new developments and new policies should be subject to environmental impact assessment;
- the requirement that industries and government departments and agencies be subject to periodic environmental audit;
- effective monitoring, permitting detection of infringements and adjustment of regulations where necessary;
- granting public access to EIA assessments, environmental audit data and monitoring results, and to information about the production, use and disposal of hazardous substances.

There must be means for these laws and measures to be effectively enforced, and sanctions against those who contravene them. The enforcement machinery must also provide for the restoration or mitigation of damage. Elements should include:

- penalties severe enough to deter non-compliance;
- liability systems that provide for compensation not only for economic losses suffered by other users of the environmental resource in question, but for ecological and intangible losses;
- the capacity to require that damaged ecosystems should where possible be restored, and that punitive damages can be imposed where restoration is impossible;
- imposition of strict liability in the event of accidents involving hazardous substances;

- a requirement that insurance or other financial provisions be made, so as to guarantee adequate and rapid compensation;
- granting citizens' groups standing in judicial and administrative procedures, so that they can contribute to the enforcement of the law and seek remedies for environmental damage;
- making agencies that are responsible for the implementation and enforcement of environmental law accountable for their actions.

Governments will need to review the adequacy of their institutional machinery for carrying out these functions at both national and local levels. They should adopt a cross-sectoral approach, preferably establishing an integrated environment protection agency with wide powers.

The development and implementation of environmental laws depends on the education and training of lawyers, administrators, industrialists, financiers and scientists. Such training should be a priority in national educational systems (see Action 6.3).

Action 8.6.	Review the adequacy of legal and administrative controls, and of implementation and enforcement mechanisms, recognizing the legitimacy of local approaches.

Many societies have rules rooted in legal tradition that require the sustainable and efficient use of natural resources. The obligation of stewardship is a feature of westernized legal systems. In nations following the common law tradition, the doctrine of waste requires owners of land to use it sustainably. Elsewhere, customary law systems demand strict rules governing the allocation and use of resources. There is, therefore, an existing legal culture into which our generation's obligations towards the world's resources can be set.

New laws should not be passed unless they fit into this existing setting, and can be enforced. Every legal instrument should be assessed for its practicability, in terms of its context, the resources available to implement and enforce it, and its acceptability to the society concerned.

The role of local authority legislation should not be underestimated. While national standards should, whenever possible, be set and adhered to (and should themselves reflect internationally-agreed rules), both federal and unitary states should accept that stricter environmental protection measures may be enacted at sub-national or local level. Local authorities should be encouraged to use their own powers to protect their own environment, especially when community involvement in the formulation and implementation of the measures makes them more effective.

Economic policy and technology

Economic policy is also an essential instrument for achieving sustainability. Once environmental resources are correctly valued and included in national assessments, and the costs of their depletion become evident, the case for conservation is greatly strengthened. Economic instruments are also valuable tools for the establishment of sustainable practices because they provide a strong incentive force, while leaving individuals and industries a freedom of choice as to the precise measures they adopt.

Action 8.7.   **Ensure that national policies, development plans, budgets and decisions on investments take full account of their effects on the environment.**

Governments could accomplish this by:

- ensuring that environmental quality and natural resources are properly valued in national accounting (see Box 14);

- incorporating sustainability in national and other economic development plans to ensure harmony of economic and environmental objectives;

- adopting a set of sustainability indicators and using them to monitor progress (see Annex 6);

- examining existing monetary and fiscal policies (such as subsidies, taxes,,exchange rates), for their impacts on sustainable resource management and environmental protection, correcting those that damage ecosystems or resources;

- evaluating the environmental costs and benefits of public investment and expenditure programmes before these are approved (see Action 8.3).

Action 8.8.   **Use economic policies to achieve sustainability.**

Both lower-income and higher-income countries should use economic instruments as a flexible and efficient means of promoting sustainability. The precise approach will depend on national circumstances, but the general arguments in the following paragraphs are widely relevant.

A key step for governments is to adopt and implement the Polluter Pays Principle and its variant, the User Pays Principle. The former requires that market prices reflect the full costs of environmental damage arising from pollution (for example, a mine or chemical factory

---

Box 12. Full social cost

The full social cost of a product includes the cost of production plus the "environmental" and "user" costs. "Environmental" cost is the cost imposed on society through any damage to ecosystems and other resources as a result of degradation and pollution. "User" cost is the value of future resource benefits foregone because they have been reduced by current use.

Uses that are sustainable can still impose a user cost if they involve harvesting at non-optimal levels. If users of a fishery or a forest alter its ecological structure so that it yields less than before, they reduce both its present and future availability. The value of that extra increment for future generations, foregone by harvesting today, is the user cost of harvesting today. If the resource is harvested unsustainably, the user cost will be even higher, depending on how much the stock available for future users is reduced.

Box 13. Economic instruments to promote conservation and sustainable development

A number of instruments are available to promote conservation and sustainable resource use.

Resource taxes are useful for limiting demand when it is not important to establish a maximum level of aggregate resource use. Since their purpose is to be an incentive for sustainable behaviour, such taxes should become revenue neutral after a period of adjustment. That is, they could replace existing taxes; or the money they raise could be returned to the taxpayer as subsidies for more sustainable technologies and practices (for example, investment in better pollution control equipment).

Resource taxes should be introduced gradually to avoid economic disruption. A pre-announced schedule of increasing the taxes over a period of 10 or more years would give the private sector time to adapt. Matching declines in the rates of other taxes would make resource taxes more acceptable. It is more important that resource taxes are equitable, easy to modify, and steer the economy in directions that are in society's interest, than that they are based on unattainably exact measures of social cost. The aim is to raise taxes on behaviour we want less of, such as depletion and pollution; and reduce them on what we want more of, such as employment of labour.

Taxes should also be differentiated to discriminate between products in the same product-group but with different environmental impacts (see Action 5.4).

Charges. Charges apply the User Pays Principle. They are useful for regulating access to shared resources. Examples are: pollution charges; tourism fees for protected areas; and water charges for irrigation. Pollution charges per unit of pollutant should be set at a higher level than the cost of removing that unit in an environmentally sound way. This would both motivate the industry concerned to prevent pollution and promote the development of anti-pollution technology.

Subsidies. Subsidies can cover costs of achieving sustainability above the amount that resource users can be expected to pay. Also, accelerated depreciation of capital investments and credits for research and development can encourage the adoption of efficient technologies. Subsidies that encourage resource depletion and environmental degradation, for example grants or taxbreaks to drain wetlands or clear forests, should be removed. Such subsidies often contradict the policies of other government sectors, and impose a double cost on society — the subsidy itself plus the cost of the damage it promotes.

Deposit/refund schemes and performance bonds. Under a deposit/refund scheme a deposit is charged on environmentally harmful or undesirable inputs and products, and refunded once the item has been disposed of appropriately. Deposit/refund works well at individual, community and industry levels. It is a useful means of ensuring that the economic cost of environmental protection reflects the true social cost; and it reduces the risk of people avoiding high charges through illegal dumping (provided the deposit is more expensive than the cost of disposing of the material in an approved way). It also provides a way of dealing with toxic wastes, when proof of guilt is difficult or expensive and proof of innocence easy.

A performance bond is a kind of deposit/refund scheme. A deposit is charged to ensure sustainable resource management and refunded on fulfillment of the management objectives. Performance bonds can be used to ensure restoration of sites of extractive and other industries having major local impacts. For example, timber companies could pay reforestation bonds, refundable once the forest had regenerated satisfactorily and reached a specified age.

continued . . .

> *Box 13 continued*
>
> **Tradeable permits.** Permits to pollute or use a resource up to an allowable level are created by law and allocated by auction or on the basis of existing use. Enterprises are authorized to buy and sell permits. Tradeable permits are better than taxes in cases when it is important to establish a maximum level of aggregate emissions or resource use. Any tradeable permit system must be based on adequate and sustainable standards with respect to ambient environmental quality and the health of renewable resource stocks. Tradeable permits are not effective when the pollutant being controlled accounts for a very small proportion of the cost of the product, since then there is no incentive to participate. Nor are they appropriate for hazardous wastes, which should be dealt with stringently. They are usually considered as a transition technique to avoid economic dislocation until stricter standards can be attained.
>
> Before a tradeable permit system is adopted, who should be allowed to participate in the market, who will gain and who will lose from it should be considered. To avoid controversy over this "polluter-buys" mechanism, money raised in this way is best earmarked for compensation for environmental damage, clean up of pollution, and restoration of degraded ecosystems.

should pay the costs of ensuring that its effluents and emissions do not damage fisheries or create a hazard to health). The result is that a strong incentive for pollution control is created. The User Pays Principle requires that prices reflect the full social cost of use or depletion of a resource (Box 12). This in turn provides an incentive for sustainable use and discourages needless depletion (for example a timber industry should pay the costs of soil loss, irregular water run-off, and loss of biological diversity that it causes, as well as the direct cost of timber extraction). Both principles also imply the removal of subsidies and other economic distortions that encourage resource depletion and environmental degradation. It may be necessary to shelter certain sections of society, especially the very poor or elderly, from the full impact of such costs through carefully targeted support schemes.

Charges, resource taxes, tradeable permits, subsidies and performance bonds can be incentives to industry to meet environmental standards in the most cost-effective way (Box 13). In effect, they use market forces so that both producers and consumers are moved toward environmental objectives. They are progressive in that they stimulate the development of sustainable technology and practice. They promote efficiency, reduce the costs of enforcement and generate revenue.

Pricing policies, standards and subsidies can be used to encourage industry to adopt technologies that use resources more efficiently. High prices for energy, water and raw materials can stimulate resource conservation. Phasing the introduction of standards that exceed the present capacity of the regulated industry, so that it can develop the necessary technology before the effective date of the legislation, is a useful procedure. Subsidies, funded by taxes on high-input technologies, provide a further means of moving industry towards low-input (and non-polluting) processes.

Finally, if governments are to understand the effects of their policies, they will need to adopt procedures for environmental and resource accounting. The standard measures of economic performance and national income are dangerously misleading. They take no account of the depreciation or depletion of natural assets or the social costs of pollution. They count expenditures to counteract environmental damage as income rather than costs. What is needed is to include the costs of environmental damage and resource depletion to derive a statement of true (sustainable) income. A problem lies in converting the values of certain natural assets to monetary terms so that they can be properly compared with values resulting from market transactions. Until there is further progress in solving this problem, sustainability indicators will need to be used (see Box 14 and Annex 6).

Action 8.9. Provide economic incentives for conservation and sustainable use.

Regulatory and economic instruments, such as taxes, charges, subsidies, tradeable permits, etc., help to correct biases caused by the underpricing of life-support systems and natural resources. They can enable industry and other resource users to meet environmental standards in the most cost-effective way, to do better than the standards require, and to add their resources to those of government to protect the environment. Incentives can also:

- harness market forces to encourage producers and consumers to achieve environmental objectives;
- stimulate the development of new environmentally-sound products and pollution-control technologies;
- reduce costs of enforcement;
- generate revenue.

Various economic and regulatory instruments can serve as incentives; none is suitable for all circumstances. Suitability should be assessed case by case. A description of the instruments available, and of the ways they work, is given in Box 13.

The knowledge base

Without a sound basis of scientific knowledge, and public understanding of its implications, policies for sustainability are unlikely to be as well formulated or widely supported as they should be. Action is needed on four broad points: strengthening research capacity; establishing machinery for monitoring the state of the environment and progress towards sustainability; improving the availability of information about the environment to the public; and ensuring that there is an effective transfer of new knowledge about the environment into the educational and training system.

Action 8.10. Strengthen the knowledge base, and make information on environmental matters more accessible.

The information needed to integrate human development and environmental conservation depends on research. National research capacity should be reviewed, and research institutions enabled to:

- identify and define key tasks;
- plan and carry out appropriate investigations;
- create a stimulating environment for research;
- participate in international programmes;
- disseminate and apply research results.

Universities and research institutions in many parts of the world have suffered from diminishing support in recent years, and this trend needs to be reversed, particularly in the environmental sciences. It is especially important to build research capacity in lower-income countries. International scientific cooperation should be strengthened for this reason.

Freedom of information should be guaranteed. Governments should:

- make information about the environment freely available;
- inform people immediately about any environmental accident that might affect them;
- open records of pollutant discharges and other monitored activities for public inspection, giving people the right to take copies for their own use at reasonable times and reasonable cost. This right should be subject to exception only in genuine cases of national interest;
- regard environmental data as a public resource, not as a financial asset.

Box 14. Including environmental cost in measures of economic performance

Sustainability is embodied in the standard definition of income: it is the maximum amount that a person or nation could consume in a given period and still be as well off at the end of the period as at the beginning. Thus income means not "current earnings" but "current earnings plus asset gains minus asset losses". Income, thus defined, equals maximum sustainable consumption. Growth in true income is by definition sustainable, because any consumption that is not sustainable cannot be counted as income.

The standard measures of national economic performance (GNP, gross national product) and of national income (NNP, net national product) do not take account of depreciation of natural assets. Yet reduction of oil and mineral reserves, deforestation, and losses of fertile soil, are likely to raise the cost of production or result in lower yields. They also record expenditures to counteract environmental damage as income, not as expenses. Thus they give an illusion of economic health. This illusion is reinforced if environmental damage increases current human medical and production costs, since these expenditures add to the income of suppliers. Finally, environmental damage can reduce production. In this case conventional accounting deals with it correctly by reducing income only if it reduces current production or increases the cost of current production. Other environmental damage (for example, the costs of ill health or reduced future productivity), is not reflected in GNP.

Natural wealth is drawn on to finance investments in industrial capacity, infrastructure, education, and so on — but the accounting process does not reflect the fact that one kind of asset has been exchanged for another. Hence it does not provide a means of assessing whether, or to what extent, the exchange has been positive or negative. A country may be heading for bankruptcy — depleting its mineral reserves, destroying its forests, polluting its air and waters, and spending the proceeds on current consumption — and still think its economy is performing well because the GNP and NNP figures look so good. This anomaly reinforces the false dichotomy between "economy" and "environment".

A new statement of true national income is needed. It might be:

True (sustainable) income = Net National Product (Gross National Product minus depreciation of human-made capital) plus increases in natural assets minus depreciation of natural assets minus defensive expenditures against environmental damage minus the costs of unmitigated environmental damage.

To enable true income to be calculated, indicators of sustainability need to be defined (Annex 6), and regular assessments made of the sustainability of economic sectors, and of environmental quality. The information could be published in the form of state-of-the-environment reports or sustainability reports and should be organized so that it can be related to the national accounts.

Information expands opportunities. It is an essential commodity, and one of the key ways to empower people, as long as it is communicated in forms that are easily understood by the people concerned.

Agencies managing information can help by:

- working together to develop standards and protocols to ensure the comparability and transferability of information between databases;

- collaborating to help establish and develop local and national databases, to meet the needs of the local users;

- paying particular attention to the need to present decision-makers and their advisers with relevant information in a comprehensible and useable form, with confidence limits clearly stated;

- developing and participating in networks for the free two-way flow of information.

Governments should establish, and continually review and improve, national monitoring systems. Continuous, long-term series of data are essential.
Monitoring should cover:

- key physical, chemical and biological features of the environment, major parameters of human development and the status of natural resources, all important in their own right or as indicators of environmental well-being and the quality of life;

- performance of policies, laws and other institutional arrangements as a prerequisite for their improvement;

- the progress of environmental protection measures, as compared with stated national plans;

- land-use changes, again in relation to stated plans and objectives;

- changes in public behaviour and attitudes, to give a better picture of political support for policy change.

International collaboration is needed to develop standard methods, identify key indicators, and promote the establishment of national monitoring and data centres, particularly in lower-income countries. A global network for environmental monitoring with information transfer points is required so that national data sets can contribute to the global overview, which can in turn provide the context for the interpretation of national results.

At the international level, satellite-based systems are needed for continuous monitoring of the distribution of major ecological formations like forests and deserts, the biomass and productivity of vegetation, and changes in land-use patterns. Although expensive and not always easy to interpret, these systems are the cheapest way of obtaining a broad overview of the state of the Earth's ecosystems. The systems should be complemented by well coordinated ground observations and the results should be evaluated by international facilities such as the UNEP Global Environmental Monitoring System (GEMS), the IUCN/UNEP/WWF World Conservation Monitoring Centre (WCMC) and the Environmental Early Warning Mechanism proposed by UNEP.

A programme of national environmental auditing should be established, with governments reporting on a regular basis on the state of their environments. This reporting should include assessment of performance in achieving targets for improved environmental quality and standard of living. It should be subject to independent scrutiny.

Box 15. Energy and assets

Chapters 2-8 have dealt with many aspects of the complex relationship between environmental conservation on the one hand and development and the economy on the other. Inputs and outputs to and from the economy within the context of the environment are shown in simplified form in *Fig.3*.

The Earth (oval figure) contains and limits everything except the energy of the Sun. Solar energy (1) drives photosynthesis in green plants; cycles water from the oceans to the atmosphere and back; circulates global air masses; warms soils. Our lives and the economy depend on these ecological processes. Solar energy (2) is also available in economically useful forms (E) — e.g., hydrocarbons, hydro, wind power, etc.

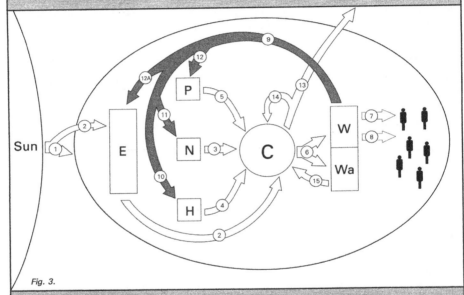

Fig. 3.

These forms of energy drive the conversion processes (C) which are central to the economy and affect the environment. In addition to energy, other inputs to conversion (production factors) are natural assets (N) — natural resources and environmental services, (flowing via 3); human assets (H) — people's skills, knowledge, intellect and vigour (flowing via 4); and physical plant and infrastructure (P) — settlements, factories, machines, systems of transportation and communication (flowing via 5).

Conversion results in loss of heat (13) some of which can be recaptured (14) and used again. The visible results (6) of conversion are material wealth (W) and material wastes (Wa). Material wealth provides the goods and services that people need (7) or want (8). Material wastes can sometimes be recycled (15) to contribute to material wealth. Material wealth is used for the investment (9) needed to maintain the process of conversion and to ensure sustainability. Investment must be allocated among the production factors.

There has been a tendency to run down natural assets to expand physical plant (12), including energy extraction facilities (12a), and to allow a high level of discretionary consumption (8). Human development (10) through education, training and health care (including family planning) is often neglected, and the failure to invest in the maintenance and rehabilitation of natural assets (11) has been close to catastrophic. Many of the actions recommended in the Stategy imply the re-allocation of investment to correct those imbalances.

9. Creating a global alliance

Thinking globally and acting locally is not enough. We must act globally as well. The environment links all nations. The atmosphere and oceans interact to provide the world's climate. Many great river systems are shared between several states. Pollution knows no frontiers, as it moves with the currents of air or water. Sustainability within a nation often depends on international agreements to manage shared resources. Nations must recognize their common interest in the world environment.

Climate change, ozone depletion, and pollution of the air, rivers and seas are worldwide threats. Neither wealth nor sovereignty can protect us from these pervasive influences. The affluent nations of the Western Pacific, Western Europe and North America — islands of wealth in an ocean of want — face a rising tide of migrants trying to escape from environmental degradation and economic stagnation. These and other factors — from long-range weapons to modern communications and international money markets — are continually eroding the significance of national frontiers.

At the same time the integrity of national frontiers — even though many are legacies of colonialism and make no ecological, ethnic or economic sense — is a principle that many governments passionately defend. A key issue for the future is whether frontiers will hold, be held by force or crumble before a tide of environmental refugees. The only chance of stabilizing the situation lies in international cooperation on an unprecedented scale to establish sustainability for all societies. Sovereign states must stop regarding themselves as self-sufficient units (which few, if any, are), and accept a future as components of a global system.

"Interdependence is one of the present day phenomena that has greatest impact on the fate of nations," declared the South Commission. "If the multiple bonds that characterize interdependence are convincingly present in any field, it is in that encompassing development and the environment. Human civilization is moving toward a global state. This is apparent in all dimensions: social, economic, cultural and political, as well as environmental. But the transition is not occurring smoothly and harmoniously: it is turbulent and beset with conflict."

International cooperation needs the backing of international law. To expand from nationalism to globalism, we need to reshape the law to reflect the need for the peoples of the world to live sustainably, and the obligations of nations towards the Earth that they share. We need to build a global alliance, and to use international law (especially treaty law) to give it effect. The new alliance must have at its heart the understanding not only that all have a role to play in safeguarding the Earth, but also that those who have more economic and social resources must contribute more.

The Third World's cumulative debt is more than $1 trillion, and interest payments alone have reached $60 billion a year. As a result, since 1984 there has been a net transfer of capital from lower-income to upper-income countries. The most indebted regions are sub-Saharan Africa, where debt now equals Gross National Product; and Latin America, where it is 60% of GNP. These massive debts can force countries simultaneously to curb living standards, accept growing poverty, and export greater amounts of scarce resources, thereby accelerating environmental destruction. Yet despite these constraints, many lower-income countries invest more money on conservation and environmental management, as a proportion of their Gross National Products, than do upper-income countries.

Most low-income countries obtain three-quarters or more of their export incomes from primary commodities. Prices of many of these, including copper, iron ore, sugar, rubber, cotton, and timber, have fallen in recent years. These prices in any case do not include the environmental and user costs (see Box 17) of producing the resources. So the natural wealth of the exporting countries is subsidizing the importers.

Political borders impede the flow of goods and services but not the much larger flow of money. Trade barriers by high-income countries cost lower-income countries two and a half times more than all the aid they get. Fluctuations and speculation in currency, commodity prices, and interest rates weaken vulnerable economies. Capital flight from Latin American nations, generally to United States and European banks, may have as big an impact as the Latin American debt. Transnational companies can move money freely, and while some have adopted an exemplary policy of maintaining the highest standards everywhere, others have played one country off against another to win cheap resources and weak environmental controls.

Official development assistance is equivalent to only 1.1% of the combined GNP of the recipient countries, and is less than the interest they pay on their debt. Much of it has given the recipients neither development nor assistance. Rather it has exported a style of managing people and resources inappropriate for the receivers and now seriously questioned by the donors. In the process, too much is kept by the donors to pay for equipment and consultants from their own countries.

To increase the capacity of low-income countries to support themselves — and in so doing to develop sustainably and protect their environments — their debts must be reduced and their terms of trade improved. Increased flows of finance are also essential, especially to Africa, Latin America, and low-income Asia. But it must be a different kind of assistance: a true partnership for sustainability.

Priority actions

A meaningful global alliance requires acceptance by every nation of its share of responsibility, and a commitment to as much action as its means permit. The alliance will also require effective, properly funded international institutions, both non-governmental and intergovernmental. In addition:

- each nation should accept the duty to live sustainably, to help others to do so, and to support new international laws that define those obligations;
- agreement must be reached on how to conserve the global commons, and to share the benefits derived from them equitably;
- upper-income (especially high-income) countries should reduce their resource consumption, especially by increasing efficiency (see Chapter 5);
- the debt burden of lower-income countries should be reduced, and their conditions of trade improved;
- development assistance should be reformed and increased;
- international institutions should be reformed and strengthened.

Strengthening international law

There is, already, a substantial body of international environmental law: a list published by UNEP in 1987 includes 118 titles. It is important that existing measures are fully supported and implemented. But additional instruments are needed, to address issues now neglected. There is also a need for a global instrument that gives expression to both the ethic of living sustainably and the obligations that stem from it.

Action 9.1.   Strengthen existing international agreements to conserve life-support systems and biological diversity.

Many international conventions deal with the environment. The following are particularly important:

Atmosphere

- Vienna Convention for the Protection of the Ozone Layer, and its (Montreal) Protocol on substances that deplete the ozone layer;
- Geneva Convention on Long-Range Transboundary Air Pollution.

Oceans

- The United Nations Convention on the Law of the Sea (UNCLOS) (not yet in force);
- The group of global and regional instruments dealing with the protection of the oceans from pollution from ships (IMO conventions), dumping of wastes (London, Oslo and Regional Seas conventions), land-based pollution (Paris, Helsinki and Regional Seas conventions), and the conservation of marine living resources (Fisheries conventions, International Whaling Convention, Convention on the Conservation of Antarctic Marine Living Resources).

Fresh waters

- Boundary Waters Convention on the Great Lakes (Canada-USA): agreements on shared rivers (Rhine, Danube).

Waste

- The Basle Convention on the Control of Transboundary Movements of Hazardous Wastes and their Disposal;
- The Bamako Convention on the Ban of the Import into Africa and the Control of Transboundary Movement and Management of Hazardous Wastes within Africa.

Protection of biological diversity

- The Ramsar Convention for the Conservation of Wetlands of International Importance especially as Waterfowl Habitat;
- The Convention Concerning the Protection of the World Cultural and Natural Heritage (UNESCO, Paris);
- The Convention on International Trade in Endangered Species of Wild Fauna and Flora (CITES) (Washington);
- The Convention on the Conservation of Migratory Species of Wild Animals (Bonn).

States should maintain their support for these and other relevant international agreements on the environment. Those that have not done so should adhere to and implement them. All Parties should enact domestic legislation, and commit resources, to carry out their obligations under each accord. Assistance should be made available to help lower-income countries with the work of implementation.

Action 9.2.   Conclude new international agreements to help achieve global sustainability.

Governments should give priority to the following:

- completion, adoption, and implementation of a convention on the conservation of biological diversity;
- negotiation of the proposed convention on climate change, meanwhile committing themselves to reducing greenhouse gas emissions (see Action 4.3);
- commitments to collaborate on safeguarding the world's forests (see Chapter 14);
- bringing into force of the UN Convention on the Law of the Sea (UNCLOS) (see Action 16.10).

Adequate funding is essential to the success of both the climate change and biological diversity conventions. Effective financial mechanisms must therefore be provided under these instruments or through other means.

Governments should also:

- give more attention to the conservation and sustainable management of shared seas and river basins, and of other shared ecosystems and living resources. Regional bodies with resource management functions should be established or strengthened (see Action 16.11). These organizations should adopt an integrated approach to management, and provide for environmental assessments of proposals with potential transboundary impacts;
- take action to improve resource conservation, especially fisheries management, outside the limits of national jurisdiction. Unregulated, unselective and probably unsustainable driftnet fishing on the high seas illustrates the need for such an international management regime (see Action 16.10);
- support the new instrument being negotiated for conservation of the Antarctic environment (see Action 9.3).

Action 9.3.   Develop a comprehensive and integrated conservation regime for Antarctica and the Southern Ocean.

Antarctica and the Southern Ocean are the home of 54 species of seabird, some numbered in millions and 21 marine mammal species, including several gravely depleted large whales. The region is one of the world's few remaining great wilderness areas; and a demilitarized and nuclear-free zone of international peace and cooperation. Scientific activity and tourism have expanded rapidly and are causing locally significant pollution. They need to be carefully regulated. Southern Ocean fish stocks are heavily exploited. Mining and hydrocarbon production could have severe impacts.

The Antarctic Treaty System contains significant gaps, and implementation of some measures needs improvement. Measures have largely been reactive; an anticipatory approach is now required. A comprehensive, integrated and legally binding conservation regime, based on the principles of this Strategy is needed. The regime should provide for adequate scientific information, monitoring, open reporting, and effective compliance procedures.

Governments should:

- support the new instrument being negotiated under the Antarctic Treaty for conservation of the Antarctic environment, and use the Antarctic Conservation Strategy as a guide to future policy in the region;

- exclude minerals activities as incompatible with Antarctic conservation;

- continue to cooperate in the development of new measures to regulate logistics, science, waste disposal, tourism and protected areas management.

Action 9.4. Prepare and adopt a Universal Declaration and Covenant on Sustainability

This Covenant should be the expression in international law of the world ethic for living sustainably (see Chapter 2). It would reflect the commitment of States to the principles of that ethic and define their corresponding rights and duties. In addition, it would set out the measures whereby the principles could be implemented.

The Covenant should:

- build on the proposal for a Universal Declaration and Convention on Sustainable Development, submitted to the UN General Assembly by the World Commission on Environment and Development (WCED) in 1987;

- build on the principles embodied in existing international Conventions and agreements that deal with aspects of environmental conservation and the sustainable use of natural resources;

- give expression to the need to safeguard the environmental rights of future generations;

- build on the principles of the World Charter for Nature and other "soft law" documents that deal with the maintenance of the productivity and diversity of the Earth, and *inter alia,* define rules for the ethical treatment of other species;

- express the commitments and corresponding obligations of States to live sustainably, and to care for their national environmental resources;

- emphasize the responsibilities of all States also to protect the global commons and shared resources;

- propose mechanisms and procedures for settling international disputes over environmental and resource issues;

- address the issue of liability of States in respect of their impact on global and shared environmental resources.

The Covenant would provide a coherent statement of global environmental policy, and a framework for existing global and regional accords and for new initiatives. It would pave the way for the consideration by States of broader environment and development issues. The framework should also extend to new financial institutions to support global action for sustainability (see Action 9.2 and Box 17).

Increasing the capacity of lower-income countries to address environmental priorities

Alliances need to be built on strength. Many lower-income countries cannot now concentrate on sustainability because their limited resources must be directed toward more immediate preoccupations. It is crucial to strengthen their capacity to adopt sustainable resource use policies so that they can join fully in the global alliance. This is likely to demand investment in institution-building, education, community action and governance as well as specific programmes of environmental management.

Action 9.5. **Write off the official debt of low-income countries, and retire enough of their commercial debt to restore economic progress.**

Official debt is what is owed to governments and governmental banks. Commercial debt is what is owed to commercial banks.

Some high-income countries have begun to forgive the debts of low-income countries, but they should all now write off completely the official debt of low-income countries and set up a fund to retire much of their commercial debt. This debt relief should be additional to other development assistance.

Debt-for-nature swaps are a useful part of the debt retirement process. The funds released by retiring debt should, however, be used to support broader strategies for sustainability, including action to stabilize population, conserve life-support systems and biological diversity, maintain and replant forests, develop renewable energy sources, and increase energy efficiency. To avoid any semblance of imposed "conditionality", arrangements should be based on a perception of need shared by donors and recipients, with funds managed by a genuinely independent international body and with the recipient countries in full control of their strategies for sustainability.

Action 9.6. **Increase the capacity of lower-income countries to help themselves.**

Economic growth and the generation of resources for sustainable environmental management in the developing lower-income countries would be greatly facilitated by:

- removing non-environmental trade barriers to their exports;

- supporting and stabilizing their commodity prices;

- encouraging investment.

Subsidized agriculture in high-income countries creates artificially low world prices, and undermines the local and export markets of lower-income countries. This makes it difficult for them to sell even those commodities for which they have a comparative natural advantage, and reduces funds available for investment in sustainable agriculture. By encouraging over-production, subsidies can also lead to degradation of farmland in high-income countries.

Subsidies should be redirected within high-income countries to those farmers who practise conservation and good husbandry, or maintain landscape quality and biological diversity, rather than those who produce the most (see Action 13.13).

Trade barriers should be scrutinized. Legitimate environmental restrictions on trade, such as health protection standards for the pesticide or heavy-metal content of foodstuffs, must be kept. But the removal of other barriers would help lower-income countries obtain greater benefits from their natural resources. The likely effects on the environment of trade liberalization should be assessed before particular actions are taken.

In addition, ways need to be found to support and stabilize the prices of commodities exported by lower-income countries. They could include international commodity agreements, stabilization funds established under the auspices of UNCTAD; and assistance to lower-income countries to diversify their commodity sectors. The International Tropical Timber Agreement (ITTA) provides one example of a commodity agreement now being developed towards support for sustainable management (Action 14.10).

Upper- and lower-income countries together should explore ways of limiting the flight of capital from the latter to the former or of at least ensuring that much of it is reinvested in the lower-income countries.

Box 16. Technical cooperation: how to make it work

Technical cooperation (TC) can be difficult, time-consuming and prone to failure, particularly if it is poorly planned or managed. The Development Assistance Committee of the Organization for Economic Cooperation and Development has drafted principles for TC which, if followed, would greatly increase the chance of success. Key points include the need for:

- clear recognition of the central responsibility of recipient countries in the planning of technical cooperation;
- better planning and integration of TC within overall and sectoral development programmes of recipient countries;
- greater emphasis on long-term institution-building;
- more careful use and selection of expatriates and fuller use of local people;
- more involvement of local executive agencies and local user associations in the design and implementation of technical cooperation programmes.

Reforming North-South financial flows, including the mode of delivery of development assistance

Debt retirement and trade liberalization should go a long way towards reversing the present unacceptable resource flow from the lower-income to the higher-income countries. But development aid remains an extremely important means of promoting sustainability. Official development assistance is now almost $50 billion a year from OECD countries (0.35% of their GNP) and over $3 billion from OPEC countries (0.79% of their GNP). Multilateral and bilateral aid agencies should increase their development assistance and use it to support the development of sustainable economies.

Action 9.7.   **Increase development assistance and devote it to helping countries develop sustainable societies and economies.**

High priority should be given to helping countries improve their knowledge, skills and institutions (see Box 16). This is the most valuable kind of aid because it increases a country's capacity to analyze and solve its own problems. Institution-building should be an integral part of most aid activities. Indeed an aid activity cannot be regarded as successful unless it has helped to improve the local institutions with which it works.

Aid agencies could further promote the development of sustainable economies by:

- providing additional funds for sustainable development programmes;
- building countries' institutional and technical capacities for project management;
- increasing assistance for social reform programmes;
- ensuring participation by affected communities in the design and implementation of projects and programmes;
- changing the mode of lending from project to programme. For example, funds could be provided for an entire forestry programme, leaving the recipient government to devise the constituent projects. The funds could be paid in instalments as agreed programme targets are met;
- increasing the number of small-scale projects with maximum grassroots participation. These generally require smaller sums of money than conventional development projects, with higher local expenditure, a higher ratio of capital costs, and greater use of local technology and expertise (see also Chapter 7). To be consistent with the previous recommendation, this should be done by supporting umbrella programmes, which could be managed by citizens' groups;
- assessing, disclosing and taking full account of the environmental impacts of programmes as well as projects.

These proposals would naturally demand a substantial increase over current levels of aid. Part of this increase can be met through the Global Environment Facility (see Box 17) or some successor institution.

Box 17. The Global Environment Facility

The Global Environment Facility has been set up on a pilot basis under an agreement made by 25 countries in November 1990 and is managed by the World Bank, the United Nations Environment Programme, and the United Nations Development Programme. The GEF will provide concessional funding for investment projects and related activities to meet four objectives:

- limitation of greenhouse gas emissions by supporting energy conservation, the use of energy sources that will not contribute to global warming, and forest management and reforestation;
- preservation of areas rich in natural diversity;
- protection of international drainage basins and seas, particularly from transboundary pollution;
- halting destruction of the ozone layer, by helping countries make the switch from CFCs and other ozone depleting substances to less damaging substitutes.

Initial commitments to the GEF are estimated at $1-1.5 billion. Clearly, these are not sufficient to meet the above objectives. The continuance of the GEF is likely to depend on its perceived ability to meet real needs in a cost-effective way.

Strengthen international commitment and capacity to achieve sustainability

An effective global alliance must harness the total resources of humanity to deal with the immense challenges of the coming decades. Intergovernmental bodies, non-governmental organizations, and the world of business, industry and commerce, must all work together. International efforts must be supported by strong national alliances that draw together committed groups of all kinds. Intergovernmental, non-governmental and business groupings must develop better methods of collaboration if they are to be truly effective.

Action 9.8.	**Recognize the value of global and national non-governmental action, and strengthen it.**

Global sustainability will be achieved only if it is pursued by individuals and communities throughout all nations. Citizens' groups, and especially those concerned with conservation and development, have a particularly important part to play because they are familiar with the issues, have the expertise to bring to bear, and have both commitment and flexibility.

Bodies such as IUCN- The World Conservation Union, which combine governmental and non-governmental sectors in their membership, can make a distinctive contribution, as can WWF with its active links with the business community. These and other partners can lead in a wide range of actions to promote sustainability including:

- convening forums at national and regional level, involving the governmental and non-governmental sectors, and business and industry;
- organizing workshops and groups of experts to evaluate key issues and provide reports, including information for the media;
- developing methodologies and strategies for sustainability;
- providing suggestions for action to governments or local communities, which they can then take up and develop further for themselves;
- undertaking demonstration projects, in partnership with government agencies or local communities as appropriate.

Governments committed to sustainability should form productive partnerships with environment, development and humanitarian NGOs and citizens' groups. Development assistance agencies should support them in lower-income countries. Governments and official agencies should encourage NGOs to build links with one another. Governments should actively encourage the involvement of NGO and business groups as equal partners in national and international meetings. A real partnership is a strategic alliance based not on funding but on openness, trust, and a commitment to shared social goals. Many more such partnerships are needed in both lower-income and higher-income countries.

Action 9.9.	**Strengthen the United Nations system as an effective force for global sustainability.**

The United Nations system has promoted and assisted better management of the environment and natural resources. But sectoralism, both in international bodies and national governments, has impeded progress. Sectoralism is particularly strong in the United Nations system because its sectoral organizations have their own autonomous legislative bodies. At the very least, governments, through parallel resolutions in the respective governing bodies, should redefine the mandates of the UN agencies and impose a collective and individual responsibility to work for sustainability in a coordinated way. Governments will achieve this only if they ensure that their own representatives to the various UN agencies pursue consistent policies. Governments should also review options for ensuring the full participation of appropriate NGO groups in their meetings, thereby strengthening partnership, and broadening the base for decisions.

The UN system should adopt an integrated approach to the environment and to sustainability. Attempts at coordination, such as the System-Wide Medium Term Environment Programme, should be guided by inter-agency, inter-sectoral policies laid down at the highest level. Consideration should be given to a system of governance in which the General Assembly would coordinate the policies of the whole system, making use of committees in place of autonomous councils to deal with matters of operational detail.

The UN system should provide annual reports along the lines of the Joint Statement on the Environment proposed by UNESCO. Such statements would be signed by the heads of UN and other participating bodies and would be addressed to top decision makers. They would cover global environmental issues requiring urgent international cooperation, providing an information synthesis, an assessment of the issues' importance, and the main policy options for action.

PART II

Additional Actions for Sustainable Living

The traditional approach to the management of the environment has been sectoral, dealing with agriculture, forestry, fisheries, nature conservation, pollution prevention, energy use and conservation, industry, human settlements planning and other components of the world system, as if they were independent entities. But too much sectoralism in resource management and in the apportionment of responsibilities between departments of government and among international agencies is responsible for many of the environmental problems that confront us today. We have to understand the environment as an interactive system that provides the foundation for development and is the ultimate determinant of sustainability and the quality of life.

For these reasons, the eight main Chapters in Part I followed an integrative approach, taking the principles described in Chapter 1 and exploring their implications for personal ethics and conduct; for social action to improve the quality of life, conserve the biosphere, and keep within the Earth's carrying capacity; and for action by individuals, local communities, governments and the international community.

We will doubtless continue to manage the main components of the environment as sectors. This will work well so long as the linkages among sectors are fully understood and if actions in one area are evaluated for their impact on others and planned to minimize adverse effects.

Part II of the Strategy considers the application of the principles described in Part I to some of the more familiar sectors of environment and policy: energy; business, industry and commerce; human settlements; farm and range lands; forest lands; fresh waters; and oceans and coastal areas. These chapters add a further 62 detailed actions to the 60 recommended in Part I.

10. Energy

Simple societies were, and still are, driven by human and animal power, and fuelled by wood, charcoal and dung. But in industrial societies energy and fuel production and use have become much more sophisticated. Commercial energy consumption has grown at a continually accelerating rate.

Commercial energy is essential for development. It is no accident that the countries that use very little are among the poorest.

But commercial energy production and use also cause serious impacts on the environment, in the form of acid drainage, methane emissions and mining wastes; oil spills from on-shore and off-shore installations and from ships; and air pollution by sulphur dioxide, nitrogen oxides and carbon dioxide when coal, oil or gas are burned. The energy industries are also major users of non-renewable resources, some of which will be of increasing value in future as feedstocks for chemical industry.

There is much waste in the commercial energy industry and in the use of its products. For example, electrical heating systems make use of high-grade heat to produce low-grade heat: that is, to make the temperature of rooms only a few degrees different from that of the adjacent environment. Many power stations shed waste heat into their environment as hot water or warm air or steam: only lately have combined heat and power plants begun in many countries to market their low-grade heat to warm nearby buildings. Many buildings are poorly insulated, wasting money and energy through the avoidable leakage of heat into the surrounding air in cool weather, and leading to over-heated working conditions in hot weather. Many industrial processes still use far more energy than is needed to power the operations they undertake. Motor vehicles consume about one third of the oil used in the world and some 40% of the energy used in the OECD countries. They are notoriously inefficient as well as major sources of pollution.

Energy efficiency, and the prevention of pollution from the burning of fossil fuels, is essential for all countries. Wasteful and inefficient energy policies characterized the development of Europe and North America. Now developed countries must reduce their emissions of carbon dioxide and other pollutants, which will require a continuing increase in the efficiency with which they generate and use energy. This will in turn require many changes in established practice. Instead of seeking to generate and sell more power we will need to manage demand so that consumption is reduced.

Planning should commence with an analysis of human needs and a consideration of how these can be met most efficiently and equitably. Future development should pay more attention to local, small-scale, devices delivering low-grade heat where it is needed. It will also need more efficient commercial energy systems. At present, while energy efficiency has been improving steadily in many high-income countries, it has been declining in several newly-industrializing countries.

Too frequently, growth in energy consumption has been treated as a yardstick of economic growth, regardless of the efficiency with which that energy has been used. We need to de-couple economic growth from growth in energy production, and recognize that if we are to achieve sustainability we must achieve the first without a matching expansion in the second. Development assistance agencies and multilateral development banks should place less emphasis on funding conventional energy supply projects and provide more help for new, renewable sources and for measures that will improve efficiency and conservation. Increased efficiency in the energy sector is therefore a key to global sustainability.

Priority actions

The needs are for:

- long-term energy strategies for all countries;
- increased efficiency in energy generation from fossil fuels, and increased use of alternative, particularly renewable, energy sources;
- increased efficiency in the distribution of energy;
- reduced energy use per person in all sectors, and major increases in the efficiency of use in the home, industry, business and transport.

Action 10.1.   Develop explicit national energy strategies.

Each government should prepare a national strategy for its commercial energy industries, covering extraction, conversion, transport and use for the next 30 years. These strategies should indicate how the target for reduction in energy consumption per head recommended in Action 5.2 would be set and achieved. They should include:

- policies for the optimal use of national fossil fuel resources, bearing in mind the need to minimize the depletion of non-renewable resources; explicit statements of the technical and economic means to husband these resources, and ensure efficiency in their use and distribution, and minimal pollution by the energy generation industry;
- policies for the development and safe use of other energy sources (see Action 10.3);
- policies and standards for the energy efficiency of processes and products, including vehicles (see Action 10.4);
- economic policies that ensure that the price of energy covers the full social cost of its production, distribution and use and gives the consumer an incentive to choose the most efficient and least damaging sources, products, and transport modes;
- use of taxes or incentives, as appropriate, to encourage greater energy efficiency in homes, and to shelter the poorer sectors of the community from the impact of steep increases in energy prices which these policies may cause (see Action 5.4);
- information campaigns to bring home to people the imperative of energy conservation and to stimulate them to choose products that meet high standards (see also Action 5.1);
- obligations on manufacturers to monitor and publish the energy efficiency of their processes and the energy costs of their products;
- provision for an annual report on the state of implementation of the national energy strategy and especially the extent to which targets are being met;
- support for citizens' groups to promote the national energy strategy.

Citizens' groups, especially environmental NGOs, and business and industry should be fully involved in the development of the national strategy. National environmental protection

Fig. 4. Energy industry - Impacts and losses

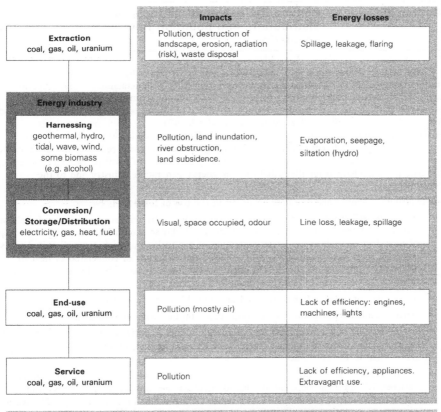

	Impacts	Energy losses
Extraction coal, gas, oil, uranium	Pollution, destruction of landscape, erosion, radiation (risk), waste disposal	Spillage, leakage, flaring
Energy industry **Harnessing** geothermal, hydro, tidal, wave, wind, some biomass (e.g. alcohol)	Pollution, land inundation, river obstruction, land subsidence.	Evaporation, seepage, siltation (hydro)
Conversion/ Storage/Distribution electricity, gas, heat, fuel	Visual, space occupied, odour	Line loss, leakage, spillage
End-use coal, gas, oil, uranium	Pollution (mostly air)	Lack of efficiency: engines, machines, lights
Service coal, gas, oil, uranium	Pollution	Lack of efficiency, appliances. Extravagant use.

The diagram illustrates a typical energy system. Energy losses and environmental impacts occur at every stage from extraction to service. Reductions in demand (the bottom of the diagram) bring about reductions in supply (the top of the diagram). Therefore, end-use and service efficiency are particularly important for saving energy and reducing environmental and economic costs. The main ways of reducing energy demand are:

• Changing behaviour: for example, doing more work at home; choosing activities that require little or no commercial energy over those that require a lot.

• Changing the structure of urban and transport systems.

• Changing the structure of economies from high-volume resource industries to high-value information and service industries.

• Increasing the efficiency with which energy is used.

Useful energy efficiencies can also be obtained at the supply end by improving energy conversion, distribution, and storage.

agencies should be given responsibility for setting energy efficiency standards and monitoring their attainment by industry. They could also be assigned the responsibility for preparation of the annual progress reports described above.

| Action 10.2. | Reduce the use of fossil fuels, wastage in energy distribution, and pollution from commercial energy generation. |

Many nations favour the use of indigenous fossil fuels, especially coal, even when this is unduly costly or brings needless environmental impact. It is understandable that a country will seek to restrict trade in energy to levels that do not constrain its ability to pursue economic goals of its own choice or reduce its ability to pursue an independent foreign policy. While self-reliance may be a legitimate goal, total self-sufficiency often makes neither economic nor environmental sense in today's interdependent world. Many countries also subsidize energy for the consumer, thus distorting the economy and reducing the incentive for careful use of energy. A first step towards economy in the use of fossil fuels is to ensure that the true price is charged for them, both to the energy generation industry and to the consumer.

Governments should also promote economy in the use of fossil fuels by:

- increasing efficiency in the energy-generating industry by imposing standards of fuel-use efficiency, based on the best available technology. These should in turn promote the use of new devices such as the latest generation of gas turbines, which are well suited to use in small, local power stations and have raised the efficiency of conversion of heat to electricity from 33% to about 50%, greatly reducing the cost of building a plant. Other technical advances include co-generation of heat and power;

- using taxes or charges (see Action 5.4 and Box 13) to promote efficiency;

- setting standards for pollution emissions based on best available technology;

- setting standards for acceptable loss of energy or fuel (especially gas) in distribution, and requiring that losses above that standard be charged against the profits of the industry rather than to the consumer.

- where possible, substituting natural gas for coal. This is because coal burning emits between 70 and 95% more carbon dioxide than gas per unit of useful energy produced. Oil is intermediate, producing 35-45% more CO_2 per unit of useful energy. The waste of natural gas by burning it off ("flaring") during oil extraction is thus deplorable, and should be reduced or if possible eliminated.

International cooperation (see Chapter 9), including development aid, should include exchanges of knowledge about the best available technology, and help with the transfer of that technology to developing countries.

| Action 10.3. | Develop renewable and other non-fossil fuel energy sources. |

No energy source can be exploited without some environmental impact. Hydropower involves building dams which sometimes displace communities, or when placed in sparsely settled mountain country, create conflicts with the conservation of landscapes and biological diversity. Wind, solar and wave power all require installations which may affect habitats or amenities. The use of plant materials ("biomass") to generate alcohol as a fuel involves cultivation and harvesting, and hence competes for land with agriculture, forestry or nature conservation. The concerns over substitution of nuclear power for fossil fuel energy sources arise both from the fear of accident, elevated following the disaster at Chernobyl, and from the fact that no nation has so far demonstrated that the wastes arising from that industry can be securely and safely disposed of.

It is important that research and development into the efficient use of renewable energy sources continues. Governments should support this work, and exchange the results through international agencies such as the International Energy Agency. Development aid agencies should help. Key elements in policy are likely to be:

- increased use of hydropower, particularly small-scale installations, but only where Environmental Impact Assessments and comprehensive benefit/cost analysis show the development to be truly cost-effective;

- promotion of the development and use of geothermal, wind and wave energy, again in localities suited to them, and only following EIA;

- promotion of small-scale solar energy systems (photovoltaic cells) for use in domestic situations and to power individual installations like pumps;

- encouragement of simple technology that uses solar energy directly for heating and drying;

- continued development of biomass-based fuels where they can be derived from crop residues, surpluses, or are produced on land not otherwise needed for food growing, or are not of higher value under natural or semi-natural vegetation;

- use of methane emitted from landfill sites for energy generation or heating;

- investment in research into possible future fuel systems, e.g. based on hydrogen;

- continued pursuit of a cautious policy regarding nuclear power, building to the highest safety standards and concentrating on safe and efficient operation of stations. Finding ways of securely disposing of intermediate and high-level wastes should not be longer delayed. Meanwhile, governments of countries with nuclear power stations should ratify the international conventions on Early Notification of a Nuclear Accident and on Assistance in the case of a Nuclear Accident or Radiological Emergency.

Action 10.4.   Use energy more efficiently in the home, industry, business premises and transport.

There is immense scope for saving energy and money through greater efficiency. This is especially true in homes, offices and business premises, and it is a process to which millions of people can contribute. In many countries about half the commercial energy supplied is used to heat the spaces in which people live and work. Such heating is often highly inefficient. Insulation standards are poor, as are controls that ensure that heat and light are supplied only when people need them. It has been calculated that increasing energy efficiency alone could reduce carbon dioxide emissions in several high-income countries by between 1% and 2% per annum. On this basis the United States could readily cut its emissions by 60% by the year 2050.

Governments should:

- establish, publish and enforce standards for energy efficiency in industry, space heating, building construction and transport;

- use charging and pricing systems to achieve improved standards of efficiency. Not only should energy prices reflect the full social and resource cost of the product, but charges should also be used as an incentive for saving energy. This would mean that a larger share of the earth's capacity to disperse carbon dioxide and other energy-related emissions could be freed to facilitate safe development in the industrializing countries;

- encourage the development and rapid introduction in lower-income countries of more efficient cooking stoves. Those that substitute kerosene, liquid petroleum gas or electricity for fuelwood or charcoal can perform as well using only 30% of the energy and avoiding the environmental degradation caused by excessive use of fuelwood. To achieve this substitution, assistance may be needed to make the higher quality fuels available to the poor;

- set performance standards for transport, covering energy use and pollution, including noise, and use fuel taxes to stimulate the development of energy-efficient vehicles and aircraft. Doubling the fuel efficiency of cars to an average of 21 km per litre would halve the amount of carbon dioxide (about 500 million tonnes) that the world's 400 million cars emit to the atmosphere annually. This performance standard could already be met, and could be doubled in future (see Action 12.3);

- ensure that transport modes are charged their full cost to the community. If road vehicles were charged at a rate proportionate to their impact on road surfaces (which rises steeply with the weight carried on each axle) there might well be radical changes in the distribution of freight between road and rail, and much greater energy efficiency (see Action 12.3);

- require all government and other public premises, including schools and hospitals, to carry out energy efficiency audits identifying where significant savings can be made, and implementing the results. Similar audits should be carried out for all commercial and industrial premises;

- ensure that the energy efficiency of all electric appliances and vehicles is clearly stated on the product or in the sales details, under clearly specified test conditions (which should be realistically related to conditions of likely use).

Action 10.5.   **Conduct publicity campaigns to promote energy conservation and the sale of energy efficient products.**

Governments, citizens' groups and industry should promote energy conservation and efficiency:

- drawing attention to and explaining the energy efficiency information given on consumer products and in the sales details of vehicles and appliances, so that people understand them and can make informed choices;

- explaining the savings householders can make through insulation and other energy saving practices in the home;

- explaining and demonstrating how energy efficiency audits should be carried out in offices, schools, hospitals, factories and other places;

- explaining to owners of office premises, and to schools, hospitals and industry the gains to be secured through more efficient use of energy, including timing controls on heating and lighting;

- explaining the reasons why energy prices are being raised, and publicizing how those most disadvantaged and in need can get help;

- including energy information prominently in "green consumer guides" (see Action 5.5), and encouraging the nongovernmental environment movement to keep energy issues prominently in the public eye;

- devising award schemes that give prominence to new energy conserving devices, and rewarding companies or groups whose performance has been outstanding.

The information campaigns should include all media, should extend into environmental education in schools (see Action 6.2), and include demonstrations of successful practice.

11. Business, industry and commerce

Many firms have recognized that caring for the environment is good business. This is not just a matter of public relations. Energy efficiency, waste reduction, and pollution prevention can increase profits. So can more resource-efficient technologies and processes, and employees who take pride in their work and their company. These factors are important in both upper-income and lower-income countries.

The lower-income countries must expand their industry to escape from acute poverty and achieve sustainability. Three quarters of the world is under-industrialized, and will need to strengthen its industries in the next 30 years. But this development must follow a different pattern from that which has blighted the environment and imposed heavy social costs in many areas of upper-income countries. Industrialization is already causing serious damage in some parts of the developing world — such as eastern China. This damage must be put right where it has happened, and avoided elsewhere.

Responsibility for ensuring clean industrialization is divided between governments, as regulators and managers of economic policy, environmental experts as the people who know most about the carrying capacity and resilience of the Earth, and industry itself, as the principal source of technological knowledge. New technology will be needed to clean up the mistakes of the past, and achieve new industrial growth without disaster. It will be largely invented by industry. New industrial development will need financing — and that will come largely from business and commerce. Protection against risks will be needed — by government, as regulators, and by the insurance industry. Terms of trade will need to be reformed so that markets may be opened for new products from the developing world.

Businesses must make the ethic for living sustainably an integral part of their corporate goal, taking care that their practices, processes, and products conserve energy and resources and have a minimum impact on ecosystems. Industries that are based on natural resources, like minerals, timber, fibre, and foodstuffs, or depend on environmental quality as tourism does, have a special responsibility.

This means:

- adopting **practices** that build concern for the Earth into the whole apparatus of business, industry and commerce, from plan to realization; that avoid damage, monitor impacts, and require consultation with local communities and the public at large;
- introducing **processes** that minimize the use of raw materials and energy, reduce waste, and prevent pollution;
- making **products** that are "environment-friendly", with minimum impact on people and the Earth.

As societies commit themselves to sustainability, practices that are now limited to a few far-seeing companies will become universal. The inclusion of environmental impact assessment in the planning of company policy, the regular conduct of environmental audits of company activities, and the recognition of environmental performance as a factor affecting senior executives' salaries are likely to be among these. Successful companies will maintain their freedom of manoeuvre by constantly innovating and improving their social and environmental performance.

The usefulness of the Polluter Pays Principle, the User Pays Principle and the Precautionary Principle has already been emphasized. The sooner they are adopted, the better the public interest and the interests of business will be served. Such action will be likely to lead to:

- continuing development of processes which are "closed", in the sense that they do not produce any wastes other than simple materials like water or inert mineral residues;
- higher standards in the waste disposal industry;
- more rigorous screening of the 1000-2000 new chemical products which are added each year to the estimated 70,000-80,000 substances already on the market. Even tighter screening must be demanded for the new products and genetically-altered micro-organisms, being developed in the biotechnology industry;
- much higher standards of landscaping during extraction by the minerals industry, stringent action to prevent dust-blow and water pollution, a more careful husbandry of minerals deposits, and very high standards of site restoration after extraction, guaranteed by bonds deposited by the firms concerned before extraction begins;
- dialogue between industry, government and the environmental movement to define good practice from an environmental standpoint, and to deter companies that may seek to externalize costs and undercut those who behave responsibly.

Many of the new technologies and processes will be perfected in the higher-income countries. International assistance must be provided to transfer them to the lower-income countries. Research to help industries in the latter countries to develop approaches suited to their environmental, economic and social conditions should be supported. Such support should continue in parallel with investment to restore the devastated environment of areas like those found in central and eastern Europe, and to improve the environmental performance of industries in the higher-income countries.

Attention should not be focussed on manufacturing alone. Activities of the service industries, the financial sector, and the tourist industry also have important relationships with the environment and natural resources.

Tourism is the world's largest civilian industry and is of great significance in the economic development of lower-income countries. It both depends on and affects cultural and natural diversity, including resources used and managed by agriculture, forestry, the water industry, the authorities responsible for protected areas, and urban development agencies. For tourism to develop sustainably, conservation and development must be integrated, and many different sectors and interests must be coordinated.

Priority actions

Industry, business and commerce must play a key part in the development of sustainable societies. Action is needed to:

- bring governments, the business sector and the environmental movement into a new dialogue;
- commit businesses to sustainability and environmental excellence, expressed in high performance standards and advanced by economic incentives;
- build public confidence in industry by thorough discussion of objectives, processes, products and practices and open disclosure of the results of monitoring. Commercial

confidentiality must be respected, but should not be used as an excuse to frustrate the release of information that is in the public interest.

Action 11.1	Promote sustainability through dialogue between industry, government, and the environmental movement.

Improving the environmental performance of the industrial sector is the joint responsibility of business and government, but both need to draw upon the expertise of environmental organizations. Government and industry should cooperate to:

- establish national, sector-by-sector discussion of the ecological context within which industry operates to facilitate the development of appropriate practices, processes and products (see Boxes 8 and 19);
- consult regional or local communities on the pattern of industrialization that best suits their circumstances (see Action 7.3). This can help avoid NIMBY (Not In My Back Yard) reactions in a local community that learns late in the day that an industry plans to locate a potentially hazardous development within its area;
- set goals for new technical development that will reduce pressure on the environment;
- agree on the best economic and regulatory framework for such new development, and on how to promote public understanding of the rationale behind new regulations and economic instruments such as taxes and charges;
- agree on the monitoring and environmental audit procedures to be followed, and on the information to be made available to the public.

Action 11.2.	Adopt high environmental performance standards backed up by economic incentives.

Governments should establish and enforce national (and, where appropriate, international) environmental goals, laws, regulations, incentives, and standards, concerning:

- occupational health and safety of workers;
- energy-efficiency, materials-efficiency, and water-efficiency of practices, processes, and products;
- an integrated approach to pollution prevention and control;
- control over the manufacture, marketing, use, transport, and disposal of toxic substances.

Allowing businesses to choose how they meet standards promotes efficiency and innovation. Regulations should therefore leave industry freedom in this respect.

In setting standards, regulatory authorities should seek the best practicable environmental option, reviewing the effects on air, water, and other media and minimizing the risk to the environment as a whole. In accordance with the Precautionary Principle, they should specify limits to the emission of hazardous substances which are as stringent as the best available technology can provide, and should consider setting even tighter standards to enter into force at a specified future date, so as to stimulate technological advance. The aim of the regulatory process should be to retain potentially hazardous substances within the factory fence. Standards should be calculated so that any permitted emissions will not harm human health or sensitive ecosystems (whichever is the more vulnerable to the pollutant), and should include a safety margin for uncertainty. Research on the concentrations of pollutants ("critical loads") that ecosystems can tolerate should be supported.

Regulatory authorities should continually revise standards in the light of technical advance. They should ensure that new industries and plants employ the best technology available, and that existing plants are up-graded as necessary and practicable. They should require that all emissions to the environment are monitored, and that the records are open to public inspection.

Governments should review existing economic incentives to industry and business, and ensure that they promote conservation of energy, materials and water and minimize pollution and waste. They should remove incentives that conflict with these objectives (see also Action 8.8 and Box 13). They should require that all proposed new industrial development is subject to Environmental Impact Assessment, and that all existing industrial activities, including the production and consumption of goods and services, are subject to environmental audit. These assessments and audits should be open to public inspection.

Action 11.3.   Commit each business to sustainability and environmental excellence.

Industry favours self-regulation. This is desirable in principle, but the environmental record of many sectors of industry needs to improve before public confidence can be assured. The more businesses show that they are committed to high standards of environmental performance, the more government's role can be limited to the definition of standards, provision of appropriate economic incentives and to monitoring, with enforcement as a last resort.

Commitment to sustainability calls for the following steps:

- develop and publish a corporate environmental policy, adopted by the company's board of directors;

- prepare an action programme to define objectives for all personnel, with guidelines on how they should be met;

- make a member of the company's board, preferably the Chief Executive Officer, responsible for environmental policy, and provide adequate professional support;

Box 18. Guidelines for sustainable industrial processes

- Use low- and non-waste technologies and transform as much as possible of the materials used into marketable products.
- Increase the useful life of products.
- Upgrade used products.
- Recover components and recycle materials when products cease to be useful.
- Use toxic chemicals only as a last resort, and if no safer alternatives can be found.
- Practise a cradle-to-grave approach to integrated waste management.
- See Box 19 for benefits of preventing pollution.

- delegate responsibility to individual line managers for ensuring that individual plants or processes are environmentally acceptable;
- make success in meeting health, safety and environmental targets an important factor in pay and promotion;
- introduce programmes of environmental education and training so that managers and others know what is expected of them, why, and how to do it;
- review progress with the environmental action plan regularly, giving praise and reward for outstanding achievement;
- invest in research and development so as to improve the company's ability to prevent pollution, reduce waste, and facilitate recycling;
- undertake business and product lifecycle analysis as an aid to improving the environmental acceptability of the production process, and to choosing new products;
- monitor emissions and environmental quality to check that the companies' controls are effective;
- institute environmental and safety audits. These could be of two kinds: a basic audit to confirm compliance with regulations, perhaps undertaken by external auditors as financial audits are; and a voluntary and confidential assessment for internal purposes only;
- help society's progress toward sustainability by becoming more involved with governmental and nongovernmental efforts outside the industry, for example by contributing expertise to the discussion of local and national objectives, and by participating actively in the dialogue under Action 11.1;
- help with technical assistance and technology transfer. A company should also help its customers to use its products in the safest and most efficient manner;
- ensure that uniformly high standards are maintained throughout the company's operations, and that technology that is not environmentally acceptable is eliminated everywhere;
- provide the lower-income countries in which the company operates with full information on the resource and environmental problems of the industry, on risks associated with processes and products, and on standards and other measures to protect health and ensure sustainability;
- become more involved in development assistance programmes, for example by contributing personnel to help industry in lower-income countries meet standards, through training seminars, and so on. Companies should help international trade associations and labour unions to develop and provide environmental training programmes adapted to the conditions of each lower-income country.

Action 11.4.   **Identify hazardous industries, and locate and operate them with stringent safeguards.**

Governments, industry and citizens' groups should cooperate to compile a list of hazardous industries; and establish strict procedures for their siting and operation.

Each jurisdiction should insist on state-of-the-art environmental protection procedures, ensuring that the action to take in an environmental emergency is widely known in the community. All employees should be thoroughly trained. Safeguards need to be greater in areas subject to natural hazards such as earthquakes.

Governments should adopt "community right-to-know" laws that require an industry to report to the local authorities and emergency services any significant quantities of hazardous substances held on its premises. Hazardous goods should be clearly labelled when transported. Emergency services should be told about the properties of and risks from such substances, and what to do if there is an accident. This information should also be available to members of the public.

Governments should cooperate regionally to prevent industrial accidents that could have an impact across national frontiers, and to deal with such accidents if they happen. All States should adopt the Basel Convention on the Control of Transboundary Movements of Hazardous Wastes and Their Disposal and other international agreements in this field (see Action 9.1).

Action 11.5.   **Develop effective national and international systems for waste management.**

All governments should ensure that they have effective national legislation on waste management and the labelling, packaging, marketing, and disposal of hazardous substances.

An integrated approach to waste management is needed. New technology should minimize the production of hazardous wastes.

New and safer substitutes for toxic chemicals should be sought continually. Governments should:

- ensure that no new substances are placed on the market until their health and environmental impacts have been thoroughly screened by an independent expert body;
- reach international agreement on procedures for such screening, and the exchange and publication of the results;
- regulate international trade in hazardous substances, including requirements for prior notification and information exchange;
- uphold the Convention on Civil Liability for Damages Caused during Carriage of Dangerous Goods by Road, Rail and Inland Navigation Vessels (UN/ECE), the Basel Convention, the London Convention on the Prevention of Marine Pollution by the Dumping of Wastes and other Matter, and other international legal instruments governing the transport of wastes and their disposal at sea. Improvements to these international legal instruments should be sought, and help given to developing countries in establishing the facilities they require.

Action 11.6   **Ensure that all industries that are based on the use of natural resources use them economically.**

The minerals industry faces a particular challenge. Minimizing the depletion of non-renewable resources demands that they not be used wastefully, and this implies that extraction rates should be slowed and reserves conserved for the future. Such action is difficult in a competitive market system. The industry should enter into dialogue with governments and develop operational plans that serve long-term as well as short-term interests.

Industries that use the products of forestry, agriculture, fisheries, or that depend as tourism does on the non-consumptive use of natural resources, have a special responsibility to care for their resource base. Already, supplies of tropical timber are threatened by the failure of governments and industry to harvest tropical forests sustainably. The whaling industry destroyed itself by mismanagement. The international ivory trade has been halted because of weak controls and widespread illegality. Industries concerned should:

- monitor the impact of their industry on the resource base and adjust harvests where this is clearly necessary (see Action 4.13);

- work with governments and conservation groups to develop plans and methods for the sustainable use of the resources on which they depend. In particular, the timber industry should co-operate with the International Tropical Timber Organization (ITTO) and with IUCN and governments to prepare management guidelines for sustainable use and adopt a system which will allow timber produced from sustainably managed forests to be identified and favoured on world markets;

- abandon methods of harvesting which are indiscriminate, damaging to the resource, or cruel. The fishing industry should regulate the use of drift nets in accordance with United Nations Resolution 44/225 and progressively phase them out in favour of less destructive implements. The fur industry should replace inhumane traps by more humane ones, following the norms of the International Organization for Standardization;

Box 19. Benefits of preventing pollution

An evaluation of 500 industrial case studies shows that the benefits for companies that reduce waste and prevent pollution can include:

- Lower costs of raw materials;
- lower energy costs;
- lower waste disposal costs and reduced dependency on waste treatment and disposal facilities;
- reduced or no future liability for clean-up of, or contamination by, buried wastes;
- fewer and lesser regulatory complications;
- lower operational and maintenance costs;
- lower employee, public, and environmental risks and expenses, both present and future;
- reduced liability insurance costs;
- better employee morale, productivity, and product quality.

In the 500 cases, wastes were reduced by 85% to 100%. The payback periods ranged from three years to one month. The firms involved include old industries and new high-tech enterprises. The methods used included: incorporation of in-line technologies, and process modifications (in which the previously used substance is replaced with a new, less polluting substance).

The technologies for some of the changes were readily available, others were newly developed proprietary processes. Some companies that developed new processes have gone on to patent them and sell or lease them to others. Thus they solved their own problems and developed a new product at the same time.

Not all waste streams can be easily reduced with current technologies; some will require intensive research to develop less polluting processes.

- discuss with communities, especially of indigenous peoples, in the areas of their operations how to prevent damage to local interests and traditional ways of life (see Action 7.3 and Box 11);

- give support, including financial backing, to international and national agreements and organizations that protect the resource base, and promote research that will allow its sustainable use.

The biotechnology industry is a special case. It is new, rapidly growing, and uses genetic material in novel ways. An international agreement is needed to establish how biotechnologies and their products should be screened for safety and environmental acceptability; to protect the interests of countries conserving the biodiversity that provides the raw materials for biotechnology; and to help lower-income countries to develop sustainable biotechnology industries. This agreement could be based on the Code of Conduct for Biotechnology, drafted by FAO at the request of the Commission on Plant Genetic Resources (see also Action 13.9).

The tourist industry is another special case. It is non-extractive: that is, it does not harvest nature, but it and its infrastructure of hotels, transport and other facilities can none the less have a major impact on the environment. Governments, conservation organizations and the industry should work together to:

- Ensure that tourism is planned and regulated so as to control its impact on nature and maintain its resource base. Developments should be subject to environmental impact assessment, and companies should undertake environmental audits. Planning for tourism must be integrated with other land uses, especially in protected areas.

- Control tourism's impact on people. Tourism's corrosion of cultures is widespread and probably unavoidable. What is avoidable is that it occurs without people's consent. The people affected by tourism must be involved in decisions on developments and able to modify proposals and to block those they see as inimical to their life-style and environment. Local communities should take decisions, and participate actively in the tourist industry, so that they derive economic benefit.

- Ensure that tourism's importance as an industry is recognized when decisions are taken about national resource use. At present, resource extraction industries (like mining) tend to be given priority. Tourism's vital stake in natural and cultural heritage is often overlooked by government and insufficiently defended by the industry itself. If managed correctly, tourism in protected areas may become a very effective instrument and source of finance for conservation.

- Balance the various subsectors of tourism (for example, ski resorts and wilderness experience) to prevent environmental damage, locate the right development in the right place, and increase the economic viability of both the industry and the local communities it works among.

- Educate tourists and operators on their responsibilities towards the environment, and raise awareness of natural beauty and the imperative for its conservation.

12. Human settlements

Humans are a social species. Throughout known history, people have lived together in groups, often linked by ties of kinship. The commonest human settlement is the village — a cluster of dwellings housing between 100 and 10,000 people, often flanked by areas of cultivation and pasture. In India in 1980, there were some 580,000 settlements, of which 575,000 were rural, and 98% of these were villages with less than 5,000 inhabitants.

While most people still live in rural areas, the proportion of urban dwellers is rising fast. Job shortages and lack of access to land in rural areas and the provision of better education and public services combined with greater opportunities for employment have led increasing numbers of people to move to the cities. Their influx, added to rapid increase in the numbers of people already living there, has made the world's city dwellers the fastest growing sector of human populations.

In 1950 only about 725 million people lived in urban settlements. By 1970 the total had reached 1350 million and UN estimates and projections set the figure at 2400 million in 1990 and 3200 million in 2000. On that basis, half of humanity will live in cities by the end of the century.

The size of cities is also growing, especially in lower-income countries. In 1950 there was only one city outside the high-income countries with over 4 million inhabitants — greater Buenos Aires. By 1980 there were 22 cities in the lower-income countries with more than 4 million people each, compared with 16 in the higher-income countries. For the year 2000 the totals are estimated at 61 and 25 respectively. And the rates of growth are striking: throughout the 1970s Mexico City and Sao Paulo each added half a million people each year, and Jakarta and Cairo grew at half that rate. The trend towards an increasingly urban population is likely to continue since it is caused by long-term structural changes in the global economy.

In most high-income countries the growth of major centres is now slowing, but areas of countryside are being urbanized. A similar phenomenon is occurring around many of the more dynamic cities in Asia and Latin America, as nonagricultural industries and service enterprises develop in rural areas. By contrast, many African cities are adopting characteristics of the countryside as more and more lower- and even middle-income groups grow part of their own food in or close to the city, due to the scarcity of jobs and inadequacy of incomes.

Cities generate and accumulate wealth, and are the main centres for education, new jobs, innovation, culture, and greater economic opportunity. But they are immense consumers of natural resources. Even though planning could prevent it, they sprawl over and sterilize land. They require enormous quantities of water, energy, foodstuffs and raw materials. They generate pollution which contaminates water, air and soil far beyond their boundaries. Thus many rural environmental problems are inextricably linked to urban demands.

The anatomy of a city is fundamental to its functioning. Transport systems link the various quarters, and join city to city. Their smooth working is essential if goods are to be moved and people to travel efficiently. Unfortunately, virtually all major cities were laid out before motor vehicles became common, and their road systems are often inadequate for present needs. In fact, many cities are grinding to a halt because of urban congestion, while noise and pollution endanger health and erode the quality of life. Hydrocarbons and nitrogen oxides, emitted by gasoline-powered cars, react in sunlight to create an acrid oxidant smog that is a hazard to human health and damages vegetation. Badly-adjusted diesel and two-stroke engines emit smoke and potential carcinogens. Where lead is still added to petrol, this provides a further health hazard. Air pollution is particularly bad in cities because of their high traffic densities, low traffic speeds, and the trapping of pollution between high buildings. Slow-moving urban traffic also wastes energy. Inter-city traffic is also imposing a massive burden on highways designed for far lighter loads than they must now bear.

Only a minority of cities have efficient, safe, clean and attractive public transport systems that people want to use. The installation of new rapid transit systems like metros and tramways is difficult and costly.

Despite being centres of industry and commerce, many cities display extreme poverty and environmental degradation. In high-income countries, as older industrial towns decline and inner city districts decay, the less educated, the poor and the elderly find themselves trapped and sometimes homeless in places where services are disappearing and crime rates are high. Ethnic minorities, immigrants, and the disabled suffer disproportionately, the victims of a growing equity gap.

In lower-income countries, the proportion of urban inhabitants suffering from poverty and environmental degradation is much greater than in high-income countries. Lack of effective policies for the sustainable development of rural economies forces young people to abandon the countryside and move to the city. It is common for half or more of a city population to live in overcrowded inner city tenements or illegal settlements. For most, water supply, sanitation, garbage collection, and access to health care are grossly inadequate. The environments in which they live are the most life-threatening in the world.

These problems are due more to failures of government at all levels than to rapid population growth. The failures of governments are not merely administrative, however: in many cases they also reflect historical and political influences. Much urban growth has outstripped the capabilities of municipal governments because national governments do not give them sufficient authority to raise revenues and manage their affairs. Government structures remain centralized, but because each city is unique its management and development decisions should reflect a high degree of local involvement. In lower-income countries many urban governments, especially in capital cities, are not elected, yet (as Chapter 7 emphasizes) representative government is perhaps the only check against neglect of the needs of poorer citizens.

Sustainable urban development depends on new partnerships of local people, citizens' groups, businesses and governments. Development plans must be equitable, sustainable, practical, sensitive to local norms and cultures and welcome to the people concerned. Citizens, politicians, urban managers and professionals should be trained to work within such a framework. The Global Strategy for Shelter to the Year 2000 provides guidelines for the required national and international action.

Cities can provide high-quality living for all their inhabitants at sustainable levels of consumption. The poverty suffered by the minority of urban dwellers in richer nations and the majority in poorer nations can be drastically reduced without a large expansion in consumption. In both instances, more effective and representative local governments, and more far-sighted national governments are required.

Priority actions

Sustainable urban development is only possible when local governments are given adequate powers, and develop effective capabilities. They need to manage change in the context of an ecological approach so that cities can support more productive, stable and innovative economies while maintaining a high-quality environment, proper services for all sectors of the community, and sustainable resource use. These conditions are most likely to be met if all interest groups participate, and if government is active, decentralized, representative, and supportive of citizen efforts.

Action 12.1. Adopt and implement an ecological approach to human settlements planning.

Communities need to adopt and implement an ecological approach to human settlements planning to ensure explicit embodiment of environmental concerns in the planning process and thus promote sustainability. This will entail:

- the planning and management of human settlements to satisfy the physical, social and other needs of their inhabitants on a sustainable basis by maintaining the balance of the ecosystems of which the settlement is an integral part;
- harmonious combination of human-produced and natural elements to provide the habitat within which urban dwellers seek their well-being.

A strategy for sustainability based on an ecological approach can be expected to:

- improve and ensure water supplies;
- minimize the problem of disposal of waste;
- reduce the diversion of high-quality land from agriculture and help maintain the productivity of land;
- develop more energy-conserving patterns of living and production of goods;
- maximize the use of available resources;
- integrate settlement maintenance and services with employment, community development and education.

Action 12.2. Develop more effective and representative local governments, committed to caring for their environments.

As called for in Action 7.4, local governments need to be able to:

- provide essential infrastructure and services, especially health care, family planning services, emergency protection, safe and efficient public transport, traffic management, water supply, sewerage and solid waste collection and disposal;
- establish legislation, regulatory systems and local offices that meet citizens' needs for guidance and support and protect them from exploitation by landlords, employers and speculators;
- encourage and support the establishment by local or national citizens' groups of neighbourhood centres to advise people on health care, hygiene, family planning, self-help housing, efficient use of energy, water and materials, and other important tasks.

Using these powers and frameworks, municipal administrations should address major problems, especially:

- illegal settlements, by giving people secure titles to land and progressive access to basic services provided by public authorities (see Box 20);

- housing shortages by encouraging people to participate in self-help housing schemes, and helping them to obtain, at affordable cost, resources such as sites, materials and credit so that they can build or improve their housing within the framework of services provided by local authorities (see Action 7.6);

- pollution, by ensuring that laws and regulations are enforced, and that industries, utilities and transport services are charged for the use of the infrastructure from which they benefit, for their impact on the environment and their use of environmental resources (see Chapter 4).

The authorities should ensure that local taxes and tariffs charge businesses and, where practicable households and individuals, the price of the infrastructure from which they benefit.

They should promote balanced development by applying development control laws stringently, implementing local plans that have been developed through wide community participation. These plans must ensure that the city's expansion avoids prime farmland and wildlife habitat. Provision needs to be made for urban parks, squares and children's play areas. Plans should also broaden the economic base by encouraging new sustainable activities that will create employment and income.

Box 20. Illegal settlements

A successful strategy for dealing with illegal urban settlements is to:

- legalize them, arranging fair compensation for owners;
- accept the inhabitants' way of building. Don't try to improve their houses. They will do that once their land is secure and they have basic services;
- provide water supply, sanitation, roads, other basic infrastructure and community facilities. This often motivates people to improve their own homes;
- identify "barefoot architects" individuals with get-up-and-go in the community to organize maintenance, help install water, electricity, sewer lines, advise on laying foundations, and so on.

Action 12.3. Develop an efficient and sustainable urban transport policy.

Most of the changes needed to reduce congestion, pollution and excessive use of energy in urban transport have already been proposed, and some have been tried out. To give people the benefit of better transport management, municipal authorities should:

- encourage a switch to public transport by providing swift, safe, clean and efficient services based on what people need. Concessionary fares to promote use of this transport should be considered, especially for the elderly and the lower-income groups;

- speed bus travel by providing segregated lanes, and also help cyclists by giving them separate, safe, routes;

- speed all road travel by establishing urban clearways on which parking, including for deliveries, is prohibited at peak periods;
- consider road pricing schemes and other devices that charge users of private vehicles the full social cost of their travel. Parking fees and taxes on parking provided at offices and factories are another means of charging road vehicles for the services they use;
- establish pedestrian areas, especially in historic city centres;
- when planning new urban regions, segregate pedestrian areas, cycleways, and access for road freight delivery, and try to cut distances between home and work. Prevent the use of residential areas as short cuts by through traffic. Good road design can greatly improve amenity and make cities cleaner and safer places;
- avoid creating satellite cities and dormitory developments that automatically increase the use of energy in transport.

Central governments and national transport enterprises should:

- provide swift and efficient inter-city public transport;
- ensure that each transport mode bears the full social cost of its operations. The economic instruments available include charges and taxes;
- impose standards for fuel use efficiency and pollution prevention that match what best current technology can attain, and use economic incentives to promote energy-efficient and non-polluting vehicles;
- set targets for the improvement of technology, including the development of vehicles that do not burn fossil fuels, and do not emit pollutants in urban streets. Electric-powered and hydrogen-powered vehicles could have advantages, if inexpensive, lightweight, high-energy density batteries and improved methods for generating and storing hydrogen can be developed.

Box 21. Moving information instead of people

Communication of information will be more and more important in future societies. Modern electronic communication, linking people and allowing swift and accurate transfer of information, may soon make many journeys unnecessary. City authorities, national governments, and telecommunications industries should collaborate to make the national communications networks as efficient as possible, thereby helping people to work from home, and reduce unnecessary travel.

Action 12.4.   Make the city clean, green and efficient.

City administrations should make municipal energy use sustainable, and improve the quality of the air, water, and urban amenities. They should ensure that local industry complies with national and local standards and regulations. Central governments should ensure that national legislative, regulatory and fiscal systems devolve enough power to local governments to allow them to implement the actions their citizens want.

Specifically, city administrations should:

- reclaim derelict land within their borders, using it for housing, public open space, food production or new industrial development;

- cooperate with local politicians, planners, businesses, and citizens' groups, to plan and create green spaces and green belts, including community forests and woodlands, as a means of ameliorating climate and providing food, amenity and habitats for plants and animals;

- promote municipal energy conservation strategies, encouraging and assisting citizens to implement the domestic policies described in Action 10.4;

- ensure that the city's own waste collection and disposal services measure up to the highest standards. Municipal governments, citizens' groups, and businesses should work together to develop and implement waste reduction and recycling plans;

- operate efficient waste water and sewage treatment processes, purifying the water for re-use, and processing sewage sludges for fertilizer;

- build partnerships with national and local citizens' groups. As Chapter 6 stressed, these groups have a key role in stimulating people to support more conserving, sustainable policies. City authorities should consult citizens' environmental groups and industry to forge common action for sustainable urban development. Such groups could have lead responsibility for public campaigns to promote the sustainable city.

Reclaiming waste

Many cities in lower-income countries are extremely efficient at conserving resources. Open spaces are used to grow food, and every item of household or business garbage that has some value is reclaimed. Such action is often driven by poverty: thousands of households survive on a meagre income from sitting through garbage at the local dump. However, in some cities, such as Shanghai, this reclamation is explicitly promoted by government policy. City authorities should foster the development of such resource-conserving activities and the employment they generate, while improving the economic returns to the people and addressing the health risks involved.

13. Farm and range lands

More people are hungry now than ever before, and their numbers are growing. Because too little food is produced where they live, or they are too poor to buy it, 950 million people in lower-income countries (excluding China) do not eat enough for an active working life. This is 19% of world population, an increase since 1980, when 16% of world population (730 million people) were not getting enough food.

Lack of food is most severe in sub-Saharan Africa and South Asia. Per capita food output in the former has been dropping at about 1% a year since the beginning of the 1970s. Agriculture in many lower-income countries has been sapped by a growing dependence on imported food, an emphasis on crops for export, inadequate provision for research and extension activities, and land degradation.

Fifteen percent of the Earth's total land surface is affected by human-induced processes of soil degradation. At least 66 million hectares of irrigated land, that is 30% of the total, are affected by secondary salinization. An estimated 6-7 million hectares of agricultural land is made unproductive each year because of erosion. This is more than twice the rate of the past three centuries. Waterlogging, salinization and alkalinization reduce the productivity of an additional 1.5 million hectares each year. Land degradation is widespread in the world's drylands, affecting 5.5 million hectares or almost 70% of their area and leading to an estimated annual loss of production worth US$42 billion. Almost 1 million hectares, much of it prime farmland in rain-fed areas, is being lost each year to urbanization.

Unsustainable pastoralism is one of the most intractable of the problems faced by dryland countries. Most efforts to introduce more productive breeds, reduce stocking densities, improve rangelands, and promote sustainable systems of water and range management have been unable to overcome traditional attitudes and practices. Degradation of grazing lands will be reversed only when livestock numbers are brought within the carrying capacity of the range, but there is strong resistance to reducing herds to sizes that the range can support. Yet the social and environmental circumstances which made much traditional pastoralism sustainable no longer exist, and sustainability demands adaptation of these systems.

Different problems exist in various areas where tropical forests have been cleared to create pastures. This process has often been encouraged by tax concessions, subsidies and granting land title to cleared areas. Loss of nutrients, erosion, and reduced water-retaining capacity combine to make many of these lands relatively unproductive and prone to further degradation. The economic incentives which drove this process in Brazil have recently been removed. Other tropical countries should follow suit.

In virtually all these regions, the increased production needed to feed increasing numbers of people must come largely through better use of the land already being farmed. Most "unused" land has little agricultural potential, because of poor soil or low rainfall. Such land is best used to maintain life-support systems and biological diversity and to provide timber, bushmeat, fuelwood, nuts and other wild resources.

In stark contrast, too much food is grown in much of Europe and North America. Such subsidized overproduction can be expensive economically and ecologically. It has reduced biological diversity, and the attractiveness of many rural landscapes. Subsidized disposal of surpluses allows food aid to areas afflicted by famine, but depresses markets for locally produced commodities, and undermines the potential for agricultural development in lower-income countries.

Other problems arise because the structure of world agriculture is changing. In high-income countries, family farms are being replaced by corporate holdings. In lower-income countries, programmes to increase agricultural production have concentrated where gains are likely to be easiest — among larger farms in relatively fertile and well watered valleys and plains. In both cases, the lot of the small farmer and the rural landless is likely to worsen unless steps are taken to provide them with viable alternatives.

Despite differences in the characteristics of farm and range lands and in agricultural practices throughout the world, there are a number of common factors. Most farmers have a sense of stewardship of the land. They understand that they must conserve the productivity of the soil, look after their water supplies, and control pests if they are to maintain their income and standard of living. They recognize the importance of maintaining the variety of their crops and livestock. They also need secure land tenure and a reasonable return on investment.

Priority actions

Action to promote sustainable agriculture is needed in both upper-income and lower-income countries. In all countries, there should be action to:

- prepare and implement strategies and plans to use agricultural land optimally;
- control the use of fertilizers and pesticides;
- conserve genetic resources;
- provide appropriate economic incentives and support.

In high-income countries, farms are being amalgamated and the economies of scale that this enlargement permits favour intensive (monocultural) agriculture, with associated questions of sustainability and impacts on biological diversity.

In the upper-income countries there is also a need to remove marginal land from intensive cropping and to eliminate excessive subsidies. In lower-income countries, priority should be given to increasing sustainable production on irrigated and rain-fed lands, increasing the self-reliance of small farmers on marginal lands, and developing new, sustainable techniques.

Strategies and plans to use farm and range lands sustainably

In many parts of the world, current farming practices are not sustainable. In many lower-income countries, agricultural productivity is hampered by poor logistical support and weak infrastructure. If food production is to be increased in a sustainable way, these deficiencies must be corrected and a favourable economic framework for agriculture established, Such actions need to be backed up by practices aimed at maintaining or enhancing fertility and productivity.

Soil and water management must be integrated so that both are conserved, conditions for root growth and crop production are improved, and environmental impacts are minimized.

The organic content of soils must be kept up. Loss of organic matter reduces the supply of nitrogen from native humus, decreases the soil's water-holding capacity, and increases its susceptibility to compaction and erosion. Fertilizers must then be applied to maintain yields. However, mineral fertilizers do not replace the biological and physical characteristics of organic matter. Nor do they necessarily replace all the essential plant nutrients.

Consequently, recycling organic matter is important in any farming system. There are many traditional ways of doing this, including using manure from livestock, composting, rotational cropping using species that fix atmospheric nitrogen, concentration of livestock to graze fodder crops and enrich the land with their dung, fallow systems, and multicropping. Such methods need to be maintained and improved, particularly in lower-income countries, where sustainable yields must not merely be maintained but increased.

Action 13.1.   Undertake a national strategy for sustainability.

Every country that needs to increase agricultural production should have a national strategy for sustainability (see Actions 17.7 and 8.2), supported by regional land use plans (see Chapter 8). A national strategy will provide a framework for planning the wide range of measures recommended in this strategy. In addition, it will be particularly important as an element in considering the effects of macroeconomic, pricing and trade policies on food production and the sustainable use of farm and range lands.

Action 13.2.   Protect the best farmland for agriculture.

In view of the scarcity of high quality arable land and the rising demand for food and other agricultural products, the land that is most suitable for crops should be reserved for agriculture. Governments should map and monitor the more productive areas of farmland and adopt planning and zoning policies to prevent the loss of prime land to urban settlements (Action 12.1). Local authorities and communities should ensure that these policies are implemented in their areas.

Uncultivated ecosystems with agricultural potential may have other values that are equally or more important. Such ecosystems include wetlands, floodplains, and areas rich in natural diversity. In countries with persistent or rising agricultural deficits, agriculture may have to be given precedence, provided the land has no serious limitations. Where it has, the potential costs and benefits of any conversion should be thoroughly assessed, and the successes after conversion, monitored. In countries with agricultural surpluses, conversion of such ecosystems to farmland will be hard to justify.

Action 13.3.   Promote effective soil and water conservation through proper land husbandry.

The primary objective of land management should be improved, but sustainable, production through good husbandry. Soil and water must be conserved, and conditions for root growth and crop production improved.

It is easier to promote soil and water conservation if farmers can benefit directly and quickly by obtaining increased yields of the crops they grow. As it happens, some ways of improving yields can also conserve water and soil. Increasing the photosynthetic leaf area and root systems — necessary to increase yields — also helps to protect the soil surface, increase infiltration of water, and reduce runoff, and can improve the regularity of streamflow.

The principles of good husbandry are:

Respect land capability. Land should be used for the purposes and crops to which it is best suited.

Conserve soil. Good practices include improving organic matter, soil structure, and crop cover; crop rotations; and the proper use of fertilizers. Maintaining soil productivity is as important as curbing erosion. Most soils have an inherent capacity for recovery after they have become degraded, and this depends especially on biological activity in the upper layers, and hence on maintaining organic matter and processes there. Farmers are most likely to give priority to soil improvement if the benefits are explained in terms of better water management and crop production.

Manage rainwater. This is the key to production and soil conservation. Plant yields are reduced more by a shortage or excess of soil moisture than they are by loss of soil. If rainfall, soil moisture, and runoff are managed well, plant growth can be maximized and the soil will remain in place.

Reduce runoff before attempting to control its flow. Reducing raindrop impact and runoff reduces selective removal of the more fertile soil fractions, maintains infiltration, and prevents the smoothing of rough soil surfaces. Efforts to reduce runoff and maintain infiltration should cover the entire catchment area, starting with the highest land.

Maintain plant cover. On cropped land, a protective mulch of leaves, litter and crop residues is the most effective biological means of minimizing soil and water losses. The more erosion-prone an area, the more urgent it is to produce, improve and maintain dense and long-lasting cover with useful plants and their residues. Terraces and other physical conservation works are valuable. But, since they simply diminish runoff rather than protect the soil from rainfall damage, they are seldom enough and may not be the first priority.

Promote cooperation between technical staff and local communities. Locally developed schemes are far more likely to succeed and last than those based on top-down planning. Few lower-income countries have effective services that work with farmers rather than tell them what to do.

Adopt practices that will both increase yields and conserve water and soil. Farmers could be offered financial assistance to cover some of the costs of conservation tillage, residue management, shelterbelts, grassed waterways, small water retention structures, soil improvement crops, and protection of highly erosive lands with permanent cover crops of forages or trees. Seedlings of trees and shrubs for shelterbelts could be provided, along with assistance in designing plantings and advice on maintenance. Seed to establish permanent cover on erosion prone lands could be provided at subsidized rates.

Action 13.4. Reduce the impact of agriculture on marginal lands already in production.

In both high- and low-income countries, there are significant areas of cultivated land and pasture that are not best suited to those uses. In high-income countries such areas should be restored to woodland or wildlife habitat. In lower-income countries this is unlikely to be practicable as many people who lack other opportunities for employment live in these areas. The solution here is likely to be the adoption of low-impact production systems, and especially those generally termed agroforestry.

Box 22. Agroforestry

Agroforestry systems include trees as a main component in a multi-crop production process. The trees protect the soil from raindrop impact and insolation. Some tree species fix atmospheric nitrogen and enrich the soil, while deep-rooted trees prevent nutrient loss from the system and draw nutrients to the surface. The interaction between the trees and other components of the system leads to good soil protection and the conservation of water and nutrients. In that sense, agroforestry systems behave rather like natural multi-layered ecosystems. The drawback is that the production of the associated crops is generally less than in monoculture systems.

The main types of agroforestry system are:
- alley cropping, where annual crops are grown between lines of trees that produce valuable mulching material;
- mixed growth of permanent crops like coffee or cacao between timber trees;
- growth of crops in fields sheltered by tree windbreaks or hedges;
- orchard systems, where the trees provide edible fruits, medicines and fuelwood, while the ground layer is cropped or grazed;
- growth of scattered trees in pasture land, to improve soil conservation and provide shade, timber or fuelwood;
- plantation systems where the ground layer is grazed by livestock;
- shifting cultivation systems, where small tilled plots are allowed to revert to forest after a number of years of cropping.

Agroforestry should be considered in all formerly forested marginal land that is now managed for production, regardless of whether the systems are in high-or low-rainfall areas, or at low or high elevation. Agroforestry systems restore tree cover to cleared land but they are not substitutes for forests, which are often more effective in maintaining environmental functions and conserving biological diversity, and may also provide a more sustainable source of income.

Action 13.5. **Encourage the adoption of integrated crop and livestock farming systems, and raise the efficiency of fertilizer use.**

Low-input mixed farming systems generally involve the integration of crop and livestock production, and can involve aquaculture as well. They were traditional in many areas that are now used for intensive crop-growing, and can still play a key role where artificial mineral fertilizers are either not available, cost too much to transport, or provide too low a return. A central feature is the collection and use of biological wastes as fertilizer (in China 50-60% of such wastes are used in this way). However, countries with high populations relative to the area of good agricultural land have to achieve high yields to attain food self-sufficiency, and this generally demands the use of synthetic as well as organic fertilizer. In China almost three-quarters of the nitrogen input now comes from synthetic chemicals.

Animals are a valuable component of many sustainable farming systems, providing food, income, and power; converting crop residues into marketable products; and recycling nutrients. Separating livestock and crop production turns animal wastes from a beneficial fertilizer into a costly pollutant.

Integrated systems have yet to gain — or regain — social acceptance in many areas suited to them, and it may take many years to change community attitudes. In addition, population pressures in some areas have already resulted in farms that are too small to maintain enough livestock. Stallfeeding is a valuable option, but still requires land to grow the feed. Most low-input systems are labour-intensive, and lack of labour is a constraint, particularly for female-headed households and in sub-Saharan Africa.

Governments and farmers should work together to re-integrate crop and livestock production in ways most appropriate to particular areas. Small farmers should be consulted in setting research priorities and involved in testing the methods and technologies that research recommends. They have a wide and detailed knowledge of their agricultural environment, of methods and technologies that work (and of those that do not), of local crop varieties and livestock breeds, and of the other plants and animals with which they interact. Researchers who use this knowledge are more likely to produce useful results. Also, the small farmers are the ones who will have to implement the results of research: if it does not work for them, it will not work at all.

Action 13.6. Increase the productivity and sustainability of rainfed farming.

This is particularly needed in dryland areas to reduce pressure to cultivate marginal lands. Rainfed farming can be improved by:

- soil and water conservation, including water harvesting and integration with aquaculture;
- developing improved cultivars, and a local seed industry to produce and distribute them;
- using improved cultivars to restore and improve traditional cropping systems;
- increasing the use of fertilizers, particularly those necessary to correct nutrient deficiencies.

Improved strains of staple crops enable farmers to get higher yields under average rainfall conditions while retaining the drought resistance required to prevent crop failure in dry years.

Traditional dryland cropping systems such as four-year rotations of fallow, cowpea, millet, and peanut were sustainable because they took account of the great variability in rainfall typical of drylands. Growing two or more crops together gives bigger yields (50% in the case of millet and cowpea) and provides the farmer with insurance against crop failure. If improved cultivars give increased yields, the fallow period needed to maintain soil productivity can be restored (although in much of Africa restoring fallow is impracticable because of population pressure).

Using fertilizers can double the yields of conventional varieties of millet and maize and prevent the fertility of poor soils from being depleted by overcropping. Phosphate fertilizers are particularly valuable in the Sahel, where soils are generally deficient in phosphorus. However, because imported fertilizers are expensive they tend to be used in dryland areas only on cash crops, at least in Africa. In other areas, low input systems (see Action 13.5) including fallow systems and the use of fast-growing trees and shrubs to provide fodder and green manure offer most promise.

Water harvesting involves shaping farm land, and sometimes also its catchment area, to slow the flow of water and so increase infiltration into the soil. There are several cheap ways of marking out contours. In low or unreliable rainfall areas, water harvesting can boost yields by

20-50% in the year of introduction, produce crops in years when crops fail without it, and greatly reduce soil erosion. Water harvesting needs to be more widely used.

Control the use of pesticides and fertilizers

In lower-income countries, an estimated 10,000 people die each year from pesticide poisoning, and about 400,000 suffer acutely. Pesticide residues travel long distances and build up in the food chain, and thus affect people and other creatures far from the places where they are applied. Pesticides kill or injure large numbers of non-target organisms, including fish, birds, insects that pollinate crops, and animals that prey on the enemies of crops. Although modern pesticides have undoubtedly played an important part in raising both crop yields and product quality, they have also left many pest problems unsolved and created new ones. More than 500 species of insects and mites are now pesticide-resistant, almost triple the number in 1965.

Fertilizers have also played a major part in enhancing farmland productivity. On the other hand, their excessive use has also caused serious problems. Here, too, there is a need to strike a new balance.

Action 13.7.   **Promote integrated pest management.**

Integrated pest management (IPM) may include:

- biological controls — encouraging predators, parasites and pathogens;
- cultural controls — such as cutting or uprooting noxious weeds, crop rotation, crop diversification, and timing of planting and harvesting dates to avoid peak pest periods;
- use of resistant or tolerant cultivated varieties;
- use of microbial pesticides, pheromones (chemicals that attract insects), release of sterilized male pest insects so that matings are infertile, and chemical controls that use minimal quantities of selective and non-persistent insecticides and herbicides.

The aim is to keep pests below levels where they cause unacceptable economic damage, and to do so in an economically efficient and ecologically sound manner. Insecticides and herbicides have a role; but they should be specific and be used selectively in support of non-chemical means of control. The habitats of crop pollinators and the natural enemies of pests should be identified and preserved.

Non-native predators, parasites and pathogens can have a disastrous impact and should not be introduced until their potential effects on the native flora and fauna have been subject to a thorough environmental impact assessment and it is certain that they can be controlled.

Countries, industries, and trade and international institutions should comply with the FAO Code of Conduct on the Distribution and Use of Pesticides. The code should be translated into local languages, adapted for a variety of media (tapes, highly pictorial leaflets, and so on), and widely distributed among farmers and extension services.

Action 13.8.   **Control the use of fertilizers, pesticides and herbicides through regulations and incentives.**

The allowable levels of pollutants (including pesticide residues) in food and drinking water and the licensing, handling and application of pesticides must be controlled by regulations that are properly enforced and monitored. This task should be assigned to national environmental protection agencies.

Several high-income countries are defining the types of agricultural practices necessary to protect ecosystems, and requiring farmers to prepare management plans showing how these practices will be adopted. In Denmark, fertilizer plans are required. In the United States, under new conservation compliance provisions, farmers who crop highly erodible soils and wish to receive price support must prepare soil conservation plans. Such plans can simplify enforcement, but they are only a first step, can be expensive to administer, and require well developed institutions and infrastructure.

High-income countries should apply the User Pays Principle to agricultural inputs. Thus a tax on fertilizer has been proposed for the European Community to reduce surplus production and encourage less intensive and more sustainable use of the land. Experience in Sweden suggests that such charges can win political acceptance, if there is a commitment to the involvement of farmers in the allocation of the money collected, and a guarantee that it will be spent on activities to benefit agriculture.

Lower-income countries should remove or reduce subsidies for pesticides and herbicides to encourage their more careful use and the adoption of integrated pest management (IPM). Indonesia has saved $150 million a year by reducing its pesticide subsidy. The reduction was accompanied by the introduction of more pest resistant rice varieties and the promotion of IPM through the extension network. However, caution is needed. If plant nutrient levels in the soil are diminishing, fertilizers will have to be used to maintain or increase production and to produce the required organic matter. If the cost of fertilizers rises, farmers may need fertilizer subsidies or higher prices for their products.

In general, subsidies should be offered only for activities from which society benefits but for which there is no other mechanism for making society pay, such as improving the landscape and protecting or enhancing wildlife habitat, or for long-term objectives, such as maintenance of soil productivity. Subsidies are often provided as part of management agreements. To be effective, such agreements should:

- be carefully designed to achieve the desired environmental benefit;
- set payments so that they provide a modest incentive to adopt sustainable practices, rather than simply compensate for the expected reduction in net income caused by the changes in the farming practice required. The total social benefits resulting from these changes should be calculated, and shared with the farmers concerned;
- limit annual payments to reimbursement of the cost of required practices.

Conserve genetic resources

Genetic variability within species is essential for agricultural development, providing the raw material of domestication, plant and animal breeding, and biotechnology. Many crops and their wild relatives still await adequate conservation. Accelerated efforts to preserve threatened breeds must be pressed forward in parallel.

Action 13.9.   Promote international action to conserve genetic resources.

Current systems of intellectual property rights (IPRs) can promote development of new varieties and increase the availability of new genetic combinations. They can also reduce genetic diversity, particularly when standards of uniformity are imposed. The impact of extending patenting to genetic resources should be carefully assessed by GATT in consultation with a wide range of governmental and nongovernmental organizations. IPRs should not be extended to genetic resources in any way that conflicts with the principle, included in the International Undertaking on Plant Genetic Resources, that genetic resources are the common heritage of humanity.

The principle of "farmers' rights" recognizes that many anonymous farmers and communities have contributed, and continue to contribute, to the development of local and traditional varieties and to conservation of genetic resources. Neither IPRs nor the marketplace assign any value to these services. Two ways of honouring farmers' rights would be to:

- ensure that IPRs do not restrict access of farmers, communities or breeders to genetic resources; and do not reward individual or corporate breeders for the contributions of farmers and communities;

- establish a mandatory fund to support genetic conservation and development programmes, particularly but not exclusively in lower-income countries.

One option is to use the fund set up under the Undertaking on Plant Genetic Resources. Since animal genetic resources should also be covered, and to avoid proliferation of funds, another option is to include a "farmers' rights account" in the global fund proposed as part of the Universal Declaration and Covenant on Sustainability (see Action 9.4).

All countries should join the Commission on Plant Genetic Resources and adhere to the International Undertaking on Plant Genetic Resources.

Action 13.10. **Expand *ex situ* efforts to conserve genetic resources (see also Action 4.12).**

The main *ex situ* genetic resource conservation needs are set out below for crops, livestock and for crops and livestock together.

Crops

- Extend long-term protection to the crops that are poorly represented in long-term gene banks, and to their wild relatives.

- Establish national plant genetic resources systems. Fewer than 30% of countries have formal national plant genetic resource programmes. These national centres need to be linked internationally.

- Pay more attention to local crops and field surveys; and to evaluation, documentation, and use of material stored in genebanks.

Livestock

- Establish a World Watch system on indigenous livestock breeds to identify when valuable or unique breeds are threatened and to promote action; strengthen the Animal Genetic Resources Data Bank; and complete the system of Regional Animal Gene Banks (FAO).

- Prepare and maintain up-to-date lists of indigenous livestock breeds, with a genetic characterization of each breed. Include conservation of rare and threatened breeds in the financial provisions of livestock programmes.

- Formulate and fund practical programmes to identify, characterize, evaluate, and monitor genetic change in indigenous and threatened breeds. Participate in the Animal Genetic Resources Data Bank and Regional Animal Gene Banks.

Crops and livestock together

- Support grassroots associations of farmers and gardeners for the maintenance of traditional and local cultivars and breeds. Involve women's groups in such conservation; and record farmers' knowledge of traditional and local cultivars and breeds.

- Develop a common information service and make other arrangements for exchange of information and germplasm among grassroots, national and international agencies.

Germplasm collection in any country should receive explicit clearance in advance by the country concerned. It should be carried out under an acceptable ethical code; one is being worked out by the FAO Commission on Plant Genetic Resources. Collected material and information about the material should be shared with the country concerned.

Action 13.11.   Provide for *in situ* conservation of wild genetic resources (see also Action 4.12).

Wild genetic resources are increasingly being used to improve established crops and develop new ones, an economic contribution worth hundreds of millions of dollars annually. Their conservation is inadequate and cannot be achieved by *ex situ* means alone. *In situ* protection has been given to a few populations of a very limited number of timber species and relatives of crop and livestock species. The importance of such protection has rarely been considered when protected areas are established.

A network of gene conservation areas is essential to provide comprehensive *in situ* protection of populations of the major genetic variants of the wild relatives of plant and animal domesticates, and other important wild genetic resources. Protected areas should constitute parts of this network, whenever possible. Given the mounting competition for land, a complete and separate network of gene conservation areas is impractical.

Therefore, *in situ* conservation of wild genetic resources, especially of plants, should be included in the mandates of agencies with land-management responsibilities, particularly those that establish and manage protected areas. Such mandates should provide for zoning all or part of a protected area as a genebank area; the sustainable collection of germplasm; and the establishment of functional links with *ex situ* conservation agencies. Managing protected areas to conserve wild genetic resources also calls for assessing the status of the resources both within and outside protected areas, monitoring the status of the populations concerned, and maintaining a record of their size, locations, habitats, and phenology. This information should be part of the national genetic resource information system.

Economic incentives and support

Some of the problems of agriculture can be eased by economic and social measures. Attempting to provide alternative employment in rural areas is a high priority in some countries. In others, there is a need to arrange incentives for needed adjustments in land use and in still other countries, balanced programmes of financial and technical support will be helpful.

Action 13.12. Attempt to increase non-farm employment for small farmers and the landless.

Governments should support programmes to generate employment during slack agricultural periods. Public works with rates of return that are too slow to attract private investors, and that are essential for sustainable development, are particularly useful. They could include: construction and maintenance of rural roads, reforestation, soil and water conservation works, installation of water pipes, construction or maintenance of flood control or irrigation channels.

Job creation in rural industries is needed to take pressure off the land and provide better incomes for the landless and near-landless. The industries include processing agricultural, aquacultural, and forest products, and the manufacture of tools and equipment for agriculture, aquaculture, forestry, water supply, construction, and so on. Care is needed to ensure that most of the employment, at reasonable rates, goes to the landless and other poor who need it most. It may be better to focus such small- and medium-scale industrial development in local towns, to take advantage of their facilities.

Action 13.13. Switch from price supports to conservation supports.

Particularly in high-income countries, governments should replace price supports for commodities with incentives to remove marginal land from production, protect uncultivated ecosystems, restore farm productivity, and adopt sustainable methods of production. These replacement subsidies would cushion farmers in high-income countries from the loss of price supports, rebuild their agricultural resource base, reduce the main cause of habitat destruction, and remove a source of harm to the agricultural economies of lower-income countries.

Adoption of sustainable agricultural practices in high-income countries needs much more emphasis. Sustainable practices that should be encouraged include organic farming, farmers' markets, cooperatives, use of animal labour instead of machines, and protection of non-agricultural habitats such as wetlands and woodland.

Box 23. Support for traditional farming

Under a provision in the European Community's farm structures regulation, the United Kingdom designates Environmentally Sensitive Areas to pay farmers to farm in traditional ways for the benefit of wildlife. Payments can be for limitations on the amount of fertilizer that can be used; restrictions on changes of agricultural land use, such as from grazing to cereals; and controls over the dates at which meadows are cut for hay. They may also include positive payments to encourage woodland protection and management or the restoration of archaeological sites. Some 400,000 hectares are now covered by ESA designation, with the funds about – $18 million a year – coming from the agricultural budget.

Action 13.14. Promote primary environmental care by farmers.

Reinforcing traditional arrangements for resource use and providing secure land tenure and access to finance are essential in promoting primary environmental care by farmers (see Actions 7.1 and 7.6).

Establishing conservation districts to develop and deliver rural conservation programmes can be very helpful. Usually organized on a watershed basis, the districts serve as local organizations for technical and financial assistance for:

- soil and water conservation;
- management of wild resources, including fisheries;
- protection of natural beauty;
- recreation and public education.

Financial incentives for primary environmental care could be directed toward: forage seed purchase, shelterbelt planting, block tree planting, water storage, crop residue management, salinity management, wildlife habitat maintenance and enhancement, wetland conservation, and drainage maintenance and enhancement.

14. Forest lands

Forests, wooded grasslands, and shrublands cover 53 million square kilometres or some 40% of the Earth's land surface. Forests with closed canopies now cover about 29 million square kilometres, four-fifths of their extent at the beginning of the 18th century.

This Strategy uses the term "forests" to describe forest ecosystems, which besides trees include soils, waters and the multitude of associated animals, micro-organisms and other plants.

Forests and woodlands range from tidal to subalpine areas, from the tropics to the subarctic. They exist in an extraordinary variety of forms: evergreen and deciduous, coniferous and broadleaved, wet and dry, closed canopy forest and open woodland. Dominant trees range from massive giants to gnarled dwarfs, with many gradations and combinations. Most cultivated and inhabited lands were once clothed in forest; and most agriculture occurs on soils that evolved under forests.

Natural and modified forests provide human beings with a wealth of benefits. Forests are an integral part of the Earth's life-support systems. They play a crucial role in regulating the atmosphere and climate. They are major stores of carbon. Boreal forests warm the subarctic zone by providing a dark mass that absorbs heat from the sun. Tropical forests may have an even bigger effect. They may help to drive the general circulatory systems of the atmosphere, influence general precipitation patterns, and distribute heat to temperate zones.

Forests moderate local climates, providing generally milder, moister and less variable conditions than places without forests in the same region. Much of the water vapour in the air over tropical forests comes from transpiration through forest plants. Forests regulate the local hydrological cycle, protecting soils from excessive erosion and reducing the silt loads of rivers, slowing runoff, and moderating floods and other harmful fluctuations in streamflow. The forest cover of drainage basins regulates the run-off of water, and may help to maintain spawning habitat for fish and sustain major fisheries. Forests also provide range for livestock production.

Forests are highly diverse ecosystems, supporting millions of species and supplying a wide range of resources. In 1985 the annual value of world production of lumber, veneer, pulpwood and fuelwood was more than $300 billion. Fuelwood contributes 19% of the energy supply of lower-income countries, and 3% of the energy consumed in high-income countries. In addition, forests yield large quantities of forage, animal and plant food, medicines, non-wood fibres, furs and skins, essential oils, gums, waxes, latexes and resins, and other non-timber commodities. The total volume and value of these commodities is difficult to quantify, but they provide substantial income and employment, and are important for the domestic economies of many communities and households.

Forest genetic resources include those used to improve the performance of trees grown for timber; wild relatives of crops and livestock, used by plant and animal breeders in agriculture and horticulture; and species with potential as new products.

Forests are an important part of the resource base of tourism. And they are of inestimable cultural value: sources of beauty and majesty for contemplation, recreation, amenity, religion, art, music, and poetry.

In building sustainable societies, two major issues arise. First, given the inexorable increase in human populations over the next few decades, how much forest will have to be converted to agriculture and other land uses to meet essential human needs? Second, how should the areas remaining under forest be managed?

Some conversion of forest is inevitable to accommodate and feed maybe another 4 billion people within the next 50 years. But extensive tracts of forest are essential for life and human welfare and should be conserved. If maintained and used sustainably they could meet the large, diverse and often conflicting demands that people make of them.

Now, however, they are being destroyed or degraded almost everywhere. Most forests have already been modified by people, and the remaining areas of natural forest are under heavy pressure.

"Old-growth" forests and "modified" forests: what they mean here

Throughout this chapter, old-growth forest means a forest where trees have never been cut down or which has not been seriously disturbed for several hundred years. Modified forest means a forest where trees have been felled (during the past 250 years), usually by loggers or shifting cultivators or where other products have been harvested, but where cover of trees or shrubs of indigenous species persists. Modified forests include managed forests, where a deliberate effort is made to enhance or sustain the yield of certain forest products, notably timber. For more on these and related terms used in this chapter, see Fig. 5.

Of the 29 million square kilometres of closed forests, 32% are boreal (subarctic), 26% temperate (in both hemispheres), and 42% tropical. Three-quarters of the open forests and shrubland are in the tropics.

Boreal and temperate forests are not declining in total extent, but they are subject to major changes in species composition and local distribution. A major cause is loss and fragmentation of old-growth forests. The temperate forests in the northern hemisphere have been heavily modified for centuries and few natural forests are left there. In addition, modified forests have been degraded due to unsustainable logging, air pollution, and fragmentation as a result of urban growth.

In some parts of Europe and North America forests are expanding across abandoned agricultural land.

Logging in many northern temperate forests has occurred over a number of rotations and appears to produce sustainable yields of timber. This is especially so with selective harvesting and small clearcuts of species that grow quickly. There is some doubt about the sustainability of large clearcuts, particularly in boreal forests or in those temperate forests with a predominance of slow-growing species.

Almost 15% of the standing timber of 17 European countries has been moderately to severely damaged by air pollution. This takes two main forms: first, acid rain derived from sulphur and nitrogen oxides emitted from power stations and other large industrial centres, and, second, oxidants produced by chemical reactions involving motor vehicle emissions. The UN Economic Commission for Europe estimates that the productivity of European forests is declining at US$30 billion a year. Acid rain and oxidants are also damaging forests in eastern North America, and are likely to do so in north-east China and other areas where industries do not adopt modern pollution prevention technology.

In the future global warming is likely to cause a northward shift of the boreal forest into areas that are now tundra, and a substantial rearrangement in temperate forest distribution in the northern hemisphere. The rates of these changes may outstrip the dispersal capacity of forest trees and so cause major ecological stress, with extensive areas of die-back and reproductive failure at the southern margins of the forest zone.

Underlying the degradation of boreal and temperate forests are two major factors. The first is a lack of a proper forest policy; most so-called forest policies are timber production policies rather than policies to maintain and enhance all forest values. The second is poorly controlled urban growth and excessive air pollution due to overconsumption of energy and raw materials, and inadequate technologies (see Chapters 4, 5, 10, 11, and 12).

Every year, at least 180,000 square kilometres (almost 2%) of tropical forests and woodlands are cleared for unsustainable shifting cultivation, settlements, ranching and other agricultural schemes; in addition, in dry regions, fuelwood cutting is seriously depleting forest resources. Another 44,000 square kilometres of tropical moist forests are logged each year and then left to regenerate.

In Latin America, the chief causes of deforestation are cattle ranching, land speculation, unplanned settlement in the wake of road building, and unsustainable shifting agriculture. These destructive changes have been favoured by policies intended to promote economic growth and land colonization.

In Africa and Asia, the main causes are unsustainable shifting agriculture, conversion to commercial agriculture, and, in dry forests, fuelwood cutting. Short- or non-fallow shifting cultivation is the single greatest cause of forest loss in the tropics.

Selective logging is the usual commercial practice in the tropics. Such logging often degrades the forest, sometimes heavily. It damages seedlings and unharvested trees. It accelerates erosion as a result of poor road location, construction and maintenance; through logging on steep slopes and faulty siting of yarding areas and through the compacting of soils by heavy machinery. It reduces species diversity through physical disruption of habitats, poaching by logging personnel and selective pressures on a few commercial species. It enhances susceptibility to fire by opening the canopy which allows the proliferation of combustible herbaceous vegetation and the drying of logging debris.

These problems are made worse by recutting before there has been adequate recovery of the forest. Clear cutting would have even more damaging effects: the solutions lie in improved selective logging practices.

Logging is seldom a direct cause of forest loss, but its incidental effects can be great, both because of its immediate disruptive effects on the habitat and especially because logging roads allow settlers to penetrate and clear the forest.

Several factors underly the destruction of tropical forests. One is inequitable distribution of land and political and economic power, enabling the wealthy to liquidate forests for profit; and forcing large numbers of the landless and near-landless to colonize the forests and to try to farm land that is unsuitable for agriculture. Another is insecure land tenure for forest dwellers leading to short term maximization of profits (See Chapter 7).

Further inequities in the international economy force lower-income countries to sell whatever they can, including their forests (see Chapter 9).

Other factors include inefficient use of existing farm land (see Chapter 13); inappropriate policy relating to the use of forests and forest lands; and macroeconomic and development policies that encourage forest destruction and discourage forest conservation.

All of this is exacerbated by high rates of population growth and increasing demand for the products of tropical forests in high-income countries (see Chapter 5).

Priority actions

The world's forest estate needs to be seen and valued as a priceless natural resource, to be sustained for the long-term benefit of humanity. Each country should:

- prepare an inventory of its forest resources and a strategy for their management;
- protect areas of natural forest, maintain modified forests and use them sustainably, and establish plantations for sustainable harvesting;
- involve local communities in forest management.

International action is needed to create and maintain markets for the products of sustainably managed forests, and assist lower-income countries to derive maximum benefits from the sustainable use of their forest resources.

Action 14.1.   Establish a permanent estate of natural and modified forest in every nation and manage it to meet the needs of all sectors of society.

Rational allocation of land should be central to development planning. Forests and other land resources in different countries vary greatly. Some forests are critical for the maintenance of water supplies; others are critical for preserving genetic resources. Some have the potential to yield timber or other forest produce. Some contain soils that are suitable for sustainable agriculture; others are totally unsuitable for cultivation.

Land must be allocated to uses that match its ecological suitability, taking due account of social and economic factors. If this is well done, the end result is potentially more valuable than what might result from any alternative process.

National objectives for forest land should be based on consultation with all sectors of the community including forest dwelling people, local and regional administrations, forestry and agricultural industries, and nature conservation organizations. On the basis of this consultation a target should be set for the amount of land to be kept under old-growth and modified forest

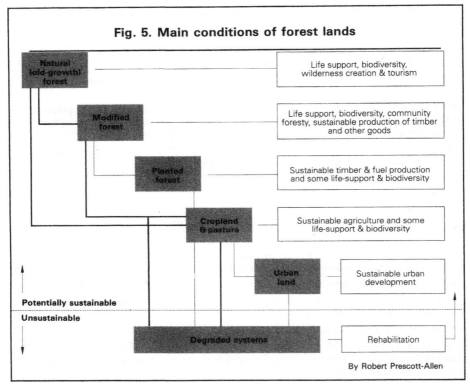

Fig. 5. Main conditions of forest lands

Natural (old-growth) forest — Life support, biodiversity, wilderness creation & tourism

Modified forest — Life support, biodiversity, community foresty, sustainable production of timber and other goods

Planted forest — Sustainable timber & fuel production and some life-support & biodiversity

Cropland & pasture — Sustainable agriculture and some life-support & biodiversity

Urban land — Sustainable urban development

Potentially sustainable

Unsustainable

Degraded systems — Rehabilitation

By Robert Prescott-Allen

1. The main conditions of forest lands are shown in the shaded boxes:

Natural forest. Forest where trees have never been cut down or have not been felled for the past 250 years. Also known as primary or old growth forest.

Modified forest. Forest where trees have been felled during the past 250 years, by logging or by shifting cultivation, and that retain an indigenous tree or shrub cover. New tree growth may entirely derived from natural regeneration or supplemented by "enrichment planting". Modified forest includes many conditions, from forests that have been selectively logged to those that have been heavily modified.

Planted forest. Forest in which all or most trees (51% or more of the woody biomass) have been planted or sown by people.

Cropland and pasture. Former forest land, now under agriculture, including agroforestry and orchards.

Urban land. Former forest land, now under buildings, roads and other human structures. Includes city parks, suburban gardens and golf courses.

Degraded land. Land whose productivity and diversity have been so reduced that they are unlikely to recover to original levels without special rehabilitation measures.

2. Steps in the conversion of natural forest to other conditions are shown to the left of the shaded boxes. The main steps today are indicated by a dark track: other significant steps by a light track.

3. Three main types of change should be distinguished:

Loss of natural forest = conversion of natural forest to modified or planted forest.

Deforestation = conversion of any forest (natural forest, modified forest, or planted forest) to non-forest conditions (cropland, pasture, or urban land).

Degradation of forests = reduction of the productivity and/or diversity of a forest, due to unsustainable harvesting of timber (removals exceeding replacements, changes in species composition), fire (except for fire-dependent forest systems), pests and diseases, removal of nutrients, pollution, or climate change.

4. Potentially sustainable uses of each condition of forest land are summarized to the right of the headed boxes. Uses of a forest are sustainable if they are compatible with maintenance of the forest in that condition. Unsustainable uses lead to conversion of the forest to some other condition. Sustainable development calls for a combination of sustainable uses of each condition.

to ensure conservation of ecological services and biological diversity and to supply the resources that only natural forests can provide. The area thus reserved will vary according to the condition of each country, but in general not less than 10% of total land area should be maintained under old-growth forest. Even this will often be insufficient to meet all conservation and development objectives unless it is buffered by extensive areas of modified forest.

In many countries natural forests are so degraded that major investments are needed to restore them in order to prevent massive extinctions of animal and plant species. In other countries, especially some Amazon Basin ones, existing forest areas are of such global significance for biological diversity and environmental functions that most of the remaining forest should be maintained in an old-growth or lightly modified state.

In some lower-income countries with high rates of population growth, forest conservation will be possible only if the people's need for agricultural land is met. This will require the carefully planned clearance of those forested areas where intensive sustainable agriculture is possible. In these countries the retention of large areas of near-natural forests can only be justified if they are used for the controlled sustainable extraction of a variety of products.

Good decisions on the allocation and management of forest land must be based upon sound forest policy. However, most forest policies are basically timber management policies and are insufficient for good forest management. The interests of communities and the many sectors that use or influence forests, from tourism to water supply, are seldom paid adequate attention; nor is maintenance of environmental services and biological diversity.

Many of the conflicts among different forest uses could be avoided if it weren't for this single-sector approach to resource management. Policies for agriculture, settlements, energy, finance and other sectors rarely recognize their impacts on forests. A change is needed now from a narrow sectoral approach to forest management to cross-sectoral policies for forest lands.

A cross-sectoral policy should:

- oblige decision makers to take account of all forest values, including environmental services and biological diversity, not just the production of timber and other commodities;

- identify all the sectors and groups that benefit from forests, define the benefits and establish objectives for sustaining and balancing them, and state how the objectives are to be achieved;

- provide mechanisms to ensure that the policies of all sectors that affect forests are consistent with national objectives for forests;

- facilitate avoidance of conflicts, integration of compatible uses, and zoning for incompatible uses so that all sustainable uses of the forest would have a place somewhere.

Decisions on the allocation of forest lands and on the policies for their management must be based upon a proper appreciation of all forest values. Each country should therefore undertake an economic evaluation of the environmental services, biological resources, timber and non-timber products provided by its forests. This will also allow for the inclusion of sustainability indicators in national accounts (see Box 14 and Annex 6); and for objective assessments of the costs and benefits of alternative uses of forests and forest lands. The non-timber benefits from natural and modified forests often provide a strong economic incentive for conserving them.

127

Action 14.2. Establish a comprehensive system of protected natural forests.

Protected natural or modified forest areas should represent the full range of variation among the forests. In turn, each area should encompass as much variation as possible to buffer against climate change, and should be surrounded by large tracts of modified, managed or planted forest. Where possible protected areas should encompass entire drainages; this will increase their protection from upstream changes and enhance their value for baseline monitoring.

Large areas of old-growth forest should be maintained in totally protected areas (IUCN Categories 1-3: see Annex 4 for an explanation of these categories). The optimal extent and location of old-growth forest depends on: the uniformity of the habitat; the size and shape of the protected areas; the quality of their management; the nature and use of adjacent lands; and the uses to which other non-protected areas are subject.

Old-growth forests are essential for the conservation of species which cannot tolerate any disturbance. Many other species will persist in modified forests. At present, we do not know the tolerances of the large majority of species. In any case, the greatest number of species can be conserved through maintaining an optimal balance of old-growth and modified forests.

In many countries the forest resources are so depleted that it will not be possible to establish an adequate system of protected old-growth forest. In this circumstance the best option for attaining conservation objectives will be to establish buffers of near-natural forest around protected areas. Such legally protected buffer zones of lightly modified forest, subject to sustainable extractive uses, should be major components of the forest estates of many lower income countries. Old growth forest and buffer zones can contribute the following benefits:

- maintenance of ecological functions;
- provision for scientific research, including baseline monitoring, and education;
- conservation of species diversity, and the habitats of fish and other wild resources;
- maintenance of genetic resources;
- wilderness appreciation and wilderness-based recreation and tourism;
- maintenance of life styles and culture of indigenous and other forest-dependent peoples who traditionally have obtained food and other non-timber goods from the area.

Action 14.3. Establish and maintain an adequate permanent estate of modified forest.

The objectives of a permanent estate of modified forest are to conserve life-support systems and biological diversity, and, within the constraints of these objectives, to provide a sustainable yield of timber and non-timber products. Such forests are an extension of the lightly-modified "buffer zone" forests discussed in Action 14.2. Depending upon the circumstances of the country they may range from forests where very light harvests of a few non-timber products are allowed, to those where forests are subject to more intensive management to enhance yields of timber. These forests provide resources, money and employment, while retaining the less easily accounted but still necessary assets of ecological services and natural diversity. Modified forests contribute the following benefits:

- maintenance of environmental services;
- production of timber, including fuelwood, and of forage, food, medicines, non-wood fibres, furs and skins, essential oils, gums, waxes, latexes and resins, and other non-timber commodities;
- substantial contributions to conservation of species diversity, the habitats of fish and other wild resources, and genetic resources;
- scientific research and education;
- general recreation and tourism.

Modified forests can continue to provide this wide array of benefits only if the dangers of deforestation on the one hand and single-purpose industrial management on the other are avoided.

Modified forest should be managed to produce a wide variety of products, including timber. This will happen only if governments create incentives for the private sector and local communities to:

- develop industries compatible with multiple-use forestry;
- refrain from overharvesting;
- invest in management to ensure the sustainability of all forest values, and limit timber production practices to those which are compatible with other forest uses.

Extractive reserves have been established in Brazil; similar projects are being developed in several African countries; Laos aims to earn 50% of its forest revenues from non-wood products by the year 2000. In many countries non-timber enterprises could equal or replace logging as major economic uses of forests.

The following measures would favour the maintenance of modified forest:

- giving communities a much stronger say in forest management;
- assigning timber-bearing land to the private sector on condition that all harvesting is sustainable and that ecological services and biological diversity are conserved. This requires an independent capacity to monitor and enforce;
- making land tenure conditional upon retaining a significant proportion of the land under forest cover;
- providing tax concessions and subsidizing the infrastructure for products harvested sustainably from modified forest and for processing such products;
- promoting export sales of products harvested sustainably from modified forest.

In the tropics, people who at present depend on unsustainable shifting cultivation should be given priority assistance during their transition to stable agricultural systems. This can be achieved through agrarian reform and promotion of agroforestry and other more intense farming methods. The pressure of shifting agriculture can also be reduced by generation of alternative employment; forest industries can play an important role in this.

Action 14.4. Increase the area of planted forest.

Plantations should be in addition to existing natural and modified forest; they should not replace them. Priority locations are degraded lands and land that is to be retired from agriculture.

Planted forest contributes to sustainability and the economy by concentrating timber production in areas close to markets and transport corridors, so reducing transport costs.

Concentration allows investment in soil improvement, which can then be more than repaid by yield increases from genetically improved trees. Thus the industry should be able to get more production out of less land and a quicker and bigger return from investments in tree breeding. Plantations can take pressure off natural and modified forests by producing large volumes of timber fast.

Plantations should be managed to high environmental standards, conserving water and soils, maintaining vegetation cover, using nutrients efficiently, and maintaining a high biomass. They should also fit in with the aspirations and needs of local people. Farm forestry should be encouraged; and more trees should be planted in urban environments and along roadsides for amenity, to improve local climate, reduce some air pollutants, and store carbon. Long-rotation carbon-sink plantations for carbon storage may have a role to play in moderating global warming. In general this function will be better achieved by regenerating natural forests because these will also provide a range of other benefits. Where carbon plantations are the chosen option they should be grown over long rotations. Although the net growth of old forest plantations is generally lower than that of young forests, the total amount of carbon stored in old forests is much higher than in young forests. Long rotations also favour accumulation of the highest possible biomass of trees, undergrowth, and humus in the soil. Timber harvested from the plantations should be used in long-lasting products, such as the structures of buildings, high-quality furniture, and perhaps high-quality books.

Short rotation fuelwood plantations are urgently needed in many tropical countries. If annual production from fuelwood plantations equalled the amount of wood used as fuel each year, substitution of fuelwood for fossil fuels would replace a source of atmospheric carbon with a closed carbon cycle.

Wood is expensive to transport because of its bulk and weight, so plantations must be located within 50-100 kilometres of where the wood is to be used. They require fertile land, so compete with other land uses. Therefore, they are most suitable where demand for fuel is high or where land is being taken out of agriculture. The latter is the case on an estimated 150,000 square kilometres in the European Community and 160,000 square kilometres in the United States.

There are many successful examples of increased fuelwood production in lower-income countries, such as Kenya and Rwanda.

Action 14.5.   **Increase national capacity to manage forests sustainably.**

In 1989, the annual volume of the international tropical timber trade was 60 million cubic metres. Assuming a yield of 1.5 cubic metres per hectare per year, this would require 45 million hectares of forest under sustained yield management. In addition, a further 200 million hectares — more than the remaining tropical moist forest area in Africa — would need to be managed sustainably to meet domestic needs for industrial wood. Fuelwood needs are in addition to this.

By 1989, only one million hectares of tropical forest were demonstrably managed sustainably. Clearly, current levels of tropical timber production cannot be maintained; too little forest remains and it is being cleared for agriculture too fast.

There is broad consensus amongst conservation groups that the unsustainable industrial exploitation of tropical forests must stop. The entire tropical timber trade could, and should, be based on sustainable management by 2000; this requires that demand is reduced to levels that can be met sustainably (see also Action 14.8).

In all countries the conditions for sustainable management are:

- establishment of a legally guaranteed permanent forest estate (Action 14.1);
- provision of training in forest ecology and management;
- provision of secure conditions for forest managers, whether they be government agencies, private corporations, local communities, or others;
- application of appropriate standards for annual allowable cut, cutting cycles, harvesting techniques and infrastructure, environmental safeguards, and so on;
- imposition of adequate control of all aspects of harvesting and forest treatments after harvesting to ensure regeneration and prevent avoidable environmental damage;
- adoption of economic and financial policies that do not require more from the forest than it can yield sustainably;
- adoption of environmental policies that protect ecological services, biological diversity, and the resource base of all forest users;
- Provision of enough information for the effective monitoring of the above conditions.

Combining profitability and sustainability

The best timber companies are capable of combining profitability and sustainability. One Swedish company has a nature conservation policy under which it conducts forestry operations on its lands in such a way as to avoid permanent adverse effects on soil and water; preserve a rich variety of plant and animal life; protect all plant and animal species that occur where it operates; protect all archaeological and historic sites; and make reasonable allowance for the wishes of the public regarding access to and use of company woodlands.

Action 14.6.   Strengthen community management of forests.

Sustainable management depends on fully involving the communities that live in or near forests in decisions about forest conservation and development. Because they live with the forest, these communities often have a strong incentive to maintain it and use it sustainably. But this incentive is sharply reduced if the communities are denied a fair share of the forest's resources, or if they feel powerless to influence key decisions made by corporations, wealthy individuals, or government officials.

In most tropical countries, governments have taken over authority for managing forests from local and indigenous communities who had their own forms of management. More than 80% of the closed forest area of lower-income countries is public land. Virtually all forest land in Canada, and large areas of forest in the USA, also are publicly owned.

Local communities that rely on the multiple benefits of modified and natural forests should be effectively involved in decisions on forest management and land-clearing. A larger share of management control of forests should be returned to local institutions. As noted in Chapter 7 (notably Action 7.1), government agencies should shift emphasis from policing the use of forest resources to providing an extension service to community management bodies. Central governments would retain sovereign taxing power, but should share the revenues with the local communities both as a matter of equity and to strengthen local interest in resource management.

Indigenous and traditional forest owners and dwellers should have full and informed consent over forest operations, and wherever possible community control over them. Local rights to lands and resources should be respected.

Action 14.7. Expand efforts to conserve forest genetic resources.

Forest genetic resources include tree germplasm and the genetic material in other forest organisms. It is necessary to conserve both. Tree genetic resources can be conserved by managing timber harvesting, by designating protected areas, or establishing genetic resource conservation stands. The genetic resources of other organisms must be conserved in protected areas. Conservation of forest genetic resources requires knowledge of the degree and distribution of genetic variation within the species concerned; and, ideally, a genetic conservation plan for each species.

Action 14.8. Create a market for forest products from sustainably managed sources and use wood more efficiently.

An important part of the strategy to conserve tropical forests is to increase the economic benefit for forest nations and communities from using forests rather than converting them to farmland. We therefore need a strong, sustainable tropical timber industry.

Economic incentives are needed to build up trade based on sustainably managed forests. A comprehensive package of measures, applying to both temperate and tropical timber producing countries, is needed to make trade conditional on sustainability. These would include systems of certification and management with provision for monitoring, and financial support for their implementation. Lower-income countries may require assistance to meet criteria (see below).

Only 24 countries account for 90% of world industrial roundwood production (see table). Development of the package of measures could begin with these countries.

Industrial roundwood production 1985-87 (000 m³)			
WORLD	1,574,499	India	23,958
USA	380,005	Romania	19,888
USSR	288,057	Poland	19,758
Canada	172,913	Czechoslovakia	17,458
China	94,974	Australia	17,029
Brazil	66,109	Spain	13,752
Sweden	48,083	Austria	12,568
Finland	38,304	South Africa	11,683
Germany	38,061	Yugoslavia	11,673
Malaysia	32,441	Chile	10,015
Japan	32,077	Norway	9,521
France	29,462	New Zealand	9,291
Indonesia	28,475	TOTAL (24 countries)	1,425,555 (90%)

Recycling and more efficient use of wood and durable uses of processed wood that will keep carbon in storage for long periods should be encouraged. Consumers should be willing to pay more for wood products from certifiably sustainable harvesting systems, and discriminate against low value, temporary uses of wood such as once-off concrete shuttering. Large amounts of wood are wasted in most construction sites and in demolition of buildings in high-income countries. This wood should be recycled.

Paper manufacturers should indicate the recycled content of all paper, and the proportions that are recycled from mill wastes (pre-consumer recycled content) and used paper (post-consumer recycled content).

Boycotts of the products whose production results from clearing forests, notably beef from forest zone ranches, may be appropriate. But blanket bans and embargoes on tropical hardwoods should be avoided. Buying tropical veneers and other valuable tropical hardwood products that have been produced sustainably would encourage maintenance and even improvement of selective wood extraction. Blanket boycotts of tropical timber are likely to favour forest clearance for low-grade shifting cultivation, because they remove economic incentives to keep even modified forests.

Selective boycotts could be beneficial where logging is flagrantly unsustainable, or affects rare species, protected areas, or the lands of indigenous peoples.

For its part, the forest products industry should:

- recognize that the only way of preventing blanket bans is by supplying sustainably managed timber;

- promote the application of internationally acceptable and verifiable operational guidelines and criteria for defining the sustainability of management in timber producing countries;

- establish labelling and tracking mechanisms to allow consumers to assess the sustainability of timber sources;

- encourage high-value end uses of tropical forest timbers.

Action 14.9.   **Set stumpage prices to reflect the timber's full value; charge licence fees that discourage exploitation of stands of marginal commercial value; and auction concessions competitively.**

The prices of forest products should reflect their full social cost (see Box 12). Revenues should be reinvested in forest conservation, research and management. Governments and other land owners commonly collect far too little forest revenue to cover the costs of management and regeneration. Or they collect enough but spend it on something else.

Timber royalties (stumpage fees etc.) should reflect market values and the costs of regeneration and ecosystem protection. In many countries, timber royalties are well below true economic values and should be raised. Low undifferentiated royalties deprive governments of revenue, increase business and political pressure for timber concessions by making them excessively lucrative, and encourage unsustainable and wasteful exploitation. Higher rates should be charged for high-value species than for low-value species.

Governments can ensure they capture as much as possible of the available resource rent by auctioning logging concessions competitively, with high minimum bid prices to guard against bid-rigging. This requires getting enough information on forest resources to assess their timber value; the cost of detailed forest exploration and inventory can be recovered through the higher revenues from fees and royalties, and through improvements in management made possible by the better information.

Income tax holidays, tax credits, accelerated depreciation, other special tax deductions, credit subsidies (artificially low interest rates and long grace periods on loans), whether given to logging and timber processing companies or to agricultural and other forest-clearing industries, often promote forest destruction and waste of resources. They deprive nations of short-term benefits and incur excessively high long-term costs. It is better to abolish them, except when they favour maintenance and sustainable use of the forest. Countries with large wood-processing industries can increase government revenues, stimulate greater efficiency in the processing industries, and reduce log exports by raising export taxes on logs. Bans on the export of unprocessed logs can encourage local timber processing and increase the value added. But export taxes are preferable to log export bans and quotas, which provoke smuggling and corruption; and to tax and tariff protection of processing industries, which cossets the industries and encourages inefficiency.

Export prices of tropical fine woods should not be so low that they permit throw-away or other short-lived uses of these woods. Tax structures and other incentives should be used to increase the economic benefits from more diversified and environmentally benign uses of forests.

Action 14.10.   **Increase the capacities of lower-income countries to manage forests sustainably and improve international cooperation in forest conservation and sustainable development.**

The three main international needs are to:

- provide lower-income countries with favourable terms of trade for sustainably produced forest products;
- provide lower-income countries with assistance in maintaining their forests and using them sustainably;
- increase international cooperation on forest conservation.

In addition to regular programmes of development assistance, the two biggest international initiatives in this area have been the Tropical Forestry Action Plan (TFAP) and the International Tropical Timber Agreement (ITTA).

The TFAP aims to halt deforestation and increase the sustainable benefits from tropical forests by improving the lives of rural people, increasing food production, stabilizing shifting cultivation, ensuring the sustainable use of forests, conserving forest ecosystems, increasing supplies of fuelwood and the efficiency of its use, and expanding income and employment opportunities.

Although it has doubled the amount of money spent on tropical forests, the TFAP has not achieved what it set out to do and there have been a number of recommendations to improve it. Of these, the authors of this strategy believe that the following are most important:

- The international coordinating unit of TFAP should be fully independent. Its chief function should be to facilitate the flow of information among all international groups having a legitimate interest in the use of tropical forest lands. It should be accountable to an independent committee representing tropical countries, funding agencies, technical experts, international non-governmental organizations, and local citizens' groups.

- The TFAP should have an open information policy. Country-level documents should be available to all parties expressing interest.

- National TFAPs should be country-based rather than donor-driven. National steering groups and secretariats, representing a broad cross-section of interests within the country, should be formed to lead the development of National Forestry Action Plans. TFAPs should actively encourage a broad political debate of forestry issues.

- Technical teams commissioned to assist the development of National Forestry Action Plans should be multidisciplinary. In addition to foresters, they should include experts in local participation, cross-sectoral linkages, land tenure, community development, farming, and ecosystem conservation.

- The TFAP should pay more attention to land tenure, and to building capabilities in tropical forest countries to foster community management of forests, and to safeguard ecological processes and biological diversity in forest development.

- The sponsors and critics of TFAP should recognize that real involvement of local communities and special interest groups is likely to slow the development and implementation of National Forestry Action Plans, but that this is a small price to pay for the long-term benefits of such involvement.

- The TFAP sponsors and secretariat should monitor, evaluate and follow up national TFAP activities. They should exert influence to ensure that the basic philosophy, goals and objectives of TFAP are respected whilst taking account of the great differences among countries.

The International Tropical Timber Organization (ITTO) is committed to an international tropical timber trade entirely based on sustainable forest management by the year 2000. The International Tropical Timber Agreement (ITTA) calls upon its signatories to develop national policies on sustainable use and conservation of their forests, including increased processing of tropical timber in producer countries.

The General Agreement on Tariffs and Trade (GATT) inhibits the achievement of these objectives by preventing countries from restricting exports of unprocessed logs; and from using trade tariffs, quotas or bans to favour trade in sustainably rather than unsustainably produced timber.

The GATT should be amended to:

- allow producer countries to practise sustainable forestry, protect timber processing industries wherever this either reduces timber consumption rates or creates employment for people who might otherwise practice low-grade agriculture on forest lands;

- enable discrimination between "like products" on the basis of the method of production (in this case, sustainable or unsustainable);

- enable countries to use any appropriate import restriction to discriminate between sustainably and unsustainably produced timber.

The ITTO should:

- seek a waiver from GATT regulations for any trade measures they indicate as contributing to conservation of forest resources;

- remind all its members, who are also contracting parties to the GATT, of the terms of the ITTA, and particularly of the desirability of encouraging producer countries to develop their own processing industries.

An international forest convention has been proposed to provide a framework for greater cooperation, to deal directly with all aspects of forest conservation and development, and to help to harmonize ecological and economic approaches to the use of forest resources. It should be used as a means of:

- establishing a global set of sustainability criteria to govern trade in forest products (Action 14.1);
- providing a framework for allowing lower-income countries to protect sustainable forest industries, and for encouraging upper-income importers to reduce tariff and non-tariff barriers to the sustainably produced processed-wood products of lower-income countries;
- sponsoring a wider range of international programmes, including a Temperate Forestry Action Programme to improve temperate and boreal forest management;
- providing a mechanism for compensation payments from high-income to low-income countries in exchange for measures to conserve forest resources of global environmental or biological significance;
- giving international legal recognition to a world register of forest sites of special importance for biological diversity conservation and provide a mechanism for funding conservation measures for these sites.

15. Fresh waters

Life on Earth depends on water. Our planet is the only one where liquid water is known to exist. Falling as precipitation and flowing through the landscape, it is a unique solvent carrying the nutrients essential for life.

Continuously moving above and below the soil surface, water maintains and links the planet's ecosystems. Some is returned directly to the atmosphere, partly via plants. The rest flows into and over the ground, permeating soil, moving through organisms, recharging underground aquifers, replenishing rivers and lakes, entering the oceans, and returning to the atmosphere.

As it cycles, "blue" water (the water in rivers and other water bodies) becomes "green" water (the water in organisms and the soil), and vice versa. How people use the land and change ecosystems affects the quality, movement and distribution of both "green" and "blue" water. And how people use water affects the quality and quantity of both "blue" and "green" water and hence the integrity of land and aquatic ecosystems.

Our use of water is creating a crisis for much of the world. Global water withdrawals are believed to have grown more than 35-fold during the past three centuries, and are projected to increase by 30-35% by 2000. Current patterns of freshwater use cannot be sustained if human populations reach 10 billion by 2050. Many countries already suffer serious water shortage. Competition among water uses is growing and exceeding the capacity of institutions to manage it. Water diversion and retention are having increasingly severe impacts on ecosystems.

In most countries, irrigated agriculture is the main consumer of water, accounting for about 70% of world water withdrawal. The irrigated land area has almost tripled since 1950. It supplies one third of the world's food; but less than 40% of the water supplied for irrigation contributes to the growth of crops. The rest is wasted. Badly managed irrigation schemes have ruined large areas of formerly fertile soils by waterlogging and salinization (see Chapter 13).

Unless effective remedial action is taken, rapid increases in water withdrawals, particularly in semi-arid and coastal zones, will cause still more widespread salinization, reduced water quality, and — in low-lying coastal areas and river basins — land subsidence.

As demand for water and energy has risen, major investments have been made in damming and diverting rivers to store water from wet season rainfall for use in the dry season or for transfer to drier lands. Large dams are often advocated as the means of increasing production from irrigated agriculture, generating hydroelectricity, assuring water supplies, and maintaining navigable waterways. Such engineering marvels have been a source of national pride and personal prestige.

But the benefits of large dams and other water engineering projects are usually not as large as foreseen and their adverse effects have been gravely underestimated. These may include: an increase in national indebtedness; disruption of riverine and coastal fisheries; erosion of the river channel and the coastal zone; displacement of inhabitants from the reservoir site; spread of waterborne diseases; saline intrusion up the estuary; destruction of long-established patterns of floodplain agriculture and livestock production; habitat degradation and reduced natural diversity; and reduced total flow because of increased evaporation from the reservoir and irrigated lands.

Throughout the world, water quality is impaired, often severely, by pollution and misuse of water and land. Waterborne pathogens are the biggest cause of death and illness in lower-income countries. Nutrients from waste water and fertilizer runoff lead to eutrophication and algal blooms, reduce suitability of ground and surface water for drinking, damage fisheries and reduce biological diversity. Salinization from irrigation, locally severe salt intrusion due to overpumping, and pollution from mining render water unfit to drink and reduce agricultural production in many countries. Heavy metal pollution, and contamination by organic pesticides, PCBs and other synthetic organic compounds, are widespread and locally serious. Acidification of waters by sulphate and nitrate deposited as acid precipitation is also a major problem in Europe, North America and parts of Asia.

The productivity and diversity of freshwater ecosystems — and especially of riverine fisheries — are threatened by agricultural, municipal and industrial pollution; changes in the water regime resulting from clearance of upper catchment basins and floodplain forests, dams, channelling of streams, and draining of wetlands; and introductions of non-native species.

Several hundred freshwater fish and invertebrate species are endangered. Aquatic genetic resources required for aquaculture are subject to selection pressures that may not result in extinction but are likely to lead to adverse genetic change. Many fish stocks are heavily exploited. Some otherwise sustainable artisanal fisheries, notably in the Amazon, are threatened by overfishing by non-local commercial fishermen.

All these problems are likely to be intensified by climate change, especially in arid and semi-arid regions. For example, a 1° to 2°C temperature increase coupled with a 10% reduction in precipitation could reduce annual runoff by 40-70%.

As populations increase, the sustainability of human use of water ultimately depends on people adapting their behaviour to the water cycle. Human societies need to develop the ability — the awareness, knowledge, procedures and institutions — to manage their uses of land, as well as water, in an integrated, comprehensive manner, in ways that maintain the quality and quantity of water supplies both for people and for the ecosystems that support them.

Lack of this ability is a key issue to be addressed by a strategy for sustainability. In general, the water cycle is cut up into tiny conceptual and managerial parts: water management is considered separately from land management, groundwater from surface water, and water supplies from aquatic ecosystems. Nowhere is there enough reliable information on water use. Information on water availability is also lacking, particularly in the tropics and subtropics. Inadequate procedures and institutions are reflected in widespread problems of water quantity and quality.

In high-income countries, legislation to control land uses that reduce water quality has yet to be fully enforced. Lower-income countries, particularly those that are rapidly industrializing, have to face new problems while trying to solve the old ones. New laws, regulations and enforcement structures are required.

Mechanisms for international collaboration are also required. The entire territory of nearly one-quarter of non-island countries is part of an international river basin. Yet more than one-third of the 200 major international river basins in the world are not covered by any international agreement, and fewer than 30 have cooperative institutional arrangements. Pollution, impoundment and diversion of water by upstream nations are likely to be a growing source of tension and insecurity.

The same activities also have major impacts on coastal waters. Since the water cycle includes fresh waters and the oceans, and since there needs to be an integrated approach to management of all land and water uses, this and the next chapter on oceans and coastal areas should be used together.

Priority actions

Sustainable use of fresh waters requires:

- better information;
- better awareness of how the water cycle works, the effect of land uses on the water cycle, the importance of wetlands and other key ecosystems, and of how to use water and aquatic resources sustainably; and better training in these matters;
- management of water demand to ensure efficient and equitable allocation of water among competing uses;
- integrated management of all water and land uses;
- improved institutional capacity to manage fresh waters;
- strengthened capacity of communities to use water resources sustainably;
- increased international cooperation on water issues;
- conservation of the diversity of aquatic species and genetic stocks.

Action 15.1. Improve the information base for sustainable water management.

Sustainable living implies that the users of water will take more responsibility for its conservation. If they are to change their attitudes and practices, they will need information and advice. There will be accompanying needs for change in the way government or private water supply agencies operate, for they will increasingly come to provide advisory and support services.

Managerial and technological innovation will be needed to develop and implement plans for the sustainable use of water and aquatic resources. Such plans should be based on long-term partnerships among the research and development community, governmental and nongovernmental agencies, and user groups.

In addition, continued support should be given to international research and training aimed at strengthening national efforts to use water resources sustainably. The main needs are:

- evaluations by drainage basin of the total economic value of the basin's water resources and aquatic ecosystems;
- estimates of water use and waste by country;
- estimates of water availability by country. Current estimates are generally unreliable. There are considerable difficulties in installing and maintaining the networks of instruments on which these estimates depend — networks for measuring precipitation, river flow, evaporation, and the quantity of water stored in the soil and aquifers. Many parts of the globe lack these networks. Others have had them for relatively short periods;
- monitoring and evaluation of policies and procedures to integrate management of water and land uses, manage water demand, and use aquatic resources sustainably;
- assessments of plausible scenarios of change in human population distribution and of climate change and of their impacts on regional water resources. This will require the ability to link global circulation models of climate and regional water-balance models.

Action 15.2. Undertake awareness campaigns and education programmes on sustainable use of water.

Awareness campaigns and education programmes are needed to persuade people to adapt their behaviour to the water cycle and to recognize that water is neither limitless nor free. The effectiveness of these efforts will be increased if the knowledge and perceptions of the target groups are drawn upon in developing the campaigns. Key points include:

- creation of basic understanding of the water cycle (where water comes from, and where it goes) through teaching in schools and colleges, and via the media;
- promotion of awareness of the water cycle among decision makers;
- explanation of the need for everybody to protect water against pollution;
- campaigns to improve hygiene and sanitation especially in lower-income communities;
- steps to improve awareness of the values of wetlands, peatlands and other aquatic ecosystems and the ways they can be used sustainably, among communities, government decision makers, schools and colleges, and the media;
- action to provide decision makers with syntheses of the best available scientific data so that they understand interactions among water users.

Action 15.3. Provide training in the management of human uses of, and impacts on, the water cycle.

Many countries do not have the capacity to take the actions recommended in this chapter. To build that capacity, training programmes are needed in the management of water and aquatic ecosystems. These should be given as multidisciplinary courses in their own right, and as part of courses in engineering, biological sciences, social sciences, and economics. Increased training at secondary school, undergraduate and graduate levels is required, as are vocational and on-the-job training.

Most institutions providing training in water issues still view water management as a sectoral issue. Greater emphasis needs to be placed on water management as a subject requiring careful integration of a number of disciplines. Training institutions should provide programmes on the integrated management of water resources and the design and implementation of water-based strategies for sustainable land use.

Action 15.4. Manage water demand to ensure efficient and equitable allocation of water among competing uses.

Governments and major water users should assign high priority to increasing the efficiency of water use. Economic instruments, and especially realistic pricing policies, should be adopted. Special attention should be given to municipal infrastructure (a lot of water is lost due to broken mains); and to water use in irrigation, applying economic incentives to encourage and produce better technologies, such as micro-irrigation. Management should be improved, waste virtually eliminated, and existing irrigation systems rehabilitated before costly new projects are considered.

Box 24. Saving water

Local rainfall is the only source of water for large segments of the world population. It is crucial that local rains are used efficiently through appropriate land use planning, water harvesting, choice and combination of annual and perennial crops, and scheduling of crop planting, so as to conserve surface and groundwater for the most important uses. Better forecasting of rains is also needed.

Greater efficiency in allocating water uses and in using water can be achieved by charging consumers the full cost of water used. Full cost includes the costs of building and operating the water supply systems; of losses in distribution; and of protecting forests, wetlands and other ecosystems required to regulate flow and maintain water quality. Providing a reasonable supply of domestic water free-of-charge would prevent this measure from harming the poor and disadvantaged members of society.

Greater emphasis needs to be placed on recycling of water (Japan and Israel provide good models). In particular:

- greater use should be made of waste water. The technologies exist. Their use should be supported and used especially in areas that lack waste water systems. For example, municipal wastewater can be used to meet some irrigation needs, particularly in arid and semi-arid zones;
- the great potential for water reuse within the chemical, pulp and paper, petroleum, coal, primary metals, and food processing industries should be realized;
- water pipes should be well maintained;
- luxury domestic uses of water (such as maintaining lawns) should be discouraged, perhaps by high charges, in arid and semi-arid zones of high-income countries.

The financial costs and environmental implications of meeting the demand for water during severe drought conditions are excessive because the infrastructure needed to supply occasional peak demands is idle for the whole of most years. Sound water management aims to guarantee economical supplies for public health and other essential uses by:

- using media advertisements and awareness campaigns to persuade people voluntarily to reduce water use where possible;
- subsequent prohibitions on non-essential uses, such as ornamental garden watering, automatic car washes, and refilling swimming pools and ornamental ponds, that are easy to police when public awareness of the need for water conservation is high.

Much of the existing licensing legislation is oriented toward water withdrawals and navigation. Uses such as recreation, and conservation of aquatic resources and ecosystems, are given little or no recognition. The legislation should be changed to recognize and provide for all uses.

Action 15.5.   **Give greater emphasis to the drainage basin as the unit of water management (see Action 4.5).**

Drainage basins are complex systems in which the effects of human activities on the hydrological cycle are rapidly passed on to communities and ecosystems downstream. All uses of water and land affect the quality and flow of water from headwaters to the coastal zone.

Water policy within each drainage basin should be based on evaluation of carrying capacity, accommodate multi-purpose approaches, and reflect the guiding principles set out below.

- Uses of surface, underground and coastal waters within the basin should be planned on the basis of assessments of water quantity and quality.

- Water use for domestic, industrial and agricultural consumption, as well as that required for the maintenance of wetland ecosystems, should not exceed the limits of sustainable supply, taking full account of the requirements for ecosystem functioning. Limits will depend on the technology, infrastructure and management capability available: in countries where these factors are poorly developed, only 10-20% of potential supply may be used sustainably; in other countries, it may be possible to use 100%.

- Standards should be established for water quality and quantity for different uses, including the maintenance of ecosystem structure and functioning. Water quality standards should combine the requirements for protecting human health and for ecosystems. Pollution by nondegradable substances must not exceed levels that would endanger human health or ecosystem function. Pollution by biodegradable substances must not exceed the assimilative capacity of receiving bodies of water. Assimilative capacity should be defined for each ecosystem. Discharge of toxic substances whose long-term impact is not known should be banned.

- The amount of irrigation water should be kept at the minimum required to leach salts from irrigated soils. Salinity must not exceed limits of utility for downstream water supply and irrigation or that required to maintain ecosystem integrity.

- Management of the quality and level of groundwater should seek to minimize environmental damage such as salinization, land subsidence, adverse nutrient release, and reduced river flow.

- To maintain the level of the water table, the natural recharge rate of groundwater should be the basis for calculating the potential pumping rate from aquifers. Removal of groundwater should not reduce the discharge of water where this supports important ecosystems elsewhere in the basin.

- The control of health hazards should be taken into account in computing water required and design criteria for irrigation developments.

- Practices that adversely affect water quality such as wetland drainage, solid waste landfills, and the use of fertilizers, pesticides and other potential pollutants should be controlled so that polluted water does not reduce groundwater quality, and surface runoff does not degrade river water quality. Policies and incentives that encourage such practices should be removed and replaced with policies and incentives that encourage environmentally sensitive land use, paying particular attention to the benefits for water quality.

- Clean technologies should be promoted, and the precautionary approach to pollution, preventing the discharge of toxic or synthetic substances whose long-term impacts are not known, should be adopted.

Action 15.6.   **Integrate the development of water resources with conservation of ecosystems that play a key role in the water cycle.**

The ecosystems of each drainage basin are linked by water. Well managed catchment forests and wetlands help maintain water flow, while floodplains and many coastal ecosystems are dependent upon the maintenance of the quality and quantity of river flow. Protecting the catchment basin and maintaining river flow is therefore essential if full benefit is to be obtained from the planet's fresh water resources.

There are a number of guiding principles, including those set out below.

- The role of the basin's ecosystems in regulating water quality and quantity, and controlling productivity of coastal and floodplain fisheries and agricultural and livestock production systems, should be assessed.

- Inventories should be made of the products and services obtained from each part of the system; and the minimum requirements to sustain these benefits should be determined.

- The short- and long-term impacts of water and land use changes in the basin on ecosystem functioning should be determined. Degradation of upper catchments, major wetlands, and riverine forests should be avoided. Appropriate compensatory measures should be designed and implemented if harmful changes are unavoidable.

- All large water management projects, and especially dams, must be subject to a full environmental impact assessment and a searching cost benefit analysis. Projects should only proceed when it can be shown that, in the long term, the project's benefits exceed the total cost of the scheme, including compensatory measures and unavoidable losses, by more than the total market and nonmarket values of the system before the project begins. The project should be monitored after completion to assess the extent to which its operational rules can be modified to enhance the scale and diversity of its products.

- The economic viability of irrigation, hydroelectricity, and other water projects depends on a well regulated flow of good quality water. Protecting the catchment basin is essential. The costs and benefits of protecting watershed forests, wetlands and other key ecosystems should therefore be made an automatic component of irrigation and other water supply projects. A study of 11 irrigation projects in Indonesia found that such costs ranged from less than 1% of the development costs of the project in cases where the catchment was more or less intact, to 5% where extensive reforestation was needed, and up to a maximum of 10% when resettlement of displayed persons was required.

Box 25. Wetlands

Wetland ecosystems — floodplains, freshwater marshes, peatlands, and estuaries — play a central role in the water cycle. They absorb floodwaters and regulate floods, helping to ensure a year round water supply; they absorb nutrients and retain sediment, thus purifying water supplies; and they buffer wind and wave action, helping to protect many coastal areas from storms. In addition to these ecological services, many wetlands yield a range of products which can be harvested sustainably, including fish, fodder, timber, and agricultural crops. Many also support important populations of wildlife, including many endangered species, and are a major recreational and tourist resource.

In the past, these multiple benefits were poorly recognized, and major development projects often sought to maximize use of only one resource. Today, however, when up to 50% of the wetlands which once existed may have been destroyed or degraded, there is growing awareness of the substantial human cost occasioned by their loss. Elsewhere many local communities that depend upon wetlands have been forced to overuse them in the face of rapid population growth and extreme poverty. These communities need help to rehabilitate or restore wetlands and institute systems for their sustainable management.

- The interface between water bodies and the land should be protected, particularly in the case of riparian forests, lake shores, and other wetland areas where exchanges between groundwater and surface water are substantial.

- Water management should identify the optimum timing requirements for different users that are compatible with ecosystem functioning.

- Critical ecosystems such as catchment forests, many rivers, lakes, wetlands, and associated aquatic ecosystems that have been severely degraded or destroyed by human activity, should be restored to a condition similar to their original state. This will increase the resource base, provide more flexibility for management and reduce problems associated with environmental degradation. However, restoration of degraded ecosystems should not be accepted as a substitute for effective conservation of natural ecosystems.

Action 15.7.   **Establish a cross-sectoral mechanism for integrated water management.**

Integrated water management requires a mechanism for coordinating national and subnational agencies with responsibilities for water and land. One option is to place overall responsibility for coordination with the environment agency (in countries where one exists). Another option would be to establish a national land use authority. With respect to water, the mechanism should be able to:

- decide on inventories of water resources to be carried out, and coordinate the monitoring of their use and quality;

- develop and apply national water quality standards;

- monitor water quality and quantity;

- liaise with all agencies dealing with natural resource management related to water;

- draft an overall strategy for the sustainable use of water resources and prepare action programmes that consider existing institutional, financial and physical constraints and options;

- direct budget funding for the development and conservation of water resources;

- develop water policy, including limitations on use of ground and surface water resources, and allocations for agricultural, urban and industrial development, recreation, fisheries, and habitat for aquatic life;

- provide for public participation in the formulation of policies and strategies;

- provide for the use of facilitation, mediation, assisted negotiations, and other techniques of alternative dispute resolution, the better to manage competition among uses;

- review legislation and regulations and monitor their enforcement;

- coordinate research.

Coordinating mechanisms should accept full public input and allow debate. It is also important to improve the effectiveness of sectoral agencies with responsibility for water uses.

Action 15.8. Establish procedures to act rapidly in response to natural and human-caused hazards.

These include floods, droughts, earthquakes, and major pollution accidents. The location of manufacturing, production and storage facilities along river banks increases the probability of contamination from major industrial accidents. The procedures to back up response to accidents should include national and international administrative safety regulations, monitoring and contingency plans, provisions for reservoir safety, and the establishment of emergency clean-up and pollution containment services. It is particularly important to prevent pollution of groundwater.

Water authorities should require industries to prepare environmental audits, and to define and put into place environmentally-oriented practices for industrial plant safety and accident prevention. Legislation should require that information on pollution incidents (pollutant, location, cause, effect, response) be reported and registered.

At the regional level, governments should harmonize national measures for the protection of transboundary inland waters against pollution resulting from hazardous activities, accidents or natural disasters and for mitigation of their impacts on the aquatic environment. The ECE Code of Conduct on Accidental Pollution of Transboundary Inland Waters provides one suitable model.

Action 15.9. Give local communities greater control over the management of aquatic resources and strengthen their capacity to use them.

This Strategy calls for the government agencies concerned to treat local communities as partners in water resources management rather than themselves trying to assume full responsibility for management. Participation by communities and individuals needs to be supported at two levels:

- through user groups or associations, for direct management of local water resources and water-based activities;
- through local government and other intermediary agencies, for contributions to higher-level policy making, programme planning, and implementation.

In many parts of the world, there have been strong traditions of managing water and aquatic ecosystems as a community resource for drinking, irrigation, grazing, fisheries or fur harvesting. But those institutions have frequently been weakened by increased population pressure on land and water, by excessive government intervention, or (especially in the case of open water fisheries) by the encroachment of powerful external commercial interests.

In such cases, restoration of the *status quo* is impossible. However, the sensitive use of participatory planning, which draws heavily on people's knowledge of land and water resources in their immediate locality, can help establish new conditions in which modified forms of community management become possible. Such methods can also be effective in places without previous community management traditions. The process is rarely easy, especially when water is scarce. However, the chances of success will be increased if either customary or new community rights to water use are formally recognized in law.

Community-level programmes to provide safe drinking water and sanitation need to be expanded. Successful programmes include the Hinduja Foundation's "Drinking Water for the

Millions" in India; and AFOTEC's "Health, education and training for low-cost water supply and sanitation technologies" in West Africa. They demonstrate that such programmes must:

- involve women and strengthen their capacity to participate, since in most countries women are solely responsible for obtaining water;
- provide appropriate technologies, developed in consultation with the communities, so that they meet their needs and can be maintained by them;
- emphasize training and education.

Artisanal fishing communities are among the poorest of groups. They are vulnerable to further impoverishment, because they often cannot protect their resource from outsiders or from habitat loss or degradation. Governments can help them by:

- confirming their customary rights to the fishery and giving them sole or priority access to it;
- restoring or establishing communal management institutions;
- delegating management of the fishery to the community, or sharing management with it;
- encouraging public input and participation;
- protecting the ecosystems on which the fishery depends.

Artisanal fishing communities should be allowed to fish sustainably in appropriate protected areas. This would enable community members to pursue a traditional life-style; and, by giving

---

Box 26. Institutions for management of transboundary waters

Examples of such mechanisms include the Mekong Committee, the Treaty for Amazonian Cooperation, and the Canada/USA International Joint Commission. Formal and informal dispute management and procedural mechanisms should be developed in the spirit of the 1966 Helsinki Rules or subsequent proposals made by the International Law Association, the Institute of International Law, the Economic Commission for Europe, and others.

Governments should also consider the development of strategies and action plans, such as the Rhine Action Plan, to address priority problems. These should pay particular attention to full evaluation of the hydrological balance of the river system, including the role of wetlands and other aquatic ecosystems.

Greater regional cooperation to prevent and control transboundary water pollution would improve coordination of national water policies and strategies in all catchment areas. Legally binding agreements would strengthen measures both at national and river basin levels to protect and use sustainably transboundary waters and related aquifers. An example is the regional convention being developed by ECE governments on the protection and use of transboundary watercourses and international lakes.

The Convention on Wetlands of International Importance especially as Waterfowl Habitat (Ramsar Convention) provides a unique mechanism for international cooperation in management of aquatic ecosystems. All countries with significant wetland resources should accede to it. High-income countries should use the Convention as a mechanism to channel money and technical assistance to lower-income countries for the management of these resources. Contracting Parties should recognize the role of sound wetland management in helping to maintain water supplies and the role of effective water management in maintaining wetland ecosystems. Wetland management policies and plans should be integrated in national water policy and planning.

the community an economic stake in the protected area, could also improve protection. Such communities should also be enabled to form protected areas within their traditional territories, or to declare their entire area a restricted fishing zone.

In many drought-prone rainfed areas of lower-income countries, returns to agriculture can be substantially increased by community-based development and management of water harvesting and small-scale storage. In most of the countries concerned, technical and management support for such work is inadequate, and appropriate new support services need to be developed by nongovernmental and governmental agencies.

Major benefits would also accrue from restoring or giving to farmers' groups primary responsibility for operating and maintaining small irrigation systems, and for enabling farmers' groups, through negotiations with irrigation agencies, to take over responsibility for managing the lower sections of large irrigation systems. Both these actions would require irrigation agencies to reduce their areas of direct jurisdiction over water management decisions and to become much more responsive, service-oriented organizations.

Communities that obtain much of their livelihood from wetlands should be given high priority for primary environmental care projects. Wetlands can support a variety of uses, in addition to regulating water flow and quality and providing habitat for wildlife. However, they are easily overexploited, and many communities that depend on them currently over-use their resources. These communities need assistance to develop or restore sustainable management systems.

Action 15.10.   **Strengthen mechanisms for more effective international cooperation to share information and experience on how to use water and aquatic ecosystems sustainably.**

With 40% of the world's population living in river basins shared by two or more nations, the achievement of sustainability calls for competing demands to be solved amicably. It is important to promote mechanisms for conflict management, dispute resolution, or arbitration differences in transboundary water resources, including establishment of funded units to facilitate negotiations (see Box 26).

Action 15.11.   **Identify and protect aquatic species that are rare or threatened.**

Fresh waters support many species of plants, fish and invertebrates that are endemic to specific sites or river basins. Their habitat makes them vulnerable to changes in water regime and pollution, and many are now endangered. Many populations of these species, notably amongst fish, and the wild strains of many food plants such as rice, are important sources of genetic material used to improve domestic strains used in agriculture and aquaculture. This genetic diversity should therefore be maintained.

The intentional and accidental introduction of exotic species of fishes is increasingly affecting native fish faunas and has resulted in numerous extinctions. Sixty per cent of native cichlids in Lake Victoria are threatened by the introduction of the Nile perch. Many aquatic plants are causing similar problems, notably water hyacinth, which has spread to 80 countries in the last century.

Important actions for controlling introduction of exotics are:

- all water engineering projects should be assessed for their potential impact upon aquatic species, and measures taken to ensure that such projects do not reduce the biological diversity of the drainage basin;
- international agreements should be signed, banning introduction of exotic species in watersheds shared with another jurisdiction without express approval by that jurisdiction;
- introductions should not be made without prior analysis of the introductions and studies of the life history of the candidate species in its native range. It should be assumed that any introduced aquaculture stock will escape to the wild. Native species should first be evaluated for aquaculture purposes before considering introduction of exotic species;
- research should be undertaken and legislation developed to reduce the number of species being transferred to new countries and drainage basins via ballast water;
- research should also characterize the genetic diversity of freshwater species used in aquaculture, and ascertain how far the original genetic strains characteristic of the unexploited stocks can or should be maintained.

Box 27. Managing ecosystems to improve the quality of fresh waters

The resources of many rivers, water bodies and wetlands have been degraded or destroyed by pollution, drainage, channelization, or overexploitation.

Lake Karla in Greece was drained in the 1960s but the short-term gain of land for irrigated agriculture is now being overshadowed by problems of salinization, falling groundwater levels, pollution from agricultural chemicals and food processing factory waste, and social unrest as a result of unjust land allocation. It is now proposed to try and rehabilitate the lake.

Lake Fetzara in Algeria, drained originally by the former colonial administration, was reinstated in the early 1980s because it provided flood storage to protect the steelworks at Annaba. This single purpose restoration has actually provided multiple benefits because the slow release of winter flood water is used for downstream irrigation, the reestablished emergent vegetation provides a steady supply of forage as the lake level falls, and thousands of greylag geese from Europe have returned to overwinter at the lake as they did before it was drained.

In the Netherlands the Oievaar plan would remove some of the low summer dykes along the Rhine. The aim is to restore periodic inundation to floodplain forests. This will diversify the habitat and reestablish a supply of ecologically essential organic detritus to the delta region. This supply had been almost entirely lost through the complete embanking of the river and its dredging for navigation.

In Denmark, in the 1960s, the delta of the Skjern River was pumped dry and dyked for agriculture. It is now being partially returned to marshes and seasonally inundated floodplain. The aim is to reduce the severe pollution of the coastal fjords and sea by nutrients. This will be accomplished partly by reducing the area of intensive agriculture, and largely through the nutrient trapping facilities of the "natural" wetlands.

Box 28. Mountains

The waters of many of the world's great rivers rise in the mountains. Mountainous regions cover over 20% of the earth's surface but only 10% of the world's people live in them. Mountain inhabitants include some of the world's economically poorest but culturally richest people. Large populations at lower elevations depend on the mountains for their supply of water. They may also use energy generated on mountain rivers as well as the products of mountain forests. Many of the world's endangered plant and animal species, including valuable medicinal plants and cultivars are located in specialized mountain microhabitats. Numerous people use mountain landscapes to meet their recreational and spiritual needs.

It is not only the high, rugged mountains that are of particular interest and concern. Relatively low ranges have the same sorts of values and may be particularly important as centres of biological diversity. They may also be more seriously threatened because of their proximity to centres of human population.

Because of their steep slopes and greater exposure to winds, rain and snow than the lowlands and plains that surround them, mountains are subject to greater environmental stress. Mountain environments are currently under great threat. In Europe, about half of the forests, many of them in mountainous regions, are being badly damaged by pollution, including acid precipitation. Increased tourism is also placing adverse pressures on the high country. Erosion, both as a natural process and as a result of land clearing and poor land management, is leading to increased sedimentation in rivers downstream, and to decreasing productivity on site.

Poverty is intense in mountain regions such as the Himalayas, Andes, Atlas and Ethiopian highlands. Traditional cultures and ways of life are threatened. There are many health problems in mountain regions, including respiratory ailments and diarrhoeas in the tropics, and cancers in the north.

Mountain environments need to be maintained in as near a natural condition as possible to maximize conservation values at the global, national and local levels. Conservation of mountainous regions requires international cooperation where boundaries traverse mountain ridges.

Priority actions should include:
- instituting comprehensive social programmes for mountain dwellers;
- maintaining large areas in a natural state;
- undertaking programmes to restore mountain forests and to promote better grassland management and restoration.

The work of the World Mountain Network which links existing mountain centres and individuals interested in conservation in mountainous regions should be supported.

16. Oceans and coastal areas

The oceans are the dominant feature of this planet, covering more than two-thirds of its surface, and playing a key part in the hydrological cycle, the chemistry of the atmosphere and the making of climate and weather. Long a source of food, a network of shipping lanes and a playground, the seas have more recently become suppliers of energy, minerals, and medicines. These contributions will grow as technology advances and the resources of the land become more scarce.

The seas are also strange and exotic. Many marine creatures are quite unlike those on land. The very unfamiliarity of names such as comb jellies, endoprocts and kinorhynchs testifies to the gulf between the human mind and marine life. Most people are unaware of how they benefit from the oceans or what they do to them. The science and management of the seas and their resources have become the job of a few specialists, but they must in future be the concern of us all.

The Earth's surface	
Open ocean (beyond the continental shelves)	65%
Coastal zone (continental shelves + coastal plains)	8%
Uplands (above the coastal plains)	27%

The vastness of the oceans suggests that people cannot harm them. But their biological wealth is concentrated along a relatively narrow strip formed by the continental shelves, coastal margins and estuaries. Here are the major fishing grounds, yielding more than 80% of the world's fishing catch. Here, too, are the seas' most productive and diverse habitats: mangroves, saltmarshes, mudflats, seagrass and seaweed beds, and coral reefs. These habitats are vital for coastal protection, and provide food and shelter for a great variety of organisms, including the fishes, crustaceans and molluscs that account for more than two-thirds of world fisheries production.

The coastal zone, between the seaward margins of the continental shelves (to a depth of about 200 metres) and the inland limits of the coastal plains (to a comparable elevation above sea level) has the highest biological productivity on Earth. It is also home to most of the world's population, who depend on its resources and largely determine its state of ecological health. Six out of ten people live within 60 kilometres of coastal waters, and two-thirds of the world's cities with populations of 2.5 million or more are near tidal estuaries. Within the next 20-30 years the population of the coastal zone is projected to almost double. These pressures, linked to ever-increasing resource consumption and the impacts of expected climate change and sea level rise, will have major effects on the coastal zone. It may well be the main arena in which the efforts to create a sustainable society will take place. It will provide the benchmarks of success or failure.

As a result of human activities both inland and in the coastal zone itself, coastal and marine ecosystems and resources are rapidly deteriorating in many parts of the world. Urban, industrial, resort, and agricultural development are often poorly planned and regulated. Engineering and development projects are modifying coastal ecosystems on a very large scale. The coastal zone also receives pollution, both by direct discharge and via river systems. It is affected by changes in salinity and sedimentation regimes as a result of damming rivers and siltation due to deforestation and other land use changes. In fact, more than three-quarters of marine pollution comes from land-based sources, via rivers, direct discharges, and the atmosphere. The rest comes from shipping, dumping, and offshore mining and oil production. Coastal waters are the sinks for nearly all human-generated pollution. And more than 90% of all chemicals, refuse and other materials entering coastal waters remain there in sediments, wetlands, fringing reefs, and other coastal ecosystems.

Human inputs of nutrients into coastal waters already equal natural sources. Within 20-30 years they are projected to exceed the natural background by several times. The result will be a considerable extension of the kind of impact now found only in enclosed areas such as the Baltic and Japan's Inland Sea. Pathogens from sewage also pose health risks to bathers and to consumers of seafood. Many stocks of shellfish have had to be declared unfit for human consumption.

Organochlorines, other synthetic organic chemicals and heavy metals are the most widespread and serious chemical pollutants. In addition, plastic and other debris such as pieces of nets, ropes, packaging materials, straps and rings entangle and kill marine mammals, turtles, fishes and birds, litter shallow waters and beaches, and are found even at abyssal depths.

Despite these impacts, the world marine fish catch increased steadily during the 1980s, reaching 84 million tonnes a year in 1988. It is not expected that, even in the long term, the total will rise above 100 million tonnes. Most demersal fish stocks are fully fished. And much of the increase of the 1980s came from bigger catches of shoaling pelagic species such as Peruvian anchovy, South American sardine, and Japanese sardine whose populations are highly variable. Indeed, overfishing, facilitated by new technology and combined with natural population fluctuations, has led to the decline of some fisheries and to greater instability in others. Over-exploitation has reduced the yields of many fisheries below the theoretically sustainable harvest. Competition is growing among small-scale, large-scale and recreational fishing. Heavy pressure could reduce the genetic diversity and adaptability of the stocks or change the species composition of the fish communities.

Many fisheries are also being put at risk by habitat degradation. The biggest threats are to stocks affected by a combination of overfishing and habitat loss. Species that spend their youngest stages in brackish or fresh water are particularly vulnerable. There is also competition for habitat between fishing and aquaculture. Improperly sited aquaculture projects have severely damaged habitats (for example, shrimp farming has devastated mangroves, which are themselves important shrimp habitat, in South America and Southeast Asia). Escape to the wild of cultured stocks can disrupt native gene pools. A more general problem with aquaculture is the spread of pests and diseases, which poses a serious risk to wild stocks, as well as to the livelihood of fish farmers.

Marine resources are usually treated as communal or state property. The ecosystems and resources of the open ocean beyond 200 miles from the coast are still open access resources; and there is no effective, comprehensive legal regime to regulate their use. Establishment of

Exclusive Economic Zones (EEZs) which brought extensive resources under the control of coastal states represents the biggest ever peaceful transfer of ownership of resources, encompassing 40% of the sea and 30% of the earth's surface. But the tradition of common property persists and even within their EEZs, most countries fail effectively to control access to and use of living resources. Many nations have signed and ratified conventions on regional seas, fisheries conventions and regional fisheries agreements, and other agreements and action plans to protect coastal and marine ecosystems and resources. But most nations lack the programmes, institutions or resources to fulfill their obligations.

UNCLOS, the United Nations Convention on the Law of the Sea would be the first comprehensive, enforceable international environmental law, covering all forms of marine pollution (land-based, atmospheric, ship-borne, and originating from activities on the sea-bed). It takes an ecosystem approach to all uses of the oceans, and provides an advanced institutional framework for international environmental, scientific and technological cooperation. It is the only convention that provides for a comprehensive, binding system for the peaceful settlement of disputes. Although many nations have signed and notified UNCLOS, their number has not been sufficient to bring it into force (see Actions 9.2. and 16.10).

Many of these problems have been addressed during the last 20 years. Billions of dollars and thousands of lifetimes have been spent worldwide to understand and regulate human impact on the sea and its resources. But the efforts have most often focussed on symptoms rather than causes. The true value of the marine environment is not understood and the full social costs of using it and the resources it supports are not taken into account. Too often, scientific data are available but are not synthesized in a way to be understood and integrated into coastal management processes. In general, we have not yet grasped the concepts needed to manage relations between people and the oceans, particularly the need to look at coastal zone ecosystems as a whole and the benefits of managing environmental impacts on a drainage basin basis.

Priority actions

The challenge for management of the oceans is to use the resources and services provided by the marine environment to meet development objectives without degrading the quality of the environment or exhausting stocks of living resources. A change in development planning which recognizes the full values of the ocean and marine resources will require new tools which allow proper evaluation of the resources and environmental services the seas provide. Restructuring of national and international institutions will also be important.

Maintenance and sustainable use of the natural wealth of coastal zones and the oceans requires:

- greater consciousness of the importance of coastal zones and the oceans and of human impacts on them;
- integrated approaches to coastal and ocean management;
- better global and regional cooperation;
- greater involvement of local communities in the management of marine resources;
- conservation of coastal and oceanic ecological processes and biological diversity; and sustainable development of marine resources.

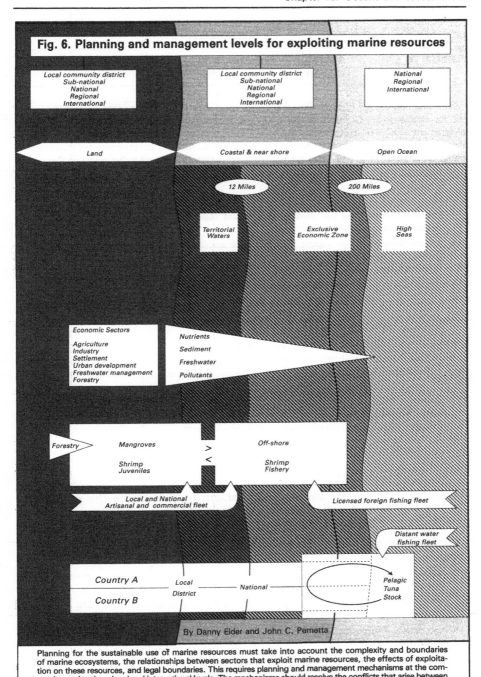

Fig. 6. Planning and management levels for exploiting marine resources

Local community district Sub-national National Regional International	Local community district Sub-national National Regional International	National Regional International

Land — Coastal & near shore — Open Ocean

12 Miles — 200 Miles

Territorial Waters — Exclusive Economic Zone — High Seas

Economic Sectors

Agriculture
Industry
Settlement
Urban development
Freshwater management
Forestry

Nutrients
Sediment
Freshwater
Pollutants

Forestry — Mangroves — Off-shore

Shrimp Juveniles — Shrimp Fishery

Local and National Artisanal and commercial fleet — Licensed foreign fishing fleet

Distant water fishing fleet

Country A
Country B

Local District — National — Pelagic Tuna Stock

By Danny Elder and John C. Pernetta

Planning for the sustainable use of marine resources must take into account the complexity and boundaries of marine ecosystems, the relationships between sectors that exploit marine resources, the effects of exploitation on these resources, and legal boundaries. This requires planning and management mechanisms at the community, national, regional and international levels. The mechanisms should resolve the conflicts that arise between sectoral uses and between users such as local and national fisheries and foreign fleets that exploit common resources such as shrimp or tuna.

Action 16.1.   Develop a national policy on the coastal zone and ocean.

National policies for conservation and natural resources management often neglect the marine environment. Governments and citizens' groups concerned with conservation, environment and development should ensure that the conservation and sustainable use of marine ecosystems and resources feature more largely in national programmes for planning, pollution control, protected areas and development control. National policies should:

- establish a mechanism to coordinate the planning and allocation of uses of the coastal zone (Action 16.2);
- provide a means of reviewing each sector's benefits from and impacts on the coastal zone and determining how the needs of each sector should be balanced and conservation and development combined;
- set out procedures for dealing with shoreline instability, including sea level rise, subsidence, saltwater intrusion, and settling of deltas during extraction of groundwater or hydrocarbons;
- reduce pollution of the sea from land-based sources;
- harmonize national marine policies and laws with UNCLOS (see Action 16.10);
- provide for cooperative action and shared use of the ocean and its resources beyond national jurisdiction.

All activities, regardless of how far inland they take place, and all policies must consider the need to protect the coastal zone and marine ecosystems. Environmental impact assessments (EIA) should specifically consider impacts on coastal and marine ecosystems (see Chapter 8).

All renewable and nonrenewable resource projects in the coastal zone and ocean should also be subject to EIA, taking full account of impacts on other users of aquatic resources and ecosystems. Oceanographers and marine ecologists should be consulted more systematically by the relevant authorities on decisions on coastal development.

Action 16.2.   Establish a mechanism to coordinate the planning and allocation of uses of the coastal zone.

Comprehensive coastal zone planning and management are essential everywhere, but priority should be given to:

- areas with dense and increasing populations, or high levels of per capita resource consumption, on coasts with restricted water circulation;
- areas where conflicts are occurring or foreseen due to pressure on coastal and marine resources;
- seas where overexploitation, pollution, or habitat loss have a major impact on resource production.

Coastal zone land use and management plans should (see Fig. 6):

- be organized by drainage basin and adjacent continental shelf ecosystem;
- include comprehensive planning of waste management on the basis of pollution prevention options that result in minimum harm to the environment and human health;

- regulate agriculture and other land uses to control erosion and siltation, and prevent chemical contamination and excessive input of nutrients;
- include local and regional management plans supported by quality criteria, assessment, monitoring and research.

Countries should use the best experience and technology to deal with coastal areas that are vulnerable to sea level rise, storm surges, flooding, or erosion. The main concern should be to maintain coastal habitats, such as mangroves and other wetlands, coral reefs, coastal barriers and lagoons, and natural coastal processes such as sedimentation and marsh growth that offer the best defences against adverse changes.

In some cases, modest engineering works may be justified. In others, changes in land use may be required. Only in cases where major population centres are threatened should substantial engineering works be considered. In almost all cases, the best coastal protection will be achieved by establishing buffer zones where uses are compatible with natural nearshore processes. The width of the buffer zones will depend on the likelihood of coastal disasters and habitat alteration.

Action 16.3. Allocate marine resource user rights more equitably among small-scale, large-scale and sport fisheries, and give more weight to the interests of local communities and organizations.

Small-scale, community based fisheries account for almost half the world fish catch for human consumption, employ more than 95% of the people in fisheries, and use only 10% of the energy of large-scale corporate fisheries (see Fig. 7). But governments often encourage large-scale and sport fisheries at the expense of small-scale fisheries because the former have more effective lobbies and are sources of foreign exchange. This policy needs review, giving more support to local community activities.

Few governments have been able to manage coastal resources sustainably. The capacity of coastal communities and organizations to manage the resources they use varies greatly with social and economic circumstances. In various parts of the world, coastal communities are mobile, moving with the resources they harvest, and resource policies need to take this factor into account. Where indigenous or traditional institutions survive and can form the basis of management, they may need to be strengthened or modified to enable them to cope with modern conditions. In other areas, the state has assumed management responsibility and communities may have become antagonistic to externally imposed management, yet depend on it for conservation of the resources. Even where traditional systems have broken down, it may still be worth while exploring opportunities for developing new management partnerships between governments and users. Education and training in conservation may then be necessary.

Sport fisheries often comprise a large portion of the take in certain areas or for certain species. The catches are often unquantified and poorly regulated, making fisheries management difficult. Management of sport fisheries should be integrated with that of other fisheries.

In situations of great pressure on coastal resources, particularly in densely populated areas, it is often necessary to reduce access to the resource and develop alternative means of livelihood. Aquaculture is one option. It is usually appropriate if a low-input system is used (small ponds, cages, pens, or tanks) so that it can be taken up by small communities, and if it is well integrated with conservation, particularly of the habitats of wild resource species.

Fig. 7. The world's two marine fishing industries - how they compare

	Large scale	Small scale
Number of fisherfolk employed	Around 500'000	Around 12'000'000
Annual catch of marine fish for human consumption	Around 29 million tonnes	Around 24 million tonnes
Capital cost of each job on fishing vessels	$ 30'000-$ 300'000	$ 250-$ 2500
Annual catch of marine fish for industrial reduction to meal and oil, etc.	Around 22 million tonnes	Almost none
Annual fuel oil consumption	1 4-1 9 million tonnes	1.4-1.9 million tonnes
Fish caught per tonne of fuel consumed	2-5 tonnes	10-20 tonnes
Fisherfolk employed for each $ 1 million invested in fishing vessels	5-30	500-4000
Fish destroyed at sea each year as by-catch in shrimp fisheries	6-16 million tonnes	None

Original in *NAGA*, the ICLARM Quarterly

Action 16.4. Use an ecosystem approach for management of marine resources.

Management of fishery resources should be based on knowledge of their size and distribution, variations in annual recruitment levels, and interactions among species. Initially, such knowledge may only be approximate but, as exploitation intensifies, further studies should be done to make the evaluations more accurate.

Because of the need to understand better the natural fluctuations of fish stocks and their relationship with environmental factors, the focus of management should be shifted toward entire ecosystems, using experience gained in the management of single stocks as well as other information. An ecosystem approach considers relationships among resources and their uses, and involves determining the carrying capacity of the ecosystem.

Lower-income regions may not have the scientific and technical resources for this approach. Also, many management problems cannot wait for the outcome of ambitious research programmes. Accordingly, a simplified way of managing from an ecosystem perspective is being developed by the International Centre for Living Aquatic Resource Management (ICLARM).

Action 16.5.	**Conduct information campaigns to raise the profile of coastal and marine issues; and include a strong marine component in environmental education in all countries.**

Governments, citizens' groups, and the media should aim for a major increase in awareness of the importance of the sea for all people and of the mounting threats to the coastal zone in particular. They should promote understanding of:

- the importance of the oceans for planetary life-support systems;
- the concept of the coastal zone, including its multiple-use characteristics;
- the vulnerability of coastal ecosystems and resources to the impacts of inland actions, including actions far upstream;
- the risks to public health due to contamination of coastal waters and seafood;
- property rights in the coastal and inshore marine environment, including limitations on fishery, mariculture and other exploitation;
- need for laws on pollution prevention, sustainable resource management, and protection of coastal and marine ecosystems and resources.

Effective campaigns and formal education need quantified information, including maps, data on marine resources and uses, and on habitat losses and other indicators of coastal degradation. Laws and international conventions should be translated into the languages of the relevant user groups and widely publicized.

Action 16.6.	**Promote marine protected areas.**

The worldwide network of coastal and marine protected areas is far less developed than its terrestrial counterpart. Governments should greatly accelerate the establishment and effective management of coastal and marine protected areas and should in particular:

- urgently develop a "system plan" for protected areas to safeguard representative coastal and marine ecosystems;
- extend these by regional system plans;

- develop guidelines for designating areas;
- prepare management plans for all such protected areas, where possible integrating them as part of a comprehensive planning mechanism for all uses of coastal ecosystems (as pioneered by the Great Barrier Reef Marine Park Authority in Australia).
- seek means of protecting localized and biologically and scientifically important oceanic ecosystems, such as sea vents and sea mounts.

Marine protected areas would serve as replenishment areas for marine resources, and should be designed to maintain the genetic diversity of key species. A global system plan should be prepared by 1992 and the full system should be in place by 2010.

Action 16.7.   Conserve key and threatened marine species and gene pools.

Subsistence whaling is important culturally and economically for a number of indigenous and lower-income communities, and must be respected as long as the whale stocks in question are not jeopardized. The moratorium on commercial whaling should be maintained. Non-destructive methods for scientific research on whales should be further developed and universally practised.

Marine turtles are widely threatened. The main actions needed are at regional and local levels. Major nesting beaches should be protected from development. Projects should be prepared with local communities to meet their development needs, and enable them to conserve and use sustainably their turtle resources.

Protection of other threatened species, such as the monk seals, is also a high priority.

International agreements should be developed to ban introduction of exotic species into seas, archipelagos or coastlines shared by jurisdictions without express approval of all the jurisdictions concerned. As noted under Action 15.11, no introduction should be made without prior analysis of the life history of the species concerned, and action should be taken to prevent the transference of species to new habitats via ship's ballast water.

Consideration should be given to banning fishing methods with a high impact on non-target species, notably dynamiting, the use of long drift nets, and the use of non-degradable fish traps.

Mechanisms need to be developed to protect relict fauna, such as the coelocanth, and the species assemblages of sea vents and sea mounts. The potential of aquaria to serve as *ex situ* genebanks, particularly of rare invertebrates, should be explored.

Action 16.8.   Place high priority on preventing marine pollution from land-based sources.

Pollution means the direct or indirect introduction by people of substances or energy into the marine environment (including estuaries) resulting in harm to living resources and ecological systems, hazards to human health, hindrance to fishing and other legitimate uses of the environment, impairment of sea water quality, and reduction of amenities.

The precautionary approach (see Chapter 4), the Polluter Pays Principle and User Pays Principle (see Chapter 8) should be applied to the prevention of marine pollution. Technology to reduce or eliminate pollution at source should continue to be improved, regulations enforced, and economic instruments strengthened. Existing pollution should be reduced as quickly as possible.

Control of land-based pollution requires major changes in agricultural and industrial practices, as well as the development of waste treatment technology and the development or expansion of treatment facilities both along the coast and far inland. The main changes needed include:

- comprehensive control of sewage discharges;

- reducing runoff of fertilizers and livestock wastes from agricultural land through the adoption of high standards of land husbandry;

- limiting industrial effluents through more efficient use of resources and use of clean production technology;

- prohibition of plastics disposal from land (it is already banned from ships by MARPOL 73/78, Annex 5).

Special attention should be paid to improving sewage treatment to reduce risks to public health from consuming seafood and bathing in contaminated water and consuming contaminated seafood.

Uses of herbicides, pesticides, nitrate and phosphate fertilizers, and synthetic organic chemicals should be rigorously controlled, and the adoption of integrated pest management should be accelerated (see Action 13.7). Sedimentation needs to be greatly reduced through controlling land clearance and limiting deforestation (see Chapters 13 and 14). The flow of nutrients to coastal waters should be maintained at acceptable levels by restricting impoundments (see Action 15.6).

Much more work needs to be done to develop water quality criteria and effluent standards, particularly for the tropics.

So far, only five conventions contain provisions for the control of pollution from land-based sources. The five conventions are: the Convention for the Prevention of Marine Pollution from Land-Based Sources, 1974 (Paris Convention), covering the northeast Atlantic; the Convention on the Protection of the Marine Environment of the Baltic Sea Area, 1974 (Helsinki Convention); the Athens Protocol (1980) to the Barcelona Convention, covering the Mediterranean; the Quito Protocol (1981) to the Lima Convention, covering the southeast Pacific (GESAMP, note 2); and the 1990 protocol to the Kuwait Regional Convention for Cooperation on the Protection of the Marine Environment from Pollution. Other regional agreements are being developed but the work needs greatly to be accelerated. The Montreal Guidelines for the Protection of the Marine Environment against Pollution from Land-based Sources, drafted by the United Nations Environment Programme, could be the basis for new regional conventions which should also cover pollution of the ocean via the atmosphere. The World Meteorological Organization is developing a technical annex covering marine pollution via the atmosphere, to be attached to the Protocol for the Protection of the Mediterranean Sea against Pollution from Land-based Sources.

Action 16.9.   **Adopt procedures for effective prevention of pollution from ships and offshore installations, and for rapid response to emergencies such as oil spills.**

Current international agreements, especially the IMO MARPOL Conventions, have greatly reduced oil pollution and the dumping of toxic materials from ships. But they need stricter enforcement, along with provision of new guidelines. In particular:

- operational discharges of oil by tankers should be stopped. These chronic oil spills account for the largest source of marine oil pollution and could easily be prevented if efficient enforcement mechanisms for MARPOL (Annexes 1 and 2) were developed;

- educational campaigns should be mounted to encourage the owners and crew of ships to dispose of plastics and other synthetic materials safely;

- all ports should establish facilities for the reception of ships' wastes;

- plastic packing materials should have degradable sections to reduce the risk of their trapping animals.

Few countries have adequate contingency plans and emergency response procedures. The International Maritime Organization is preparing a convention on emergency preparedness and response. However, governments and industry need to establish clear and effective procedures. Those of the Shetland Oil Terminal Environmental Advisory Group in the United Kingdom are a model which could be followed more widely.

Action 16.10. **Ratify or accede to the United Nations Convention on the Law of the Sea (UNCLOS) and other international legal instruments and develop an effective regime for sustainable use of open-ocean resources.**

UNCLOS provides a comprehensive, enforceable framework for conservation and sustainable use of the seas and the basis for international cooperation toward this end. Although some 45 nations are applying the treaty, it is not yet in force, since this requires ratification or accession by 60 states. Governments, international bodies, and citizens groups should persuade governments that have not yet done so to ratify or accede to UNCLOS. The UNCLOS Secretariat should make greater efforts to bring the Convention into force and secure adherence by the major marine states. Consideration of amendment should await its coming into force.

UNCLOS states the obligation of States to cooperate to conserve the living resources of the high seas. However, none of the existing international mechanisms provides sufficient direct control of resource conservation and fisheries development outside Exclusive Economic Zones. Unregulated driftnet fishing on the high seas illustrates the need for an international management regime to ensure that uses of the open ocean are sustainable.

The regime should require a moratorium on exploitation of newly discovered resources of the open ocean and deep sea-bed, including fans, vents and mounts, and of known resources not yet being used. All exploitation should be subject to environmental impact assessment, and the moratorium should be maintained until adequate provision is made for conservation of the resources concerned.

A number of other global instruments deal either with marine pollution (for example, the London Dumping Convention, certain regional Conventions and IMO Conventions controlling pollution from ships) or conservation of living marine resources (for example, the Geneva Convention on the Living Marine Resources of the High Seas). States that have not yet done so should adhere to them. States should also adhere to regional conventions established for their areas and consider negotiating new regional instruments where these do not yet exist.

Action 16.11. Expand and strengthen international cooperation, both regionally and among funding agencies and intergovernmental organizations.

Regional cooperation can take a variety of forms, including regional seas programmes and regional fisheries bodies. No single model is appropriate for every region. Existing regional programmes should reexamine their priorities and how they are set.

Adequate trust funds should be established for each of the regional seas programmes. New ways of generating the necessary funds may have to be devised, including the introduction of regional environmental taxation.

Regional fisheries bodies provide a means of promoting cooperation in fisheries research, conservation and development, including assembling and exchanging data on fish stocks, catches, landings, and fishing effort; finding solutions to the allocation of shared stocks; and undertaking joint research. Governments should make a stronger commitment to these bodies. Since their declaration of exclusive economic zones, countries have been more protective of their data and have reduced the effectiveness of international organizations.

In all regions there is need for greater scientific cooperation focussed on an ecosystem approach. Regional centres for the joint development of environmentally safe and socially relevant marine technology should be established within each regional seas programme, in accordance with Articles 276 and 277 of UNCLOS. Regional action plans need to be developed for the Arctic Ocean, Black Sea, South Asian Seas, North Pacific, Southwest Atlantic, South China Sea, and the Sea of Japan.

Development assistance for marine matters needs to be cross-sectoral and based on the ecosystem approach to planning and management. The large number of individual intergovernmental marine programmes results in gaps and duplication. Governments should consider ways of consolidating the programmes and better coordinating the remainder.

Action 16.12. Promote inter-disciplinary research and exchange of information on marine ecosystems.

Interdisciplinary research is particularly needed on the capacity of coastal seas and regional ecosystems to withstand various levels of human activity.

The required research on marine ecosystems must be inter-disciplinary, and demands the interaction of scientists with different training and experience, for example, oceanographers, fishery scientists, meteorologists, ecologists, and social scientists. Research for coastal zone management requires the integration of terrestrial, estuarine and marine sciences. The social, economic and political dimension of resource use also needs to be studied.

The projects of the Group of Experts on the Effects of Pollutants (GEEP) of the Intergovernmental Oceanographic Commission's Global Investigation of Pollution in the Marine Environment (GIPME) exemplify an interdisciplinary approach to evaluating the biological effects of pollutants.

Long-term monitoring is required to keep track of changes in marine ecosystems. The results of monitoring should be analyzed and used to improve policies and management. Integrated environmental databases, such as Geographical Information Systems (GIS), are essential for translating a variety of data into useful information for decision makers.

Development assistance agencies and research institutions in high-income countries should assist lower-income countries to strengthen their marine science capabilities, including the establishment of laboratories that can reliably measure agricultural and industrial contaminants.

PART III

Implementation and Follow-up

Part I set out the nine principles on which a sustainable society must be based, and the Chapters in Parts I and II elaborated them. Taken together, the two Parts send a clear message that changes in the behaviour of individual people, communities and nations are essential if humanity is to live in harmony within the world of nature.

Caring for the Earth sets out broad lines of advance, but strategies do not implement themselves. Most important will be how people and communities respond: what they do to make the change to living sustainably, and how fast they move.

In the single Chapter that forms Part III, guidelines are proposed to help the users adapt the Strategy to their own needs and capabilities. It suggests ways towards implementation. It also describes how the partner organizations propose to follow up the Strategy themselves, working with the community of users.

A document like the present one is neither the start nor the end of a process. Already many documents have pointed the way towards sustainability. Already many actions have been taken. The world has advanced a great deal in its understanding of environmental needs and priorities since the nations of the world met at Stockholm in 1972 in the United Nations Conference on the Human Environment and since the World Conservation Strategy was published in 1980. The Preparatory Committee for the United Nations Conference on Environment and Development, to be held in Rio de Janeiro in June 1992, is elaborating an agenda of action – "Agenda 21" – for the coming century. The present Strategy is intended to help us move towards that century with confidence, emphasizing issues that must be addressed if humanity's progress is to be assured.

Part III begins with a check-list of 122 actions elaborated in the two preceding sections of this Strategy. It adds a further 10 actions, of which the last — on monitoring and evaluating the Strategy — is the key to the follow-up action the partners will be taking. Part III also sets out a series of targets: of achievable, concrete steps that could be taken by specified dates. The list of targets is not exhaustive, and the partners themselves expect to add to and refine it as monitoring and evaluation proceed. The targets are stated here as a first step — and a challenge to all who take seriously the need to move towards sustainability.

17. Implementing the Strategy

Caring for the Earth poses challenges. There are no easy solutions. The problems we face cannot be solved overnight by some new vision on the part of world leadership. Action by governments and strengthened international institutions is clearly a part of the solution; in fact, it is essential, but it is not enough. The attitudes and practices of individuals — the action on the ground — count just as much. And governments and community leaders will do their share only if they are both supported and pressed to action by individuals and citizens' groups.

Caring for the Earth is addressed to the whole world community. The world leaders who will participate in the UN Conference on Environment and Development are an important audience, but so are non-governmental organizations and professional groups, religious leaders and educators, business people, farmers and fisherfolk – all those who find in its statements an echo of their own concerns and convictions. It is not necessary that they agree with every statement between these covers. It is not necessary that they find all the actions in the Strategy relevant to their circumstances. It is necessary that they take and follow up those actions which they believe to be right and timely, and that they do so with a sense of urgency. The world is running out of space and time.

The organizations that joined in partnership to prepare this Strategy commit themselves to do their utmost to secure its implementation. They will help governments and NGOs to play their parts. They will plan and coordinate their efforts, adjusting their budgets and programmes to give priority to the vital tasks that must be undertaken if we are truly to care for the Earth.

Agenda

Chapters 2-16 list 122 actions which need to be taken if a sustainable society is to be established. There are 10 additional actions in this chapter. A check-list of all the actions begins on page 174.

The establishment of targets for achievement is a means of both focussing action towards concrete ends and evaluating its results. This is a time-honoured and deliberate practice in business and one that many individuals also follow.

Targets for achieving some of the results at which this Strategy is aimed are set out in Box 31, following the check-list of actions.

Priority actions

Individuals and groups should now:

- study the check-lists of actions and targets, and determine which have the highest priority for them as individuals, as members of citizens' groups and local communities, and as citizens of their nations;

- review what changes they should make at home and at work in their own approach to life and in the policies of the groups to which they belong;
- promote the Strategy within their local groups, communities and nations;
- begin to plan specific actions based on the Strategy;
- work for reorientation of national and international policies and institutions to implement the Strategy.

The partner organizations will:

- assist as much as they can in implementation of the Strategy;
- monitor and evaluate implementation of the Strategy;
- review, update and amend the proposed targets through an interactive process with users of the Strategy;
- publish annual reports on implementation.

Study the Strategy and prepare for change

The Strategy argues for fundamental changes in how people live. Not all the actions fit every person's circumstances. None of the actions can be implemented easily or instantly. Hence the first thing is for readers to take the Strategy seriously enough to read it carefully and critically. They can then work out what it means for each of them as an individual and as a member of one or several communities.

Action 17.1.   Study the Strategy and consider its implications.

All readers of this Strategy should consider its message from an individual standpoint. They should begin with the nine principles for living sustainably, set out in Chapter 1, and the ethic of sustainable living in Chapter 2. These provide benchmarks against which to assess their own codes of belief. Some people may want to challenge some of the assertions, and may find it helpful to contact local environment or development groups, and discuss their concerns with them.

Groups concerned with conservation, development, and humanitarian aid should also study the message. They might give particular attention to working with the coalitions to promote the world ethic for sustainable living proposed in Chapter 2, and the measures that need to be taken to enhance the quality of life outlined in Chapter 3 and to change personal attitudes and practices as suggested in Chapter 6. They should also review the ability of their own local communities to care for their environments, using Chapter 7 as a guide, and evaluate the changes that may be needed. Finally, they should remind themselves of what is needed to care for the Earth and manage sectoral activities, as described in Chapters 4 and 5 and Chapters 10-16 (Part II).

Governments, government agencies and local administrations should look hard at all the chapters, but especially Chapters 3, 4, 5, 7, 8, 9 and the sectoral surveys in Part II. They will find that many of the proposed actions have implications for their ways of doing things. Even if the prescriptions in the Strategy pose a difficult challenge, they should consider carefully the arguments for change.

Action 17.2.   **Evaluate the implications of the Strategy for the policies and approaches of citizens' groups, NGOs, local communities, governments and international bodies.**

The first phase should be to identify and implement solutions that can be carried out quickly. This action follows immediately from Action 17.1, and involves:

- every citizens' group reviewing its plans and priorities and adjusting them to take account of new insights;
- local communities and local governments reviewing the priorities in their areas, and adjusting community development and conservation plans accordingly;
- governments' reviewing the adequacy of their policies and administrative capabilities in the many sectors addressed in the Strategy, and their ability to undertake the many tasks proposed for them.

National leaders could appoint groups of experts to examine the most important environmental problems and their underlying causes, and prescribe actions to deal with them. The focus would be on measures including investments that would make a significant difference and could be taken within two years.

A second phase of policy review should consider how, in the longer term, to address the main environment and development problems in a comprehensive, cross-sectoral and integrated fashion. It should:

- involve a wide range of people, in and out of government;
- span all major sectoral units within government and government agencies, and reach through local government to grass-roots citizens' groups;
- promote dialogue among government, industry and conservation and development NGOs;
- lead to the reformulation of development plans, conservation strategies, laws, regulations, pollution prevention policies, and economic policies in accordance with the goal of sustainability;
- specifically consider the application of principles such as the Precautionary Principle, the Polluter Pays Principle and the User Pays Principle, and techniques like Environmental Impact Assessment in national and local circumstances;
- lead on to the preparation or review and revision of national strategies such as Environmental Action Plans and National Conservation Strategies, and the development of a national strategy for sustainability (see Action 17.7).

Promote the Strategy

A concerted effort is needed to inform and educate people about the need for and principles of living sustainably and about the priority actions contained in the Strategy. Governments could be in the lead, but they may need encouragement and support. Public opinion is a powerful force for change, especially in democracies protected by the rule of law.

Action 17.3.   **Promote the Strategy through broadly based national and international publicity campaigns.**

The Strategy needs promotion by all sectors of the community, but there is a special role for non-governmental organizations and citizens' groups. They should:

- mount broad campaigns to persuade people and groups to change their attitudes and practices (see Box 9, Chapter 6);
- catalyze and support actions by individuals and communities;
- persuade governments to take action;
- work with governments, business and other sectors where they have begun action.

Action 17.4.   **Promote the Strategy within government.**

National leaders — heads of government — have a key role in mobilizing action toward a sustainable society. Steps that they can take include:

- convincing their inner circle of the importance of altering national policies to achieve sustainability, and of their determination to move in this direction;
- adopting sustainability — and the ways of working towards it — as consistent themes in speeches, and stimulating the public and private media to take up these themes;
- making the coordination of action for sustainability a responsibility of the national leader's office;
- launching a national strategy for sustainability (see Action 17.7);
- insisting that their states play a responsible part in the quest for global sustainability.

Parliaments and national legislative assemblies can play a major part by:

- taking up public debate on the principles of sustainability, and building consensus on the national and local actions that need to be taken;
- establishing a national vision of the future that spans political parties, and takes a long-term view. This may require setting up mechanisms to mediate conflicts among interest groups;
- reviewing and strengthening national legislation for sustainable resource management, environmental care, pollution prevention, etc. (see Chapter 8);
- involving citizens' groups in hearings and policy formulation, and taking any necessary steps to protect their political freedom;
- ensuring that national policies are extended by international actions which promote global sustainability (see Chapter 9).

In countries with federal systems, the above paragraphs also apply to the leaders, governments and parliaments of the provinces, states or territories.

Steps in implementing the Strategy

Enough has been said to make it clear that the Strategy will fail if all it leads to is talk. There has been too much of this in recent years, with thunderstorms of rhetoric followed by droughts of inaction. The test of the Strategy is the actions to which it will give rise.

Action 17.5. Provide communities with the opportunity to prepare local strategies for sustainability.

Preparation of local strategies enables communities to express their views on conservation and development issues, defining their needs and aspirations, and formulating a plan for the development of their area to meet their social and economic needs sustainably (see also Chapter 7).

Local strategies enable the communities involved to define and achieve the kind of development that is most appropriate for them. If approved by the responsible government, each such strategy could form the basis of land-use policies and a land-use plan for the area. Local strategies could usefully be undertaken as part of a national or subnational strategy, but if neither of these is available there is no reason why local strategies should not be done independently.

The geographical scope of a local strategy should be defined by the community (or communities) undertaking it. A local strategy can provide:

- a forum and process through which the community can reach consensus on the goals, scale and pace of development, including the preferred nature, size and structure of the future economy of the area;
- a means by which the community can agree: (a) measures to conserve the environment and ensure that each sector's resource base is secure; (b) measures to promote each sector's development; (c) an integrated plan of action to ensure that the two sets of measures are in harmony, and will provide a balance among sectors and a future economy consistent with the needs and values of the community;
- a mechanism for developing a constructive dialogue and reaching agreement with other affected communities and interests on the area's future.

Guidance on local strategies is given in Annex 8.

Action 17.6. Organize governmental agencies to implement the Strategy.

The key implementing agencies in many nations are the sectoral and specialist ministries, departments, authorities and inspectorates. They will lead in many of the actions in this Strategy. They should:

- consider how to integrate environment and development in their organization and procedures (see Chapter 8);
- develop inter-sectoral links, and where necessary alter mandates and practices so that the government agencies respond to inter-sectoral issues (Action 8.1);
- review programmes and projects already under consideration for sustainability, adjusting these where necessary;
- ensure that the structure and policies of their foreign affairs and development assistance organizations enable them to participate effectively in the global alliance (see Chapter 9).

Action 17.7.   Undertake national and subnational strategies for sustainability.

National Conservation Strategies (NCSs) were proposed by the World Conservation Strategy as a means for countries to integrate conservation and development and take a comprehensive, cross-sectoral approach to conservation and resource management. By identifying the country's most urgent environmental needs, they assist decision makers in determining priorities, allocating limited resources, and building the institutional capacity to handle complex environmental issues. NCSs are prepared by nationals of the countries concerned, usually by governments in collaboration with citizens' groups, universities and research institutions, the private sector, and a wide array of other interest groups.

Environmental Action Plans (EAPs) are similar to NCSs, but are sponsored by the World Bank. EAPs are produced by teams or working groups consisting primarily of nationals from governmental agencies and citizens' groups. The Bank has provided technical assistance, funds for working materials and local and international consultants, and support for studies and national workshops.

Every country that has done an NCS or an EAP should review its adequacy as a strategy for sustainability. Other countries should directly undertake a national strategy for sustainability. Subnational jurisdictions within federal countries should also undertake such strategies (see Action 8.2).

In reviewing strategies and action plans, the following criteria should be borne in mind:

• each strategy or plan is unique: each should reflect local conditions, local needs, and the circumstances under which the strategy was prepared;

• conservation and development problems should be tackled in a comprehensive and integrated fashion;

• strategies should include a fundamental reexamination of policies, laws and institutions;

• the comprehensiveness of a strategy should enable countries to understand better how the problems they face relate to each other.

Further guidance on national strategies is given in Annex 8.

Action 17.8.   Build up the global alliance.

The global alliance outlined in Chapter 9 is crucial to the human future. Few, if any, nations have the resources and skills to achieve sustainability on their own — and those tempted to try could do so only by retreating into isolation. The global alliance is, in fact, so important that some of the relevant actions of Chapter 9 are consolidated here. Following the UN Conference on Environment and Development, governments should:

• strengthen and streamline the United Nations machinery to ensure a co-ordinated approach to environmental issues, based on an agenda whose priorities are determined by the widest practicable process of dialogue (see Action 9.9);

• build new machinery to ensure that dialogue at the national and international levels reflects the knowledge, skills and concerns of all sectors of society, including non-governmental organizations, business, commerce, industry, indigenous peoples, and religious groups (see Action 9.8);

- establish new international financial mechanisms that will support technical cooperation and promote the transfer and application of the best available technology in all parts of the world, and so create the best possible conditions for sustainable resource use and protection of the global environment;
- review and adapt the world's trading system so that markets are more open to the produce of lower-income countries, and so that, taken in conjunction with the elimination or rescheduling of debt and the increase in development assistance, net resource flows are reversed and run from the higher-income to the lower-income countries (see Actions 9.5, 9.6 and 9.7);
- strengthen the global machinery for monitoring and research, so that the policies of nations are increasingly based on a common body of reliable knowledge (see Action 8.10).

Action 17.9.   Fund the transition to sustainability.

Many of the priority actions — such as the proposals for integrating conservation and development — require doing things differently and more efficiently, but will not require new money. Laws and economic incentives to force changes in technology and economic restructuring will generate new investment opportunities. Thus financing much of the change to a sustainable society can be generated by the process of change itself.

Nonetheless, a number of priority actions will need new money: to assist lower-income countries to adopt resource-efficient and environment-friendly technologies; to double the supply of family planning services; improve education; provide basic health care and sanitation; rehabilitate degraded environments; conserve biological diversity; sustain agricultural productivity; expand reforestation; and increase energy efficiency and develop renewable sources of energy. The sums required are difficult to estimate but will certainly be large. One estimate is given in Annex 7. It calls for total expenditures of $77 billion/year in 1992, rising to $161 billion/year in 2001. The total for the decade would be $1,288 billion.

Much of this expenditure will lead to savings, or will provide a sufficient return to justify the investment in conventional terms. For example, family planning services will reduce health costs, and increasing energy efficiency is more cost-effective than building a new power plant.

The money needed for environmental investment in both upper- and lower-income countries could come from a combination of sources:

- reordering budgetary priorities among sectors to favour social and environmental priorities, by cutting spending on inefficient parastatals and stopping investment in unsustainable mega-projects;
- privatizing some government activities;
- making development spending more efficient;
- using savings realized from improved administrative and delivery mechanisms;
- reducing military expenditure (see Action 3.6 and Box 4);
- private sector investments;
- royalties;
- private, NGO, and corporate contributions;
- taxes and charges (see Chapter 8);
- multilateral and bilateral assistance programmes (see Chapter 9).

Box 29 sets out some of these options in detail.

Box 29. Ways of financing new investment in environmental care

Transfers from military budgets. Land degradation and soil erosion, deforestation, global warming, competition for water, human population growth, and movements of refugees pose major threats to national and regional security. Current world military expenditures of $900 billion per year do nothing to protect countries from these threats. Tackling them in peaceful ways would be a legitimate use of military budgets, which could cover the entire cost of this Strategy and still be huge. For example, if the world military budget were cut by amounts to meet the estimates given in Annex 7, military expenditure would still be $853 billion in 1991 (a reduction of 5%), and as high as $739 billion (a reduction of 18%) at the end of the century.

Private sector investment services could generate private investments in conservation. The service would be similar to that of an investment bank, gathering long-term capital, spreading risks, arranging access to technology, and improving incentives for investments in sustainable development of biological resources.

Earthcare Bonds. These could be either redeemable or non-redeemable. Proceeds from their sale would be used to build up a capital fund for investment, the proceeds of which would be used to finance some of the actions described in the Strategy after providing modest returns to the bond holders. Aggressively marketed to individuals and organizations wishing to make an affordable contribution to conservation and human development, and managed by a reputable international organization, such a scheme could yield a significant and continuing flow of income.

Royalties. Patents and plant breeder's rights compensate the final developers of a biological product, but do not compensate — and may penalize — the interim developers of the product or the conservers of its germplasm. Interim developers include farmers, and breeders of lines that contributed to the patented product; and conservers of germplasm include people who have spent money or forgone immediate gain to conserve gene pools that have contributed to the product.

A surcharge on royalties from patented biological materials would be equitable and could be collected through existing mechanisms for royalty collection and distribution. A surcharge of 1% on current royalty payments would yield an estimated $5 million per year. This sum could be paid into the fund administered under the International Undertaking on Plant Genetic Resources, which is intended to support conservation of germplasm, and thereby to compensate farmers, if only partially and indirectly. Alternatively, it could contribute to the proposed biodiversity fund.

Private, NGO, and corporate contributions. Private and non-governmental contributions to financing implementation of this Strategy should be sought, even though they will probably be relatively small.

But there is a rationale for greater commercial sponsorship of conservation. Corporations in 10 major industries — beverages, chemicals, clothing, food and confectionery, paper and wood products, pharmaceuticals, rubber and plastics, soaps and cosmetics, textiles, tobacco — depend wholly or partly on plants and animals for their raw materials. A significant proportion of these plants and animals is wild. The corporations benefit collectively from conservation of flora and fauna, but do not pay for it. Hence it would be appropriate for them to contribute directly to the costs of establishing and managing protected areas and other measures to maintain the wild gene pools, species, and habitats that form the biological resource base of their industry.

Lotteries and other fund raising schemes could raise substantial sums from individuals for some of the priority actions proposed in this Strategy. The schemes could include a tax on tickets at big international and national events, such as the Olympic Games and World Fairs and Expositions; telethons and other fund raisers; and an international lottery.

High-income countries can be expected to meet all of their environmental investment needs; and middle-income countries that are not highly indebted should be able to meet a substantial proportion of them. As the self-reliance of lower-income countries is increased (see Chapter 9), they should also be able to meet some of their environmental investment needs. In the meantime, low-income and highly indebted countries will need considerable assistance, particularly with the costs of measures from which the global society will gain long-term benefits, but which compete with the countries' immediate needs for investment in development.

Following up the Strategy

Monitoring and evaluation are often the weakest parts of strategies, action plans, and programmes. They are neglected, partly because they appear to divert resources from the "real work". In fact they are essential for effective action, since without them we do not know if we are dealing with the most important issues or whether the actions are effective.

Action 17.10.   **Monitor and evaluate the Strategy and its targets.**

When facing uncertainty and change — as in a strategy for sustainability — it is vital to track the evolution of issues, to monitor actions to address them, and to find out which work, which do not, and why. Without monitoring and evaluation, we cannot learn from experience, since no body of experience is available from which to learn. For example, no provision was made for continuous monitoring and evaluation of the World Conservation Strategy. Consequently, it has not been possible to base this Strategy on a full analysis of the 10 years of its implementation.

The partners recognize that the test of the Strategy's success is what happens after it is published. They will therefore monitor three levels of response:

- **Promotion.** Activities of the partners, sponsors, collaborators, and others to promote the Strategy;
- **Adoption.** Formal undertakings by governments, organizations, communities, and enterprises to implement the Strategy;
- **Implementation.** Implementation of the priority actions, at international, national, and (where practicable) local levels.

The list of targets for achieving a sustainable society on pp. 178-84 is tentative, in respect of both what it does and does not include, and the precise dimensions of each target. Some of those which are quantified strike the right balance between ambitiousness and practicality; others may aim too low or too high. Targets that have not been expressed quantitatively may need further refinement. For the resolution of very difficult issues — for example those related to the global economy, development cooperation and transfer of technology — there is clearly a need for further debate before realistic targets can be established.

The monitoring and evaluation process will be conducted through a centre established by the partners. It will create a database to receive reports and answer enquiries from partner users of the Strategy. The partners intend to publish a periodic Implementation Report, which will include suggestions for new or revised targets and indicators of sustainability as well as data on progress towards those previously established.

Box 30. Check-list of actions

Chapter 1. Building a sustainable society

Action 1.1. Develop new strategies for sustainable living, based on the nine principles

Chapter 2. Respecting and caring for the community of life

Action 2.1. Develop the world ethic for living sustainably.
Action 2.2. Promote the world ethic for living sustainably at national level.
Action 2.3. Implement the world ethic for living sustainably through action in all sectors of society.
Action 2.4. Establish a world organization to monitor implementation of the world ethic for living sustainably and to prevent and combat serious breaches in its observation.

Chapter 3. Improving the quality of human life

Action 3.1. In lower-income countries, increase economic growth to advance human development.
Action 3.2. In upper-income countries, adjust national development policies and strategies to ensure sustainability.
Action 3.3. Provide the services that will promote a long and healthy life.
Action 3.4. Provide universal primary education for all children, and reduce illiteracy.
Action 3.5. Develop more meaningful indicators of quality of life and monitor the extent to which they are achieved.
Action 3.6. Enhance security against natural disasters and social strife.

Chapter 4. Conserving the Earth's vitality and diversity

Action 4.1. Adopt a precautionary approach to polution.
Action 4.2. Cut emissions of sulphur dioxide, nitrogen oxides, carbon monoxide, and hydrocarbons.
Action 4.3. Reduce greenhouse gas emissions.
Action 4.4. Prepare for climate change.
Action 4.5. Adopt an integrated approach to land and water management, using the drainage basin as the unit of management.
Action 4.6. Maintain as much as possible of each country's natural and modified ecosystems.
Action 4.7. Take the pressure off natural and modified ecosystems by protecting the best farmland and managing it in ecologically sound ways.
Action 4.8. Halt net deforestation, protect large areas of old-growth forest, and maintain a permanent estate of modified forest.
Action 4.9. Complete and maintain a comprehensive system of protected areas.
Action 4.10. Improve conservation of wild plants and animals.
Action 4.11. Improve knowledge and understanding of species and ecosystems.
Action 4.12. Use a combination of *in situ* and *ex situ* conservation to maintain species and genetic resources.
Action 4.13. Harvest wild resources sustainably.
Action 4.14. Support management of wild renewable resources by local communities; and increase incentives to conserve biological diversity.

Chapter 5. Keeping within the Earth's carrying capacity

Action 5.1. Increase awareness about the need to stabilize resource consumption and population.
Action 5.2. Integrate resource consumption and population issues in national development policies and planning.
Action 5.3. Develop, test and adopt resource-efficient methods and technologies.
Action 5.4. Tax energy and other resources in high-consumption countries.
Action 5.5. Encourage "green consumer" movements.
Action 5.6. Improve maternal and child health care.
Action 5.7. Double family planning services.

Chapter 6. Changing personal attitudes and practices

Action 6.1. Ensure that national strategies for sustainability include action to motivate, educate and equip individuals to lead sustainable lives.

continued . . .

Action 6.2. Review the status of environmental education and make it an integral part of formal education at all levels.
Action 6.3. Determine the training needs for a sustainable society and plan to meet them.

Chapter 7. Enabling communities to care for their own environments

Action 7.1. Provide communities and individuals with secure access to resources and an equitable share in managing them.
Action 7.2. Improve exchange of information, skills, and technologies.
Action 7.3. Enhance participation in conservation and development.
Action 7.4. Develop more effective local governments.
Action 7.5. Care for the local environment in every community.
Action 7.6. Provide financial and technical support to community environmental action.

Chatper 8. Providing a national framework for integrating development and conservation

Action 8.1. Adopt an integrated approach to environmental policy, with sustainability as the overall goal.
Action 8.2. Develop strategies for sustainability, and implement them directly and through regional and local planning.
Action 8.3. Subject proposed development projects, programmes and policies to environmental impact assessment and to economic appraisal.
Action 8.4. Establish a commitment to the principles of a sustainable society in constitutional or other fundamental statements of national policy.
Action 8.5. Establish a comprehensive system of environmental law and provide for its implementation and enforcement.
Action 8.6. Review the adequacy of legal and administrative controls, and of implementation and enforcement mechanisms, recognizing the legitimacy of local approaches.
Action 8.7. Ensure that national policies, development plans, budgets and decisions on investments take full account of their effects on the environment.
Action 8.8. Use economic policies to achieve sustainability.
Action 8.9. Provide economic incentives for conservation and sustainable use.
Action 8.10.Strengthen the knowledge base, and make information on environmental matters more accessible.

Chapter 9. Creating a global alliance

Action 9.1. Strengthen existing international agreements to conserve life-support systems and biological diversity.
Action 9.2. Conclude new international agreements to help achieve global sustainability.
Action 9.3. Develop a comprehensive and integrated conservation regime for Antarctica and the Southern Ocean.
Action 9.4. Prepare and adopt a Universal Declaration and Covenant on Sustainability.
Action 9.5. Write off the official debt of low-income countries, and retire enough of their commercial debt to restore economic progress.
Action 9.6. Increase the capacity of lower-income countries to help themselves.
Action 9.7. Increase development assistance and devote it to helping countries develop sustainable societies and economies.
Action 9.8. Recognize the value of global and national non-governmental action, and strengthen it.
Action 9.9. Strengthen the United Nations system as an effective force for global sustainability.

Chapter 10. Energy

Action 10.1. Develop explicit national energy strategies.
Action 10.2. Reduce the use of fossil fuels, wastage in energy distribution, and pollution from commercial energy generation.
Action 10.3. Develop renewable and other non-fossil fuel energy sources.
Action 10.4. Use energy more efficiently in the home, industry, business premises and transport.
Action 10.5. Conduct publicity campaigns to promote energy conservation and the sale of energy efficient products.

continued . . .

Chapter 11. Business, industry and commerce

Action 11.1 Promote sustainability through dialogue between industry, government, and the environmental movement.
Action 11.2. Adopt high environmental performance standards backed up by economic incentives.
Action 11.3. Commit each business to sustainability and environmental excellence.
Action 11.4. Identify hazardous industries, and locate and operate them with stringent safeguards.
Action 11.5. Develop effective national and international systems for waste management.
Action 11.6 Ensure that all industries that are based on the use of natural resources use them economically.

Chapter 12. Human settlements

Action 12.1. Adopt and implement an ecological approach to human settlements planning.
Action 12.2. Develop more effective and representative local governments, committed to caring for their environments.
Action 12.3. Develop an efficient and sustainable urban transport policy.
Action 12.4. Make the city clean, green and efficient.

Chapter 13. Farm and range lands

Action 13.1. Undertake a national strategy for sustainability.
Action 13.2. Protect the best farm land for agriculture.
Action 13.3. Promote effective soil and water conservation through proper land husbandry.
Action 13.4. Reduce the impact of agriculture on marginal lands already in production.
Action 13.5. Encourage the adoption of integrated crop and livestock farming systems, and raise the efficiency of fertilizer use.
Action 13.6. Increase the productivity and sustainability of rainfed farming.
Action 13.7. Promote integrated pest management.
Action 13.8. Control the use of fertilizers, pesticides and herbicides through regulations and incentives.
Action 13.9. Promote international action to conserve genetic resources.
Action 13.10.Expand ex situ efforts to conserve genetic resources.
Action 13.11.Provide for in situ conservation of wild genetic resources (also see Chapter 4).
Action 13.12.Attempt to increase non-farm employment for small farmers and the landless.
Action 13.13.Switch from price supports to conservation supports.
Action 13.14.Promote primary environmental care by farmers.

Chapter 14. Forest lands

Action 14.1. Establish a permanent estate of natural and modified forest in every nation and manage it to meet the needs of all sectors of society.
Action 14.2. Establish a comprehensive system of protected natural forests.
Action 14.3. Establish and maintain an adequate permanent estate of modified forest.
Action 14.4. Increase the area of planted forest.
Action 14.5. Increase national capacity to manage forests sustainably.
Action 14.6. Strengthen community management of forests.
Action 14.7. Expand efforts to conserve forest genetic resources.
Action 14.8. Create a market for forest products from sustainably managed sources and use wood more efficiently.
Action 14.9. Set stumpage prices to reflect the timber's full value; charge licence fees that discourage exploitation of stands of marginal commercial value; and auction concessions competitively.
Action 14.10.Increase the capacities of lower-income countries to manage forests sustainably; and improve international cooperation in forest conservation and sustainable development.

Chatper 15. Fresh waters

Action 15.1. Improve the information base for sustainable water management.
Action 15.2. Undertake awareness campaigns and education programmes on sustainable use of water.

continued . . .

Action 15.3. Provide training in the management of human uses of, and impacts on, the water cycle.

Action 15.4. Manage water and demand to ensure efficient and equitable allocation of water among competing uses.

Action 15.5. Give greater emphasis to the drainage basin as the unit of water management (see also Action 4.5).

Action 15.6. Integrate the development of water resources with conservation of ecosystems that play a key role in the water cycle.

Action 15.7. Establish a cross-sectoral mechanism for integrated water management.

Action 15.8. Establish procedures to act rapidly in response to natural and human-caused hazards.

Action 15.9. Give local communities greater control over the management of aquatic resources and strengthen their capacity to use them.

Action 15.10. Strengthen mechanisms for more effective international cooperation to share information and experience on how to use water and aquatic ecosystems sustainably.

Action 15.11. Identify and protect aquatic species that are rare or threatened.

Chapter 16. Oceans and coastal areas

Action 16.1. Develop a national policy on the coastal zone and ocean.

Action 16.2. Establish a mechanism to coordinate the planning and allocation of uses of the coastal zone.

Action 16.3. Allocate marine resource user rights more equitably among small-scale, large-scale and sport fisheries, and giving more weight to the interests of local communities and organizations.

Action 16.4. Use an ecosystem approach for management of marine resources.

Action 16.5. Conduct information campaigns to raise the profile of coastal and marine issues; and include a strong marine component in environmental education in all countries.

Action 16.6. Promote marine protected areas.

Action 16.7. Conserve key and threatened marine species and gene pools.

Action 16.8. Place high priority on preventing marine pollution from land-based sources.

Action 16.9. Adopt procedures for effective prevention of pollution from ships and offshore installations, and for rapid response to emergencies such as oil spills.

Action 16.10. Ratify or accede to the United Nations Convention on the Law of the Sea (UNCLOS) and other international legal instruments and develop an effective regime for sustainable use of open-ocean resources.

Action 16.11. Expand and strengthen international cooperation, both regionally and among funding agencies and intergovernmental organizations.

Action 16.12. Promote inter-disciplinary research and exchange of information on marine ecosystems.

Chapter 17. Implementing the Strategy

Action 17.1. Study the Strategy and consider its implications.

Action 17.2. Evaluate the implications of the Strategy for the policies and approaches of citizens' groups, NGOs, local communities, governments and international bodies.

Action 17.3. Promote the Strategy through broadly based national and international publicity campaigns.

Action 17.4. Promote the Strategy within government.

Action 17.5. Provide communities with the opportunity to prepare local strategies for sustainability.

Action 17.6. Organize governmental agencies to implement the Strategy.

Action 17.7. Undertake national and subnational strategies for sustainability.

Action 17.8. Build up the global alliance.

Action 17.9. Fund the transition to sustainability.

Action 17.10. Monitor and evaluate the Strategy and its targets.

Box 31. Targets

Chapter 2. Respecting and caring for the community of life

By 1993:

Establishment of a network to link national coalitions for the world ethic for living sustainably (Action 2.1).

Establishment of the international organization to prevent and combat serious breaches of the world ethic (Action 2.4).

By 1995:

Establishment of national coalitions in 50 countries (Action 2.1).

Adoption by 50 Governments of national statements upholding the Covenant and the world ethic (Action 2.2).

Adoption by religious leaders, educators, economists, scientists, technologists and policy makers, through their worldwide professional organizations, of statements upholding the world ethic, and of practical guidelines for its implementation within their professional context (Action 2.3).

By 2000:

Establishment of national coalitions in 100 countries. Continuance of the other actions noted above (Actions 2.1, 2.2, 2.3, 2.4).

Chapter 3. Improving the quality of human life

By 2000:

A 2-3 % annual increase in average per capita earnings in lower-income countries (Action 3.1).

Immunization of all children against the main childhood diseases (Action 3.3).

Reduction of childhood mortality to at least half that of 1990 or to 10 per 1000 babies born alive, whichever is lower (Action 3.3).

Elimination of severe malnutrition and 50% reduction in moderate malnutrition (Action 3.3).

Provision of universal access to safe water and 80% access to sanitation (Action 3.3).

Provision of universal primary education for children, a halving of 1990 school dropout rates, and a halving of adult illiteracy with female illiteracy no higher than male illiteracy (Action 3.4).

Surveys in all countries to define areas vulnerable to natural disaster, adjustment of land use establishment and development policies, and establishment of early warning systems, shelters and disaster relief plans (Action 3.6).

A 20% reduction in annual global military and naval expenditure, and redirection of effort to social and environmental priorities (Action 3.6).

Formulation of a Quality of Life index that provides an effective measure of development (Action 3.5).

Chapter 4. Conserving the Earth's vitality and diversity

By 2000:

Adoption by all governments of the precautionary approach to pollution prevention (Action 4.1).

Reduction of sulphur dioxide emissions by at least 90% (based on 1980 levels) and nitrogen oxide emissions by 75% (based on 1985 levels) commitment to reducing hydrocarbon and further reductions of sulphur dioxide and nitrogen oxides emissions and progress towards regulatory systems that ensure no ecosystem receives more than its critical load in all higher-income countries (Action 4.2).

continued . . .

Manufacture and use of chlorofluorocarbons should have ceased in higher-income countries, with a rapid decline in lower-income countries (Action 4.3).

A plan for coping with climate change drawn up in all countries (Action 4.4).

Net global forest depletion should have ceased (Action 4.8).

Strategies for the conservation of national biological diversity established in all countries.

Targets for the proportion of their territory that they will maintain as natural and as modified ecosystems, together with plans for the target's achievement, should be adopted by all countries (Action 4.6).

Biodiversity conservation regions where economic activities and biodiversity conservation can be combined, should be designated by at least 50 countries.

Every country should have a system of protected areas covering 10% or more of each of its main ecological regions (Action 4.9).

All countries should accept responsibility for species found only in their territory, set targets for reducing the percentage of native species threatened with extinction, and adopt strategies for the conservation of their species diversity (Action 4.10).

Guidelines for sustainable wildlife use should be adopted in all countries (Action 4.10).

By 2005:

All high-energy and medium-high energy countries should have reduced their carbon dioxide emissions by at least 20% (from 1990 levels), and adopted a further target of 70% reduction before 2030 (Action 4.3).

Integrated systems for land and water management should be operative in at least 50 countries (Action 4.5).

By 2010:

CFCs should neither be made nor used anywhere in the world (Action 4.3).

Plans to limit other greenhouse gas emissions should be implemented in all upper-income countries (Action 4.3).

A comprehensive world *ex situ* and *in situ* genetic conservation system should be in operation (Action 4.12).

All depleted fisheries should be recovering and no fishery should be overexploited (Actions 4.13, 16.7).

Marine pollution should have been reduced so that no fishery poses a public health hazard because of contamination with pathogens or chemicals (Action 16.8).

A global system of coastal and marine protected areas should be established (Action 16.6).

Chapter 5. Keeping within the Earth's carrying capacity

By 2000:

Countries with per capita energy consumption above 80 gigajoules should reduce per capita energy consumption toward that level. The rate of reduction should be 1% per year until 2000, and 2% per year thereafter (Action 5.4).

Countries with per capita energy consumption of around 80 gigajoules should stabilize consumption at that level or below.

All high-consumption countries should set targets and a timetable for reducing consumption of raw materials per person (Action 5.4).

Countries with total fertility rates (TFRs) of 2.2-3.1 should reduce them to 2.1.

Countries with TFRs of 2.1 or less should maintain or reduce them (and in any case not increase them above 2.1).

At least double and preferably triple annual expenditures on family planning (Action 5.7).

By 2010:

Countries with TFRs of 4.2 and above should seek to halve them (Action 5.7).

Countries with TFRs of 3.2-4.1 should reduce them to 2.1.

continued . . .

Chapter 6. Changing personal attitudes and practices

By 1995:
Clearinghouse for information on environmental education established (Action 6.2).
By 2000:
National plans to promote sustainable living adopted in at least 50 countries (Action 6.1).
Support for environmental education and training doubled (from 1990) by development assistance agencies (Action 6.2).
By 2005:
Incorporation of environmental education in school curricula in all countries (Action 6.2).
By 2010:
Support for environmental education and training quadrupled (from 1990) by development assistance agencies (Action 6.2).
National plans to promote sustainable living adopted in all countries (Action 6.1).

Chapter 7. Enabling communities to care for their own environments

By 1995:
Secure commitments by development assistance agencies to support community action plans and programmes (Action 7.6).
By 2000:
Review in all countries, especially in conjunction with national strategies for sustainability, the ability of communities to care for their own environments.
Handbooks published drawing on the results, to help communities follow successful examples (Action 7.5).

Chapter 8. Providing a national framework for integrating development and conservation

By 2000:
Systems of national environmental law, backed by effective enforcement machinery, completed in all countries (Actions 8.4, 8.5).
Reviews of economic and administrative policy completed in all upper-income countries, with adjustments where necessary (Actions 8.6, 8.7, 8.8, 8.9).
Integrated global system, including the Environmental Early Warning Mechanism, created to monitor a set of agreed indicators of human development, human freedom, environmental quality and ecological sustainability (Action 8.10).
System of sustainability reporting established in all countries (Action 8.10).
Adoption by all countries of a national strategy for sustainability that is guided by information on the quality of human life and the environment and has the enhancement of both as its chief goal (Action 8.2).
By 2005:
Introduction of effective EIA procedures in all countries (Action 8.3).
By 2010:
Extension of the economic and administrative review process to all lower-income countries (Actions 8.6, 8.7, 8.8, 8.9).

Chapter 9. Creating a global alliance

By 1995:
Adoption and implementation of a comprehensive conservation regime for Antarctica (Action 9.3).

continued . . .

By 2000:
Completion and adoption by at least 50% of all countries, of the Universal Declaration and Covenant on Sustainability (Action 9.4).
Adherence to CITES, the World Heritage Convention, the Ramsar Convention, the Bonn Convention and the Undertaking on Plant Genetic Resources by 75% of nations (Action 9.1).
Completion, adoption and implementation of the Conventions on the conservation of biological diversity and on global climate by 50% of nations (Action 9.2).
Entry into force of UNCLOS (Action 9.2).
Effective integration of action on environmental issues within the UN system (Action 9.9).
Official debt of low-income countries eliminated, and their commercial debt reduced by 60% (Action 9.5).
Substantial enhancement of terms of trade for lower-income countries in world markets (Action 9.6).
Doubling of development assistance over the 1990 levels, effectively deployed to promote sustainability (Action 9.7).
Publication of an annual Statement on the Environment by the UN agencies, in partnership with other appropriate international organizations (Action 9.9).

By 2010:
Universal Declaration and Covenant and adherence to the major conservation Conventions adopted by 90% of all nations.
Conventions on the conservation of biological diversity and on climate change adopted by 75% of nations.

Chapter 10. Energy

By 2000:
National energy strategies that provide for achievement of targets for energy consumption per head as set out in Action 5.4 prepared by all countries.
All countries should be publishing annual reports on the implementation of national energy strategies and on specific action taken to promote efficiency in the use of fossil fuels, develop alternative sources, use energy more efficiently in the home, at work and in transport, and share their knowledge in these fields with other countries (Actions 10.1, 10.4).
All States with nuclear power stations should have ratified the international Conventions on Early Notification of a Nuclear Accident and on Assistance in the case of a Nuclear Accident or Radiological Emergency (Action 10.3).

Chapter 11. Business, industry and commerce

By 2000:
Collaborative policy forums that bring government, industry and environmental experts together to discuss the role of industry in establishing a sustainable society established in all countries (Actions 8.1, 11.1).
The Precautionary, Polluter Pays and User Pays Principles adopted in all countries, which will have set standards based on best available technology (see p. 97).
Corporate environmental policies published by at least 75% of major and multinational companies (Action 11.3).
Basle Convention on the Control of Transboundary Movement of Hazardous Wastes and Their Disposal ratified by all countries (Action 11.5).

Chapter 12. Human settlements

By 1995:
National strategies for shelter, incorporating an ecological approach to human settlements planning prepared by 50% of countries (Action 12.1).

continued . . .

At least 50% of cities of over one million population in high-income countries and 25% of cities of that size in low-income countries will have implemented policies that will have led to measurably swifter, safer and more efficient transport systems and to a 25% reduction in ambient air pollution (Action 12.3).

Multilateral and bilateral development assistance agencies will have begun coordinated programmes aimed at accelerating the provision of water and sanitation services in the countries with the lowest present level of services (Actions 3.3, 12.1 and 12.4).

By 2000:

National strategies for shelter, incorporating an ecological approach to human settlements planning prepared by all countries (Action 12.1).

All cities of over one million inhabitants in high-income countries and 50% of cities of that size in low-income countries will have implemented policies that will have led to measurably swifter, safer and more efficient transport systems and to a 50% reduction in ambient air pollution (Action 12.3).

Ready access to safe water in all countries and to sanitation services in 80% of countries (Actions 3.3, 12.1 and 12.4).

Local governements will be fully representative of the communities that they serve and empowered by senior governments to supply needed community services in at least 75% of countries (Actions 7.1, 7.4 and 12.2).

By 2010:

All cities in high-income countries and all cities over one million inhabitants in low-income countries will have implemented policies that produced measurably swifter, safer and more efficient transport systems and a 50% reduction in ambient air pollution (Action 12.3).

Ready access to safe water and sanitation in all countries.

Local governments will be fully representative of the communities that they serve and empowered by senior governments to supply needed community services in all countries (Actions 7.1, 7.4 and 12.2).

Chapter 13. Farm and range lands

By 1995:

All countries that need to adjust their capacity for food production should have begun to prepare national strategies for sustainability and regional land-use plans in agriculturally significant areas (Actions 8.2, 13.1 and 17.7).

All high-income countries should have begun programmes to promote and provide information about good land-husbandry practices and integrated pest management (IPM), including minimizing the use of fertilizers, pesticides and herbicides (Actions 13.3, 13.7 and 13.8).

At least 40% of countries will have national plant genetic resource programmes and will have prepared up-to-date annotated lists of livestock breeds (Action 13.10).

By 2000:

All countries that need to adjust their capacity for food production will have begun to implement national strategies for sustainability and will be using regional and land-use plans as a tool for land-use adjustment (Actions 8.2, 13.1 and 17.7).

In high-income countries, good land-husbandry practices and IPM will be applied on 80% of agricultural land; the use of fertilizers, insecticides and herbicides will have declined by 25% per unit of production (from 1990 levels). In low-income countries, programmes to promote and provide information about good land-husbandry practices and IPM will have begun.

continued...

All countries will have adopted strategies for the conservation of their biological diversity (including cultivars and domesticates) and extended it comprehensive protection.

Payment of subsidies for the production of surpluses beyond those required for a food security stockpile will have ceased.

By 2010:

In all countries food production will have been adjusted to contribute substantially to the aggregate needed to meet human needs.

In high-income countries good land-husbandry practices and IPM will be applied on all agricultural land; the use of fertilizers and pesticides will have declined by 50% per unit of production (from 1990 levels). In low-income countries, good land-husbandry practices and IPM will be applied on 80% of agricultural land. The use of fertilizers and pesticides will have declined by 30% per unit of production (from 1990 levels).

A comprehensive world *ex situ* and *in situ* genetic conservation system will be in operation.

Chapter 14. Forest lands

By 2000:

A system of sustainability critera for timber production established and the international timber trade based entirely on systems of forest management which sustain all forest values (Actions 14.1, 14.10).

A well-managed and securely funded network of protected areas established throughout the world (boreal, temperate, and tropical) to protect substantial samples (in general, not less than 10%) of all types of old-growth forest (Action 14.2).

A state of no net deforestation achieved while moving towards realistic targets for expanding the global forest estate.

Cross sectoral policies adopted by at least 50 countries to maintain all forest values.

Chapter 15. Fresh waters

By 1995:

All countries that experience water scarcity will have begun to prepare a water management strategy, giving particular attention to managing demand and increasing the efficiency of water use (Actions 15.4 and 15.7).

All high-income countries will have established cross-sectoral mechanisms for integrated water-management and enabled the formation of management units based on drainage basins and the application of an ecological approach (Actions 15.5, 15.6 and 15.7).

Negotiations will have begun on agreements for the management of major transboundary waters not now covered by such agreements (Action 15.10).

By 2000:

All countries that experience water scarcity will have increased the efficiency of water use by 20% from 1990 (Actions 15.4 and 15.7).

At least 50% of low-income countries will have established cross-sectoral mechanisms for integrated water management based on drainage basins and the application of an ecological approach (Actions 15.5, 15.6 and 15.7).

New agreements for the management of four major transboundary waters will have been concluded (Action 15.10).

By 2010:

All countries that experience water scarcity will have increased the efficiency of water use by 30% from 1990 (Actions 15.4 and 15.7).

At least 80% of low-income countries will have established cross-sectoral mechanisms based on drainage basins and the application of an ecological approach (Actions 15.5, 15.6 and 15.7).

(continued)...

New agreements for the management of an additional five major transboundary waters will have been concluded (Action 15.10).

Chapter 16. Oceans and coastal areas

By 2000:
All depleted fisheries should be recovering and no fishery should be overexploited (Action 4.13, 16.7).

By 2010:
No fishery should pose a risk to public health because of contamination with pathogens or chemical pollutants (Action 16.8).
A global system of coastal and marine protected areas should be established (Action 16.6).

Annexes

Annex 1. Net primary production pre-empted or destroyed by human activities

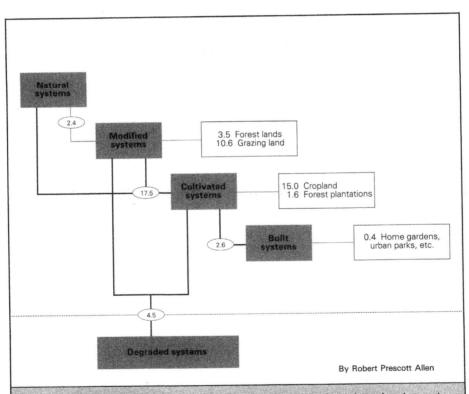

Natural systems	
2.4	
Modified systems	3.5 Forest lands 10.6 Grazing land
17.5	
Cultivated systems	15.0 Cropland 1.6 Forest plantations
2.6	
Built systems	0.4 Home gardens, urban parks, etc.
4.5	
Degraded systems	

By Robert Prescott Allen

Net Primary Production (NPP) is the amount of energy left after subtracting the respiration of primary producers (mostly plants) from the total amount of energy (mostly solar) that is fixed biologically. NPP is the total food resource on Earth, providing the basis for maintenance, growth, and reproduction of all consumers [animals] and decomposers [fungi].

All data are in petagrams (Pg) of organic matter a year (1 Pg = 10^{15} grams or 10^9 tonnes).

continued . . .

Pre-empted = used directly by people or used in human-dominated ecosystems by communities of organisms different from those in corresponding natural ecosystems.

Destroyed = potential NPP lost as a result of human activities.

It is estimated that 58.1 Pg (or 39%) of terrestrial NPP and 2.2 of aquatic NPP is pre-empted or destroyed by people. Figure 1.1 breaks down the figure for terrestrial NPP by ecosystem condition and steps in the conversion from one condition to another. Note, however, that the source of these estimates (Vitousek et al. 1986) does not distinguish natural and modified systems, so application of the data to this classification is not exact. The classification is explained Fig 1, p. 34.

27.0 Pg of NPP pre-empted or destroyed through conversion of ecosystems from one condition to another:

Natural to modified (2.4 Pg/year)

Loss of productivity due to conversion of forest to pasture (1.4 Pg/year).

Biomass killed or consumed by human-caused fires on natural grazing land (1.0 Pg/year).

Natural or modified to cultivated (17.5 Pg/year)

Natural or modified forest biomass pre-empted or destroyed by land clearing and shifting cultivation (8.5 Pg/year).

Reduction of productivity due to conversion of natural or modified systems to agriculture (9.0 Pg/year).

Cultivated to built (2.6 Pg/year)

Loss of productivity due to conversion of land to built systems (2.6 Pg/year).

Degradation of arid lands (reduction in productivity by at least 25%) (4.5 Pg/year).

31.1 Pg of NPP pre-empted by human activities in ecosystems that have already been converted:

Modified systems (14.1 Pg/year)

Forest lands: timber harvests for wood, pulp or fuel, excluding harvests from plantations (2.2 Pg/year) + forest biomass destroyed by timber harvesting but not used (1.3 Pg/year).

Grazing land: NPP of derived grazing land (land converted from forest to pasture), including consumption by livestock (9.8 Pg/year) + energy consumed by livestock on "natural" grazing land (0.8 Pg/year). "Natural" grazing land is here assumed to be modified, not natural as defined by this classification.

Cultivated and built systems (17.0 Pg/year)

The NPP of cultivated systems (16.6 Pg/year) and built systems (home gardens, urban parks, golf courses, etc.) (0.4 Pg/year) is regarded as entirely pre-empted by people.

Data source: Vitousek, P.M., P.R.Ehrlich, A.H.Ehrlich, & P.A.Matson. 1986. Human appropriation of the products of photosynthesis. *BioScience* 36 (6): 368-373.

Annex 2. Classification of 160 countries by income

Key

Low-income = real GDP per capita less than PPP$1,000*

Middle-income = real GDP per capita PPP$1,000 to $9,999

  Lower-middle-income = real GDP per capita PPP$1,000 to $5,499

  Upper-middle-income = real GDP per capita PPP$5,500 to $9,999

High-income = real GDP per capita PPP$10,000 or more

Lower-income = low-income + lower-middle-income

Upper-income = upper-middle-income + high-income

Numbers = real GDP per capita (1985-88) in PPP$ rounded to the nearest $100 ($50 rounded down)

  * PPP$ = purchasing power parities expressed in international dollars. Usual expressions of GNP and GDP convert national currency figures to US dollars using official exchange rates, which does not take account of the relative domestic purchasing powers of currencies. The UN International Comparison Project (ICP) has developed measures of real GDP on an internationally comparable scale using purchasing power partities (PPP) instead of exchange rates as conversion factors, and expressed in international dollars.

Data source

United Nations Development Programme. 1991. *Human development report 1991*. Oxford University Press, New York & Oxford.

| LOWER-INCOME | | UPPER-INCOME | |
| LOW-INCOME | MIDDLE-INCOME | | HIGH-INCOME |
	Lower-middle-income	Upper-middle-income	
Afghanistan 700	Albania 4300	Bahrain 9500	Australia 14,500
Angola 800	Algeria 2500	Barbados 6000	Austria 12,300
Bangladesh 700	Antigua &	Cyprus 8400	Bahamas 10,600
Bhutan 700	Barbuda 3900	Czechoslovakia 7400	Belgium 13,000
Burkina Faso 600	Argentina 4400	Greece 6400	Brunei
Burundi 500	Belize 2600	Hungary 5900	Darussalam 14,600
Central African R 800	Benin 1000	Ireland 7000	Canada 17,700
Chad 500	Bolivia 1500	Korea, R 5700	Denmark 13,600
Comoros 800	Botswana 2500	Kuwait 9300	Finland 14,000
Djibouti 700	Brazil 4600	Libyan Arab	France 13,600
Equatorial Guinea 700	Bulgaria 5100	Jamahiriya 7200	Germany 13,400
Ethiopia 300	Cambodia 1000	Malta 7500	Hong Kong 14,000
Gambia 600	Cameroon 1700	Oman 9300	Iceland 16,800
Guinea 900	Cape Verde 1400	Portugal 6000	Israel 10,900
Guinea-Bissau 700	Chile 4700	Saudi Arabia 9300	Italy 13,000
India 900	China 2500	South Africa 5500	Japan 13,600

LOWER-INCOME		UPPER-INCOME	
	MIDDLE-INCOME		
LOW-INCOME	Lower-middle-income	Upper-middle-income	HIGH-INCOME
Liberia 900	Colombia 3800	Spain 8200	Luxembourg 14,300
Madagascar 700	Congo 2100	Uruguay 5800	Netherlands 12,700
Malawi 600	Costa Rica 4300	USSR 6300	New Zealand 11,300
Mali 500	Côte d'Ivoire 1400	Venezuela 5600	Norway 13,800
Myanmar 700	Cuba 2500		Qatar 11,800
Nepal 800	Dominica 3000		Singapore 10,500
Niger 600	Dominican R 2400		Sweden 14,900
Rwanda 700	Ecuador 2800		Switzerland 17,200
Sao Tomé &	Egypt 1900		United Arab
Principe 600	El Salvador 1900		Emirates 19,400
Tanzania,	Fiji 3600		United Kingdom 13,100
United R 600	Gabon 4000		USA 19,800
Togo 700	Ghana 1000		
Uganda 400	Grenada 2800		
Zaire 400	Guatemala 2400		
Zambia 900	Guyana 1500		
	Haiti 1000		
	Honduras 1500		
	Indonesia 1800		
	Iran, Islamic R 3600		
	Iraq 3500		
	Jamaica 2600		
	Jordan 2600		
	Kenya 1000		
	Korea, Dem. R 2000		
	Lao PDR 1000		
	Lebanon 2200		
	Lesotho 1400		
	Malaysia 5100		
	Maldives 1000		
	Mauritania 1000		
	Mauritius 5300		
	Mexico 5300		
	Mongolia 2000		
	Morocco 2400		
	Mozambique 1100		
	Namibia 1500		
	Nicaragua 2700		
	Nigeria 1000		
	Pakistan 1800		
	Panama 3800		
	Papua New Guinea 2000		
	Paraguay 2600		
	Peru 3100		
	Philippines 2200		
	Poland 4200		
	Romania 3000		
	St Kitts & Nevis 3100		
	St Lucia 2900		
	St Vincent 2100		
	Senegal 1200		
	Seychelles 3400		
	Sierra Leone 1000		
	Solomon Is 2500		
	Somalia 1300		
	Sri Lanka 2100		
	Sudan 1000		
	Suriname 3800		
	Swaziland 2100		
	Syrian Arab R 4500		
	Thailand 3300		
	Trinidad & Tobago 4600		
	Tunisia 3200		
	Turkey 3900		
	Vanuatu 1600		
	Viet Nam 1000		
	Western Samoa 1900		
	Yemen 1600		
	Yugoslavia 4900		
	Zimbabwe 1400		

Annex 3. Average life expectancy at birth in 160 countries

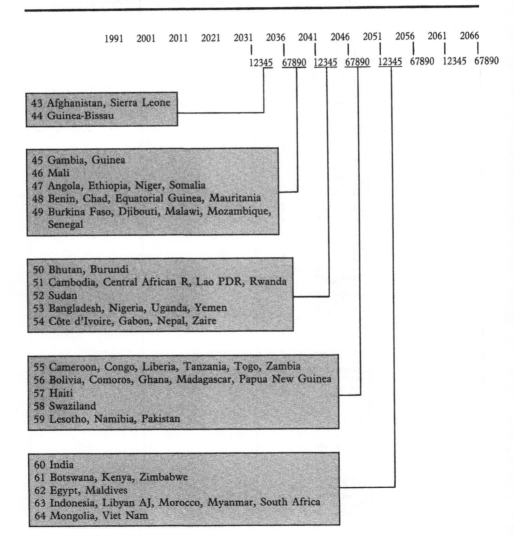

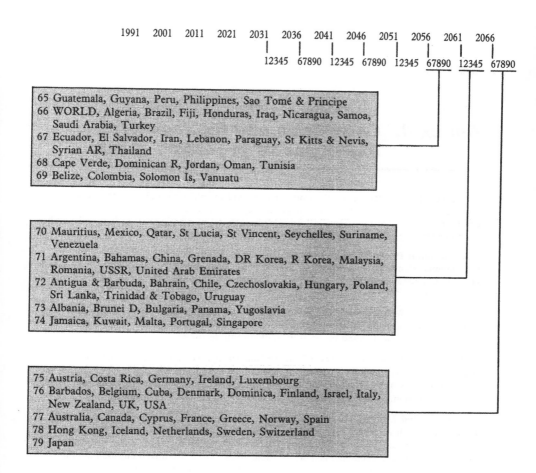

1991	2001	2011	2021	2031	2036	2041	2046	2051	2056	2061	2066
				12345	67890	12345	67890	12345	67890	12345	67890

65 Guatemala, Guyana, Peru, Philippines, Sao Tomé & Principe
66 WORLD, Algeria, Brazil, Fiji, Honduras, Iraq, Nicaragua, Samoa, Saudi Arabia, Turkey
67 Ecuador, El Salvador, Iran, Lebanon, Paraguay, St Kitts & Nevis, Syrian AR, Thailand
68 Cape Verde, Dominican R, Jordan, Oman, Tunisia
69 Belize, Colombia, Solomon Is, Vanuatu

70 Mauritius, Mexico, Qatar, St Lucia, St Vincent, Seychelles, Suriname, Venezuela
71 Argentina, Bahamas, China, Grenada, DR Korea, R Korea, Malaysia, Romania, USSR, United Arab Emirates
72 Antigua & Barbuda, Bahrain, Chile, Czechoslovakia, Hungary, Poland, Sri Lanka, Trinidad & Tobago, Uruguay
73 Albania, Brunei D, Bulgaria, Panama, Yugoslavia
74 Jamaica, Kuwait, Malta, Portugal, Singapore

75 Austria, Costa Rica, Germany, Ireland, Luxembourg
76 Barbados, Belgium, Cuba, Denmark, Dominica, Finland, Israel, Italy, New Zealand, UK, USA
77 Australia, Canada, Cyprus, France, Greece, Norway, Spain
78 Hong Kong, Iceland, Netherlands, Sweden, Switzerland
79 Japan

Key

The table shows how long a child born in 1991 may expect to live.

- Years from 2031 to 2070 are shown in five-year periods along the horizontal bar at the top.
- The numbers on the left in each box are the life expectancies at birth (1990 data) in the countries concerned.

Data sources

- Sadik, N. 1991. *The state of world population 1991.* United Nations Population Fund, New York.
- Supplemented by: United Nations Development Programme. 1991. *Human development report 1991.* Oxford University Press, New York & Oxford.

Annex 4. Categories and management objectives of protected areas

I. Strict Nature Reserve. To protect nature and maintain natural processes in an undisturbed state in order to have ecologically representative examples of the natural environment available for scientific study, environmental monitoring, education, and for the maintenance of genetic resources in a dynamic and evolutionary state.

II. National Park. To protect outstanding natural and scenic areas of national or international significance for scientific, educational, and recreational use. These are relatively large natural areas not materially altered by human activity where extractive resource uses are not allowed.

III. Natural Monument/Natural Landmark. To protect and preserve nationally significant natural features because of their special interest or unique characteristics. These are relatively small areas focused on protection of specific features.

IV. Managed Nature Reserve/Wildlife Sanctuary. To assure the natural conditions necessary to protect nationally significant species, groups of species, biotic communities, or physical features of the environment where these may require specific human manipulation for their perpetuation. Controlled harvesting of some resources can be permitted.

V. Protected Landscapes and Seascapes. To maintain nationally significant natural landscapes which are characteristic of the harmonious interaction of man and land while providing opportunities for public enjoyment through recreation and tourism within the normal life style and economic activity of these areas. These are mixed cultural/natural landscapes of high scenic value where traditional land uses are maintained.

VI. Resource Reserve. To protect the natural resources of the area for future use and prevent or contain development activities that could affect the resource pending the establishment of objectives which are based upon appropriate knowledge and planning. This is a 'holding' category used until a permanent classification can be determined.

VII. Anthropological Reserve/Natural Biotic Area. To allow the way of life of societies living in harmony with the environment to continue undisturbed by modern technology. This category is appropriate where resource extraction by indigenous people is conducted in a traditional manner.

VIII. Multiple Use Management Area/Managed Resource Area. To provide for the sustained production of water, timber, wildlife, pasture and tourism, with the conservation of nature primarily oriented to the support of the economic activities (although specific zones may also be designated within these areas to achieve specific conservation objectives).

Two additional categories are international labels which overlay protected areas in the above eight categories:

IX. Biosphere Reserve. To conserve for present and future use the diversity and integrity of biotic communities of plants and animals within natural ecosystems, and to safeguard the genetic diversity of species on which their continuing evolution depends. These are internationally designated sites managed for research, education and training.

X. World Heritage Site. To protect the natural features for which the area is considered to be of outstanding universal significance. This is a select list of the world's unique natural and cultural sites nominated by countries that are Party to the World Heritage Convention.

Ed. note: This system of categories is presently under revision.

Annex 5. Classification of countries by consumption of commercial energy per person and total fertility rate

Notes to Table on following pages

Consumption of commercial energy per person (1987, in gigajoules [joules 10^9]). "Commercial energy" includes fossil fuels, peat, and hydro, nuclear and geothermal power. It does not include fuelwood, charcoal, crop residues, dung, biogas, or solar energy.

High energy = 160 gigajoules or more/person

Medium-high energy = 80-159 gigajoules/person

Medium-low energy = 40-79 gigajoules/person

Low energy = less than 40 gigajoules/person

Sources: Sao Tomé & Principe, Seychelles, Brunei D, Hong Kong, Maldives, Vanuatu, Western Samoa, Antigua & Barbuda, Bahamas, Belize, Dominica, Grenada, St Kitts & Nevis, St Lucia, St Vincent (1986 data): GEMS Monitoring and Assessment Research Centre. 1989. *United Nations Environment Programme environmental data report*. Blackwell, Oxford (UK) & Cambridge (USA).

All other countries (1987 data). World Resources Institute, United Nations Environment Programme and United Nations Development Programme. 1990. *World resources 1990-91*. Oxford University Press, New York & Oxford.

Total fertility rate (1990). "Total fertility rate" is the average number of children born alive by a woman in her lifetime.

High TFR = total fertility rate of 4.2 and above

Medium-high TFR = total fertility rate of 3.2-4.1

Medium-low TFR = total fertility rate of 2.2-3.1

Low TFR = total fertility rate of 2.1 or less

Sources: Sao Tomé & Principe, Brunei D, Solomon Is, Vanuatu, Western Samoa, Antigua & Barbuda, Bahamas, Dominica, Grenada, St Kitts & Nevis, St Vincent: United Nations Development Programme. 1991. *Human development report 1991*. Oxford University Press, New York & Oxford. All other countries: Sadik, N. 1991. *The state of world population 1991*. United Nations Population Fund, New York.

Within each box, countries are listed in alphabetical order within regional groups. The regional groups appear in the following order:

Sub-Saharan Africa

North Africa & West Asia

South & East Asia

Pacific

North & Central America (including Caribbean)

South America
Europe & USSR

The following data appear after the name of each country:
First number, consumption of commercial energy per person (1986/1987, in gigajoules)
Second number, total fertility rate (1990)

Commercial energy data for Botswana, Lesotho, Namibia and Swaziland are combined with data for South Africa, these countries being part of the South Africa Customs Union. The figure for consumption of commercial energy per person for these countries is given in square brackets. It is assumed that this figure represents South African consumption fairly closely; but that consumption per person in the other countries is much lower.

* Total fertility rate data for Germany (German Democratic Republic and Federal Republic of Germany) and for Yemen (Yemen Arab Republic and Peoples Democratic Republic of Yemen) are combined.

High energy/high TFR	High energy/ medium-high TFR	High energy/ medium-low TFR	High energy/low TFR
Oman 245 7.1 Qatar 642 5.5 Saudi Arabia 185 7.1 United Arab Emirates 552 4.3	Bahrain 430 3.9 Kuwait 269 3.5 Brunei D 193 3.6	Trinidad & Tobago 169 2.7 USSR 194 2.3	Australia 201 1.8 Canada 291 1.6 USA 280 1.9 Belgium 163 1.7 Bulgaria 173 1.8 Czechoslovakia 185 2.0 Finland 167 1.7 German DR 231 1.5* FR Germany 165 1.5* Luxembourg 326 1.5 Netherlands 213 1.6 Norway 199 1.7
Medium-high energy/ high TFR	Medium-high energy/ medium-high TFR	Medium-high energy/ medium-low TFR	Medium-high energy/ low TFR
South Africa [83] 4.2 Libyan AJ 83 6.7	Venezuela 88 3.5	Israel 82 2.8 Ireland 101 2.4	Japan 110 1.7 Singapore 140 1.8 New Zealand 113 1.4 Austria 118 1.5 Denmark 157 1.5 France 109 1.8 Hungary 112 1.8 Iceland 157 2.0 Italy 105 1.4 Poland 141 2.1 Romania 136 2.0 Sweden 147 1.9 Switzerland 111 1.6 UK 150 1.8

Medium-low energy/ high TFR	Medium-low energy/ medium-high TFR	Medium-low energy/ medium-low TFR	Medium-low energy/ low TFR
Algeria 42 4.9 Mongolia 53 4.7		Cyprus 72 2.3 DPR Korea 79 2.4 Mexico 50 3.1 Argentina 56 2.8	Hong Kong 52 1.4 R Korea 52 1.6 Bahamas 68 1.9 Cuba 42 1.9 Greece 72 1.7 Malta 52 1.9 Spain 62 1.7 Yugoslavia 71 1.9

Low energy/high TFR	Low energy/ Medium-high TFR	Low energy/ Medium-low TFR	Low energy/low TFR

Angola 3 6.3
Benin 1 7.1
Botswana [83] 6.4
Burkina Faso 1 6.5
Burundi 1 6.8
Cameroon 8 6.9
Cape Verde 0 5.4
Central African R
  1 6.2
Chad 1 5.8
Comoros 2 7.0
Congo 12 6.3
Côte d'Ivoire 6 7.4
Djibouti 11 6.5
Equatorial Guinea
  2 5.9
Ethiopia 1 6.8
Gabon 34 5.3
Gambia 4 6.3
Ghana 4 6.3
Guinea 2 7.0
Guinea-Bissau 2 5.8
Kenya 3 6.8
Lesotho [83] 5.8
Liberia 4 6.7
Madagascar 1 6.5
Malawi 1 7.6
Mali 1 7.1
Mauritania 23 6.5
Mozambique 1 6.2
Namibia [83] 5.7
Niger 2 7.1
Nigeria 5 6.6
Rwanda 1 8.0
Sao Tomé & Principe
  0 5.4
	Seychelles 25 3.4
	
	Egypt 20 4.0
	Lebanon 39 3.4
	Tunisia 19 3.4
	Turkey 29 3.3
	
	India 8 4.1
	Malaysia 38 3.5
	Myanmar 2 3.7
	Philippines 8 3.9
	Viet Nam 3 3.7
	
	Dominican R 12 3.3
	Grenada 9 4.0
	
	Brazil 22 3.2
	Ecuador 18 3.9
	Peru 17 3.6
		China 22 2.2
		Indonesia 8 3.1
		Sri Lanka 4 2.5
		Thailand 14 2.2
		
		Fiji 11 3.0
		
		Costa Rica 15 3.0
		Dominica 13 2.7
		Jamaica 31 2.4
		Panama 17 2.9
		St Kitts & Nevis
		  21 3.6
		St Vincent 10 2.9
		
		Chile 28 2.7
		Colombia 24 2.9
		Guyana 14 2.4
		Suriname 36 2.8
		Uruguay 19 2.3
		
		Albania 38 2.7
			Mauritius 16 1.9
			
			Antigua & Barbuda
			  25 1.7
			Barbados 38 1.8
			
			Portugal 39 1.7

Low energy/high TFR	Low energy/ Medium-high TFR	Low energy/ Medium-low TFR	Low energy/low TFR
Senegal 4 6.2			
Sierra Leone 2 6.5			
Somalia 2 6.6			
Sudan 2 6.3			
Swaziland [83] 6.5			
Tanzania 1 7.1			
Togo 2 6.6			
Uganda 1 7.3			
Zaire 2 6.1			
Zambia 7 7.2			
Zimbabwe 21 5.3			
Afghanistan 4 6.8			
Iran 38 4.7			
Iraq 22 5.9			
Jordan 31 5.5			
Morocco 10 4.2			
Syria 30 6.3			
Yemen AR 5 7.5*			
PDR Yemen 27 7.5*			
Bangladesh 2 5.1			
Bhutan 1 5.5			
Cambodia 1 4.4			
Lao PDR 1 6.7			
Maldives 5 7.0			
Nepal 1 5.5			
Pakistan 7 5.9			
Papua New Guinea 9 4.8			
Solomon Is 7 6.4			
Vanuatu 7 5.6			
Western Samoa 12 4.8			
Belize 18 5.8			
El Salvador 5 4.5			
Guatemala 5 5.4			
Haiti 1 4.8			
Honduras 6 4.9			
Nicaragua 9 5.0			
St Lucia 15 4.2			
Bolivia 9 5.8			
Paraguay 8 4.3			

Annex 6. Indicators of sustainability

A sustainable society enables its members to achieve a high quality of life in ways that are ecologically sustainable. To measure progress toward a sustainable society, we need indicators of quality of life and of ecological sustainability.

Requirements of indicators

The concepts of quality of life and of ecological sustainability are broader than their measurement. By definition, indicators can measure only components of either. The search for reliable and efficient indicators of sustainability is just beginning. The indicators should be quantitative and some at least should be convertible to a monetary value so that they can be related to the national accounts. They should not be too difficult or expensive to measure. The following list of possible indicators is by no means comprehensive. Some do not meet these criteria.

Quality of life

The United Nations Development Programme has adopted two indices to measure human development or the quality of human life: a Human Development Index (HDI) and a Human Freedom Index (HFI).

HDI has three components:

- Longevity, measured by life expectancy at birth. Long life is valued because it increases the opportunity for a person to pursue goals and develop abilities and is associated with good health and adequate nutrition.

- Knowledge, or educational attainment, measured by adult literacy and mean years of schooling. This helps people to realize their potential and take advantage of opportunities.

- Income, measured by per capita Gross Domestic Product, adjusted to account for national differences in purchasing power and the distorting effect of official exchange rates (real GDP), and adjusted further to reflect diminishing returns from income.

HFI is a modification of Charles Humana's *World Human Rights Guide*, which uses 40 indicators to measure freedom. A "one" is assigned to each right or freedom that is protected and a "zero" to each right or freedom that is violated.

Ecological sustainability

A society is ecologically sustainable when it:

- conserves ecological life-support systems and biodiversity;

- ensures that uses of renewable resources are sustainable and minimizes the depletion of nonrenewable resources;

- keeps within the carrying capacity of supporting ecosystems.

Conserving life-support systems and biodiversity

Conserving life-support systems needs a combination of preventing pollution, restoring and maintaining the integrity of the Earth's ecosystems, and developing a comprehensive system of protected areas. Conserving biodiversity requires these measures plus action to restore and maintain species and genetic stocks.

Primary indicators measure the condition of the ecosystem or species concerned. Secondary indicators measure human impacts. Tertiary indicators measure actions to reduce impacts. Whether the indicator is primary, secondary or tertiary is shown by a number in brackets.

1. Progress in preventing pollution

Annual emissions of carbon dioxide, methane, CFCs, sulphur oxides, nitrogen oxides: total, per capita, and per unit of GDP. [2]

River quality: dissolved oxygen; nitrate concentration. [1]

Wastewater treatment: percentage of population served by wastewater treatment plants (primary, secondary and tertiary). [3]

Industrial accidents: number, number of deaths, per unit of GDP. [2]

2. Progress in restoring and maintaining the integrity of ecosystems

Percentages of land area that are natural, modified, cultivated, built, degraded. [1]

A subset of the above would be percentage of land under forest, and percentages of forest land that are natural (old growth), modified, planted, degraded. [1]

Percent of natural and modified ecosystems or vegetation types in fragments greater than 10,000 hectares. [1]

3. Progress in developing a comprehensive system of protected areas

Percentage of each ecological region that is covered by protected areas. [3]

4. Progress in restoring and maintaining species and genetic stocks

Number of species, and percent threatened with extinction, percent threatened with extirpation, percent with stable or increasing populations, and percent with significantly declining populations. [1]

Number of endemic species, and percent threatened with extinction [1], and percent in protected areas. [3]

Percent of threatened species with viable populations in *ex situ* facilities. [3]

Domesticated species diversity index (number of crop and livestock species raised in a region as percent of number grown 10 or 50 years previously). [1]

Domesticated varietal index (number of varieties of each crop and breeds of each livestock species raised in a region as percent of number 10 or 50 years previously). [1]

Crop and livestock uniformity index (relatedness of crop varieties and livestock breeds). [1]

Percent traditional varieties in *ex situ* collections. [3]

Genebank status index (percent of collection regenerated within past 15 years). [3]

Ensuring uses of renewable resources are sustainable and minimizing the depletion of nonrenewable resources

1. Importance of the sector for income (value added) and employment

Determining the total value-added contributed by the sector provides a basis for calculating the dollar value of changes in the status of the sector's resources and ecological infrastructure (see below).

2. Status of the sector's resources

A sector's resources are the natural assets that it uses directly: trees in the case of the timber sector; and hydro, oil, natural gas, coal, and wood in the case of the energy sector. Two sets of data are needed: the size of the current stock; and flow data (changes in production, consumption, and the size of the stock).

3. Status of the sector's ecological infrastructure

A sector's ecological infrastructure consists of the ecological processes and biological diversity that support it: for example, soil, water, and the genetic diversity of crops and livestock in the case of the agriculture sector. For living-resource sectors (timber, fisheries and aquaculture, other harvesting, agriculture and horticulture, tourism and recreation, and some of the energy sector), measures are needed of the status of the hydrological cycle (quality, quantity and reliability of water supply); soil structure and fertility; air quality and climate; and the ecosystem, species, and within-species diversity required for long-term production. For nonliving-resource sectors (mining and most of the energy sector), measures are needed of the quality, quantity and reliability of the water supply, and on air quality and changes in the reliability of climate.

4. The sector's compatibilities and conflicts with the sustainability of other sectors

Items 2 and 3 above measure what might be called the sector's internal sustainability. We also need to assess its external sustainability — its impacts on other resource sectors, on the businesses outside the resource sectors, on human health and infrastructure, and on the integrity of the biosphere or planetary ecosystem.

5. Main socioeconomic influences on the sector's sustainability

Several factors make it easier or more difficult for a sector to be sustainable. The chief ones are:

- The ratio of benefits to a given stock of resources. One of the ways of achieving sustainability is to increase the benefits from a given stock of resources. Conversely, a decline in benefits from a stock of resources is a sign of unsustainability. Two benefits that should be looked at are jobs and total income (corporate, personal, municipal, provincial). Indicators include trends in earnings and production, the ratio of jobs and income to production, and changes in value added per unit of resource.

- The extent to which the resource users pay the full costs to society of their decisions. Indicators include the proportions of development and conservation costs paid by the industry, government, and other parties (including future generations); and the net charge (tax) paid or subsidy received by the sector, once the total amount of taxes has been subtracted from the total amount of subsidies.

- Effective participation of communities and interest groups in the decisions that most affect them. Do the communities and interests that depend on the sector have an effective say in how the sector's conservation and development are planned and managed?

- Adoption of an approach to decision making that tries to foresee and prevent problems. How well are the compatibilities and conflicts with other sectors and interests being anticipated and managed?

Keeping within the carrying capacity of supporting ecosystems

The following indicators would measure the effectiveness of action to reduce consumption and stabilize population:

- per capita consumption of food, water, timber, minerals.
- per capita use of energy.
- energy use per unit of GDP.
- generation of municipal waste, per capita, and per unit of GDP.
- generation of industrial waste, per capita, and per unit of GDP.
- generation of nuclear waste, per capita, per unit of GDP, and per unit of energy.
- population trend.
- Total Fertility Rate.
- population density.

Annex 7. Estimated cost of implementing major aspects of this Strategy (US$ Billions)

Year	Stabilizing Population			Reducing Deforestation & Conserving Biodiversity	Forest & Tree Planting	Energy Conservation		Protecting Topsoil on Cropland	Retiring Third World Debt	Total
	Family Planning Services	Education & Health Improvements	Financial Incentives			Increasing Efficiency	Developing Renewables			
1991	3	6	4	1	2	5	2	4	20	47
1992	4	8	6	2	3	10	5	9	30	77
1993	5	10	8	3	4	15	8	14	40	107
1994	5	11	10	4	5	20	10	18	50	133
1995	6	11	12	5	6	25	12	24	50	151
1996	6	11	14	6	7	30	15	24	40	153
1997	7	11	14	7	8	35	18	24	30	154
1998	7	11	14	8	8	40	21	24	20	153
1999	8	11	14	8	8	45	24	24	10	152
2000	8	11	14	8	9	50	27	24	10	161
Total	59	101	110	52	60	275	142	189	300	1288

Estimates for all columns, except biodiversity, from Worldwatch Institute, adjusted to start in 1991. The table does not account for all priority actions.

Education and health improvements. Providing elementary education for 120 million school-age children not now in school = $6 billion/year at $50/child. Providing literacy training for women above school-age = $2 billion/year. Immunizing the 55% of the world's children unprotected from diphtheria, measles, polio and tuberculosis = $2 billion/year. Health education for mothers = $1 billion/year.

Reducing deforestation. Estimated to cost $800/currently deforested hectare to initiate forest management programmes and stimulate sedentary cultivation (McKinsey & Company. 1989. "Protecting the global atmosphere: funding mechanisms". The Netherlands). Other biodiversity conservation actions not yet included in estimate.

Forest and tree planting. Assumes a total of 150 million hectares to be planted — some as plantations, but most by farmers (agroforestry) — to meet needs for fuelwood, soil and water conservation, and lumber and pulpwood. Costs range from $200-$400/hectare for agroforestry to more than $2,000/hectare for commercial plantations. Assumes an average cost of $400/hectare.

Protecting topsoil on cropland, Cost of converting highly erodible cropland to grassland or woodland = $16 billion/year from 1995. Assumes world area of cropland that cannot sustain cultivation with any economically feasible soil-conserving agricultural practices is 128 million hectares, and cost of conversion equals that in USA of $50/hectare. Global soil conservation effort estimated to cost an additional $8 billion/year by 1995.

Retiring Third World debt. See Chapter 3 for an explanation.

Source of Worldwatch Institute estimates: Brown, L.R., and Wolf. C. 1988. Reclaiming the future. In: Brown L.R. *et al. State of the world 1988: a Worldwatch Institute report on progress toward a sustainable society.* Norton, New York & London.

Annex 8. Strategies for sustainability

This annex outlines how to undertake a strategy for sustainability at national and local levels. "National" includes "subnational" in the case of countries with federal systems. More detailed guidance will be made available by the Working Group on Strategies for Sustainability of IUCN's Commission on Environmental Strategy and Planning.

Strategies for sustainability are a means to achieve a sustainable combination of development and conservation in an integrated fashion. They are partly a highly participatory form of planning and policy-making. But they go further by including the actions needed to turn the plans and policies into results. They are most useful at national and local levels, but international strategies also can be undertaken.

Since each society has unique conditions and needs, and will design its strategy accordingly, what follows is intended as general advice, not as hard-and-fast rules.

Components of a strategy

Successful strategies have four components in common:

- consultation and consensus building;
- information assembly and analysis;
- policy formulation;
- action planning and implementation.

Demonstration projects may also be undertaken so that participants can see concrete results from the strategy while it is being developed.

1. Consultation and consensus building

Consensus means general agreement on a course of action.

This component provides a forum and process through which participants can build a consensus on the sustainable development of their region. It may include public meetings and workshops, opinion surveys, written and spoken submissions, and group discussions within communities. It is the means by which anybody concerned — communities, government, industry, other interest groups, and individuals — can participate in developing the strategy.

The aim is to find out people's knowledge, concerns, interests, and what results they would most like from the strategy. It ensures that the strategy builds and reflects a consensus of all participants on:

- sustainable development objectives;
- the issues that need to be resolved and the information required for sound decisions;
- policies, procedures and actions to achieve sustainable development.

It also increases the chance that all parties will implement the strategy, by enabling them to contribute effectively to it and by giving them a stake in the strategy's implementation.

2. Information assembly and analysis

Effective strategies are built on facts. This component of a strategy assembles and analyzes the information necessary for sound decisions on economic development, environmental conservation, and their integration.

Information is needed on:

- The people. Status and trends in population, employment, and resource use. Values and perceptions. Interactions among communities and interest groups. Common interests and compatibilities. Avoidable and unavoidable conflicts.
- The economy. Status and trends of the main economic sectors, particularly the resource-based sectors (energy, timber, mining, fisheries, aquaculture, tourism); their social and economic importance; their sustainability, both in their own terms and in relation to other sectors; their interactions with each other; their potential for increased sustainable development; what is required to conserve their resource base (the ecosystems and natural resources they depend on).
- The environment and natural resources. Status and trends of life-support systems, biodiversity, renewable resources, and nonrenewable resources; what is required to maintain, enhance and restore them, and use them sustainably.
- Institutions, laws, policies that promote or obstruct sustainable development.

Three main sources of information are used:

- submissions from government agencies, communities, industries, other interest groups, research and educational institutions, and the general public. These are obtained through the consultation and consensus building component;
- available reports by government agencies and nongovernmental sources (universities, industries, and other interest groups);
- background studies commissioned for the strategy.

The nature and scope of the issues and interests that participants decide should be covered by the strategy govern how much information is needed. However, this is not a major research effort. It is a matter of assembling and analyzing available facts, and separating what is known from what is a matter of opinion. Important questions may emerge that require research. The strategy may encourage such research as a separate project, but does not wait for the results of that research.

3. Policy formulation

This component is developed on the basis of the information analysis, through consultation and consensus building. It sets out agreed policies to achieve sustainable development and in particular to:

- develop an economy that is sustainable and consistent with the needs and values of the participants;
- coordinate and allocate resources among economic sectors;
- promote each sector's sustainable development and secure its resource base;
- maintain and enhance life-support systems and biodiversity;
- improve decision-making and resolve conflicts that may arise in the future, including a mechanism for making decisions in the event of an impasse;
- reduce resource waste, and achieve a sustainable level of resource consumption.

4. Action planning and implementation

An action plan sets out how the participants will implement the agreed policies. It may be divided into two parts: strategic directions, which describe broadly what needs to be done; and specific actions to be taken over the next two years or so. A budget is usually given for the specific actions. The action plan includes a procedure for monitoring and evaluating implementation and its results.

5. Demonstration projects

Most people have great difficulty grasping unfamiliar abstractions like sustainability or sustainable development. Model sustainable development projects can demonstrate the meaning and practicality of sustainability. Such projects could simultaneously help define more precisely the strategy's objectives, build public support for their achievement, test the feasibility and effectiveness of proposed actions, and explore practical ways of reducing conflicts and enhancing compatibilities among resource uses.

Demonstration projects are also a means of implementing parts of the strategy on which there is early consensus, and which can be organized and funded before preparation of the rest of strategy is completed. Early implementation is essential to avoid the impression that the strategy is all talk and no action.

Organization of a strategy

National and subnational strategies can be developed in two years, but may take longer. Local strategies usually take less time: 12-18 months, depending on their complexity. A local strategy by a single municipality can be developed within a year. Strategies involving several communities are likely to require more time, because of the need to reach agreement among them all.

The results of a strategy are the agreed policies and the actions taken to put the policies into practice. A key step in the development of a strategy is the preparation of a strategy document. This provides a summary description and analysis of the people, economy, environment, and institutions of the area; and sets out the agreed policies and action plan.

The basic organization of a strategy consists of a steering committee and a secretariat. The steering committee should be representative of the main participants in the strategy. It is responsible for overall direction of the strategy, and ensuring the full participation of all interest groups.

The secretariat undertakes the day-to-day management of the strategy's development. It is responsible for organizing consultation and consensus building, assembly and analysis of information, and drafting the strategy document. The secretariat also produces a newsletter or equivalent to keep everyone informed of the strategy's progress.

Strategy documentation should be in the local language and in a form and style with which people feel comfortable. For instance, in communities where literacy is low and issues are communicated orally, documentation could be entirely on tape (including video tape if the funds are available). In such a case, tape recorders (and plenty of batteries) should be made widely available.

Organization of a national strategy

A national strategy should be a government policy statement, not a public advisory statement; but it should reflect a true partnership between the governmental and nongovernmental sectors. The cabinet (or equivalent) should be committed to its implementation and the government should lead its preparation. However, the strategy should result in commitments to action by interest groups and other nongovernmental agencies, as well as by government; and it should be prepared jointly by government and the public. As far as possible, national strategies should be developed by nationals. If expatriate experts are needed, they should play a minor role.

The **commissioning authority** of the strategy (the body that permits strategy preparation to go ahead and that will receive the strategy document) should be a central agency of government, not a line agency.

The **approval authority** (the body that will approve the strategy's policy and action recommendations) should be the cabinet and legislature (or equivalents).

A high level (Minister, Deputy Minister or equivalent) **steering committee** should be responsible for:

- overall direction of the strategy;
- keeping cabinet (or equivalent) informed of emerging policy issues;
- ensuring the full participation of all sectors and interest groups.

It should be large enough to ensure the full involvement of the key government agencies and the major nongovernmental interest groups; yet small enough to function effectively as a body.

A small full-time **secretariat** must undertake day-to-day management of the strategy's preparation. It would be responsible for:

- organizing the consultation and information programme;
- coordinating the preparation of sectoral and other studies;
- drafting the strategy document;
- identifying potential demonstration projects;
- keeping the steering committee fully informed of progress.

The size of the secretariat will depend on the size and complexity of the country to be served.

Participants in the strategy's preparation and implementation should include all government agencies, industry and business, women's and other nongovernmental interest groups, indigenous peoples, trades unions, local governments, professional societies, universities, research institutions, schools and other educational bodies, and interested members of the public. The more people that engage in the strategy, the greater the chance of its success. Their participation should begin with the setting of the strategy's objectives.

Strategy process

Strategies go through three phases: start-up; preparation; and implementation.

Start-up

The start-up phase covers:

- promotion and explanation of the concept of a strategy for sustainability, including assessment of the need for a strategy and the feasibility of its preparation;
- mobilizing support for the strategy's preparation;
- definition of the scope and components of the strategy;
- preparation of a project proposal, including workplan and budget;

- decision by government to proceed with the strategy;
- provision of funding;
- organization of the next phase, including formation of the steering committee and secretariat.

Governments or NGOs can initiate the process. In either case governments must become involved at an early stage.

Preparation

Preparation begins with briefings of all parties on the purpose, scope, process and timetable of the strategy. The briefings should include public meetings, which would also seek the views of the people of the area on the objectives and guiding principles of the strategy.

The strategy document should be drafted by the secretariat from:

- background studies prepared by government agencies, universities and research institutions, interest groups, working groups, and consultants;
- briefs submitted by interest groups and members of the public;
- the findings of opinion surveys, public meetings, and workshops.

Background studies are needed to analyze:

- natural resources and ecosystems, their current and potential contributions to development, problems affecting them, and management status;
- the effectiveness of existing legislation and institutions for natural resource management and sustainable development.

Many of the studies could be prepared by the government agencies responsible for the resources concerned. This would make use of the expertise and skills of the agencies, as well as provide them with an opportunity to consider their responsibilities from a broader perspective than usual, taking account of their cross-sectoral and longer term implications.

Universities and research institutions also have a major role in the preparation of studies. In addition, consultants can be commissioned to write papers on subjects on which they are specially knowledgeable, that would benefit from a second opinion, and/or that go beyond the mandates of particular agencies.

Interest groups and members of the public should be invited to submit briefs, outlining their views on:

- development and conservation needs of their sector or interest;
- key resource and environment issues within their own sector or interest;
- key interactions, including compatibilities and conflicts, with other sectors and interests;
- ways of taking advantage of compatibilities and reducing and resolving conflicts;
- what the sector or interest group concerned will do to meet its development and conservation needs, respond to compatibilities with other sectors, and reduce and resolve conflicts;
- what the government should do.

Opinion surveys are an effective way of obtaining people's views on:

- their interpretation, in the form of attainable objectives, of the goals of the strategy, and the extent to which they have been attained;
- the values of the environment and natural resources of the area, identifying those places, species of plants and animals, and uses of resources and ecosystems that the people of the area particularly value and which they feel contribute to the quality of their lives;

- the main resource and environment issues, the environmental changes they have witnessed, the resource and environment problems that concern them, and how they feel they could be solved.

Two opinion surveys — one at the start of the strategy's preparation and one at the end — would reveal the extent to which involvement in the strategy's preparation had changed people's attitudes.

Workshops should be organized to review the sectoral, regional and other background studies, as well as cross-sectoral groupings of studies (for example, forest resources and ecosystems, and coastal zone resources and ecosystems). The concerned interest groups should be invited to form working groups for this purpose. Public meetings should be held to review the first draft of the strategy documents.

There should also be a strategy newsletter and regular media briefings to keep participants informed of progress.

Strategies are ambitious undertakings and the process can lose direction or get bogged down. There are ways of avoiding this:

- Concentrate initially on formulation and approval of a broad but effective statement of principles and objectives that can provide the conceptual foundation and umbrella for more detailed policy development.
- Concentrate on consultation and consensus building, placing priority on creating supportive attitudes and opinions as the first step.
- Once there is agreement on principles and objectives to provide the framework for subsequent integration, prepare and approve sectoral components in sequence or in parallel.

Preparation of the strategy is completed when government and other partners formally adopt a strategy document consisting of a policy and action plan.

Implementation

The implementation phase of a strategy is the period when the bulk of the agreed and recommended actions are taken. The success of these actions depends heavily on the skill and thoroughness with which the preparation phase is carried out.

Indicators of progress and monitoring

Each strategy's action plan should provide for an independent body to monitor and evaluate implementation of the strategy, at two levels:

- **Implementation of the action plan**
    a. Projects funded and other actions taken to implement the action plan.
    b. Changes in legislation and institutions as a result of the strategy.
    c. Concrete evidence of increased awareness/understanding of/consensus on the issues covered by the strategy by specific sectors, interest groups, communities, and the general public.
- **Results**
    d. Ecological results. Changes in the status of ecological processes, biodiversity, and renewable resources.
    e. Socioeconomic results. Changes in social and economic conditions.

Indicators of progress and a time-frame should be selected for each item.

Glossary

Terms are defined in the sense that they are used in *Caring for the Earth*. Terms that are cross-referenced are indicated by CAPITALS.

Biological diversity or Biodiversity. The variety of life in all its forms, levels and combinations. Includes ECOSYSTEM DIVERSITY, SPECIES DIVERSITY, and GENETIC DIVERSITY.

Biosphere. The thin covering of the planet that contains and sustains life. Some writers distinguish the biosphere (life), hydrosphere (water), atmosphere (air), and lithosphere (rock, the crust of the earth). As used here, the biosphere includes the atmosphere and hydrosphere and that part of the lithosphere that contains and sustains living organisms.

Built ecosystem. ECOSYSTEM dominated by buildings, roads, airports, docks, dams, mines, and other human structures. Includes urban and suburban parks, gardens, and golf courses.

Carrying capacity. Capacity of an ECOSYSTEM to support healthy ORGANISMS while maintaining its productivity, adaptability, and capability of renewal.

Conservation. The management of human use of ORGANISMS or ECOSYSTEMS to ensure such use is sustainable. Besides SUSTAINABLE USE, conservation includes PROTECTION, MAINTENANCE, REHABILITATION, RESTORATION, and ENHANCEMENT of populations and ecosystems.

Cultivated ecosystem. ECOSYSTEM where human impact is greater than that of any other species, and most of whose structural components are cultivated.

Degraded ecosystem. ECOSYSTEM whose diversity and productivity have been so reduced that they are unlikely to recover without REHABILITATION or RESTORATION measures.

Development. Increasing the capacity to meet human needs and improve the quality of human life.

Ecological process. A continuous action or series of actions that is governed or strongly influenced by one or more ECOSYSTEMS.

Ecosystem. A system of plants, animals and other ORGANISMS together with the non-living components of their environment.

Ecosystem diversity. The variety and frequency of different ECOSYSTEMS.

Enhancement. Increasing the capacity of en ECOSYSTEM or population to fulfill a particular function or yield a specified product.

Genetic diversity. The variety and frequency of different genes and/or genetic stocks.

High income. Real gross domestic product per person of PPP$10,000 or more.

Life-support system. An ECOLOGICAL PROCESS that sustains the productivity, adaptability and capacity for renewal of lands, waters, and/or the BIOSPHERE as a whole.

Lower-income. Real Gross Domestic Product per person of PPP$5,499 or less.

Low-income. Real Gross Domestic Product per person of less than PPP$1,000.

Maintenance. Keeping something in good health or repair.

Modified ecosystem. ECOSYSTEM where human impact is greater than that of any other species, but whose structural components are not cultivated.

Natural capital, natural wealth, natural assets. The stock of LIFE-SUPPORT SYSTEMS, BIODIVERSITY, renewable RESOURCES, and nonrenewable resources.

Natural ecosystem. ECOSYSTEM where since the industrial revolution (say 1750) human impact (a) has been no greater than that of any other native species, and (b) has not affected the ecosystem's structure. Human impact excludes changes of global extent, such as climate change due to global warming.

Non-governmental organization (NGO). Any organization that is not a part of federal, provincial, territorial, or municipal government. Unless otherwise indicated, includes private voluntary organizations, corporations, educational institutions, and labour unions.

Organism. A living being or form of life that is a cell or is composed of cells. Any member of the kingdoms Prokaryotae (bacteria), Protoctista, Fungi, Animalia, or Plantae.

PPP. Standardized indices of Gross Domestic Product per capita using purchasing power parities instead of exchange rates as conversion factors.

Preservation. Keeping something in its present state.

Primary Environmental Care (PEC). The organization, strengthening, and application of an individual's or community's abilities to care for its environment.

Protected area. An area dedicated primarily to PROTECTION and enjoyment of natural or cultural heritage, to MAINTENANCE of BIODIVERSITY, and/or to maintenance of LIFE-SUPPORT SYSTEMS (see Annex 4 for categories).

Protection. Securing something for a particular purpose.

Resource. Anything that is used directly by people. A renewable resource can renew itself (or be renewed) at a constant level, either because it recycles quite rapidly (water), or because it is alive and can propagate itself or be propagated (organisms and ecosystems). A nonrenewable resource is one whose consumption necessarily involves its depletion.

Rehabilitation. To return a degraded ecosystem or population to an undegraded condition, which may be different from its original condition. See also RESTORATION.

Restoration. To return a degraded ecosystem or population to its original condition. See also REHABILITATION.

Species diversity. The variety and frequency of different species.

Strategy. A combination of communication and consensus building, information assembly and analysis, policy formulation, and action planning and implementation, to enable a society to conserve its NATURAL CAPITAL (conservation strategy) and to achieve SUSTAINABILITY by integrating economic development and conservation of natural capital (strategy for sustainability).

Stumpage. A tax based on the quantity (and ideally the full worth) of timber from publicly owned lands.

Sustainability. A characteristic of a process or state that can be maintained indefinitely.

Sustainable development. Improving the quality of human life while living within the carrying capacity of supporting ecosystems.

Sustainable use. USE of an ORGANISM, ECOSYSTEM or other RENEWABLE RESOURCE at a rate within its capacity for renewal.

Total fertility rate (TFR). The average number of children born alive to a woman in her lifetime.

Upper-income. Real Gross Domestic Product per person of PPP$5,500 or more.

Use. Any human activity involving an ORGANISM, ECOSYSTEM, or nonrenewable RESOURCE that benefits people. The activities range from those having a direct impact on the organisms, ecosystems, or nonrenewable resources concerned (such as fishing, farming, mining) to those having no impact (such as appreciation and contemplation).

Notes and sources

Foreword

IUCN/UNEP/WWF. 1980. *World Conservation Strategy: Living Resource Conservation for Sustainable Development*. International Union for Conservation of Nature and Natural Resources, United Nations Environment Programme and World Wildlife Fund, Gland, Switzerland.

United Nations General Assembly Resolution 42/186 of 11 December 1987 on the *Environmental Perspective to the Year 2000 and Beyond*. United Nations Environment Programme (UNEP), Nairobi, 1988.

World Commission on Environment and Development (WCED). 1987. *Our Common Future*. Oxford University Press, Oxford.

Chapter 1

Daly, H.E., Post, J., Piddington, K., Pratt, J., Warford, J., English, J. and Partow, Z. Undated. Sustainable development: towards an operational definition. Informal document. The World Bank, Washington, DC.

Jacobs, P. and Munro, D. (Eds). 1987. *Conservation with Equity: Strategies for Sustainable Development*. IUCN, Gland, Switzerland.

Pearce, D., Markandya, A. and Barbier, E.B. 1989. *Blueprint for a Green Economy*. Earthscan, London.

UNEP. 1988. *Environmental Perspective to the Year 2000 and Beyond*. United Nations Environment Programme, Nairobi.

WCED. 1987. Op. cit.

Chapter 2

The IUCN Ethics Working Group contributed to preparation of this chapter, including Box 2.

The proposal for a world organization (Action 2.4) is based upon an idea advanced by Dr M.S. Swaminathan, President of IUCN, 1984-1990. In: IUCN. 1991. *Proceedings of the 18th Session of the General Assembly of IUCN*, Perth, Australia, 28 November-5 December 1990.

The Universal Declaration of Human Rights was adopted by the General Assembly of the United Nations in 1948. To give legal form to the provisions of the Declaration, the United Nations has adopted the International Covenant on Economic, Social and Cultural Rights and the International Covenant on Civil and Political Rights.

The World Charter for Nature was adopted in 1982 by the General Assembly of the United Nations. For its text and history see: Burhenne, W.E. and Irwin, W.A. 1983. *The World Charter for Nature. A background paper.* Beiträge zur Umwelt-gestaltung A90. Erich Schmidt Verlag, Berlin.

Berry, R.J. 1989. Science, Mankind and Ethics. Concluding address to the Sixth Economic Summit on Bioethics, Brussels, Belgium, 10-12 May 1989. In: Bourdeau, Ph., Fasella, P.M. and Teller, A. 1990. *Environmental Ethics: Man's Relationship with Nature — Interactions with Science.* Office for Official Publications of the European Communities, Luxembourg.

Delors, J. 1989. Opening address to the Sixth Economic Summit on Bioethics, Brussels, Belgium, 10-12 May 1989. In: Bourdeau, Ph. *et al.* 1990. Op. cit.

Engel, J.R. and Engel, J.G. (Eds). 1990. *Ethics of Environment and Development.* Belhaven Press, London.

IUCN. 1988. Declaration of Fontainebleau. Statement adopted on the occasion of the Fortieth Anniversary of the founding of IUCN. *IUCN Bulletin* 20(1-3) 1989.

Chapter 3

Berry, R.J. 1989. Op. cit.

Dankelman, I. and Davidson, J. 1988. *Women and Environment in the Third World.* Earthscan Publications, London, in association with IUCN.

Durning, Alan B. 1990. Ending Poverty. In: Brown, Lester R. *et al.* 1990. *State of the World 1990.* A Worldwatch Institute Report on Progress Towards a Sustainable Society. W.W. Norton, New York and London.

Renner, Michael. 1990. Converting to a Peaceful Economy. In: Brown, Lester, R. *et al.* 1990. Op. cit.

South Commission. 1990. *The Challenge to the South.* Oxford University Press, Oxford.

United Nations Development Programme (UNDP). 1990. *Human Development Report 1990.* Oxford University Press, New York and Oxford.

UNDP. 1991. *Human Development Report 1991.* Oxford University Press, New York and Oxford.

UNEP. 1990. *The State of the Environment: Children and the Environment.* United Nations Environment Programme, Nairobi.

UNEP. 1991. *Environmental Data Report.* Third Edition. Prepared for the United Nations Environment Programme by the GEMS Monitoring and Assessment Centre, London, UK, in cooperation with the World Resources Institute, Washington, DC, and the Department of the Environment, London. Basil Blackwell, Oxford.

World Resources Institute (WRI). 1990. *World Resources 1990-91.* A Report by the World Resources Institute in collaboration with the United Nations Environment Programme and the United Nations Development Programme. Oxford University Press, New York and Oxford.

Chapter 4

Conference Statement and Task Group Recommendations of the Second World Climate Conference, Geneva, Switzerland, 29 October-7 November 1990.

Global Environment Monitoring System (GEMS). 1988. *Assessment of freshwater quality.* United Nations Environment Programme, Nairobi, World Health Organization, Geneva.

Holdgate, M.W., Bruce, J., Camacho, R.F., Desai, N., Mahtab, F.U., Mascarenhas, O., Maunder, W.H., Shibab, H. and Tewungwa, S. 1989. Climate Change: Meeting the Challenge. Report by a Commonwealth Group of Experts. Commonwealth Secretariat, London.

Hunter Jr., M.L., Jacobson Jr., G.L., and Webb III, T. 1988. Paleocology and the coarse-filter approach to maintaining biological diversity. *Conservation Biology* 2(4):375-385.

Intergovernmental Panel on Climate Change (IPCC). 1990a. Policymakers summary of the scientific assessment of climate change. Report prepared for IPCC by Working Group I, June 1990. World Meteorological Organization and United Nations Environment Programme, Geneva and Nairobi.

IPCC. 1990b. Policymakers summary of the potential impacts of climate change. Report prepared for IPCC by Working Group II, June 1990. WMO and UNEP, Geneva and Nairobi.

IPCC. 1990c. Policymakers summary of the formulation of response strategies. Report prepared for IPPC by Working Group III, June 1990. WMO and UNEP, Geneva and Nairobi.

Lovelock, J.E. 1979. *Gaia: A new look at life on earth.* Oxford University Press, Oxford.

Mackinnon, J., Mackinnon, C., Child, G. and Thorsell, J. 1986. *Managing Protected Areas in the Tropics.* IUCN, Gland, Switzerland.

McCormick, J. 1989. *Acid Earth: the global threat of acid pollution.* Second edition. Earthscan, London.

McNeely, J.A. 1988. *Economics and Biological Diversity: Developing and Using Economic Incentives to Conserve Biological Resources.* IUCN, Gland, Switzerland.

McNeely, J.A., Miller, K.R., Reid, W.V., Mittermeier, R.A. and Werner, T.B. 1990. *Conserving the World's Biological Diversity.* IUCN, Gland, Switzerland, WRI, CI, WWF-US and the World Bank, Washington, DC.

Miller, K.R. 1980. *Planificación de parques nacionales para el ecodesarrollo en Latinoamérica.* Fundación para la Ecología y para la Protección del Medio Ambiente, Madrid.

Prescott-Allen, C. and Prescott-Allen, R. (in preparation). Wildlife and rural development. Case studies in sustainable rural development using native biodiversity.

Salm, R.V. and Clark, J.R. 1984. *Marine and Coastal Protected Areas: a Guide for Planners and Managers.* IUCN, Gland, Switzerland.

United Nations. 1989. Law of the Sea. Protection and preservation of the marine environment. Report to the Secretary-General. United Nations General Assembly document A/44/461, September 1989.

World Wide Fund for Nature (WWF). 1990. Climate Change. Position Paper. WWF, Gland, Switzerland.

World Resources Institute (WRI). 1988. *World Resources 1988-89. An Assessment of the Resource Base that Supports the Global Economy.* World Resources Institute and the International Institute for Environment and Development in collaboration with the United Nations Environment Programme. Basic Books, New York.

WRI. 1990. Op. cit. Chapter 22, Freshwater, p.170.

WRI/IUCN/UNEP. 1991. *Biodiversity Strategy and Action Plan.* Draft prepared by WRI, IUCN and UNEP.

Chapter 5

Dankelman, I. and Davidson, J. 1988. Op. cit.

Elkington, J. and Hales, J. 1989. *The green consumer guide.* Gollancz, London.

Family Health International. 1990. *A penny a day.* Family Health International, Research Triangle Park, NC, USA.

Holdgate, M.W., *et al.* 1989. Op. cit.

IUCN Task Force on Population and Conservation for Sustainable Development. 1987. *Population and sustainable development.* IUCN, Gland, Switzerland.

Knodel, J., Havanon, N. and Sittitrai, W. 1989. Family size and the education of children in the context of rapid fertility decline. Research Report 89-155. Population Studies Center, University of Michigan, Ann Arbor.

Pollution Probe Foundation. 1989. *The Canadian green consumer guide.* McClelland and Stewart, Toronto.

Sadik, N. 1989. *Safeguarding the future.* United Nations Population Fund, New York.

Sadik, N. 1990. *The State of World Population 1990.* United Nations Population Fund, New York.

Chapter 6

Contributions to this section have come from a workshop: "Communicating the World Conservation Strategy", convened by M.A. Partha Sarathy, Chairman, IUCN Commission on Education and Training, April 1990, Bangalore, India.

Engel, R.J. 1990. The ethics of sustainable development. In: Engel, J.R. and Engel, J.G. (Eds). 1990. Op. cit.

UNESCO/UNEP. 1987. *International Strategy for Action in the Field of Environmental Education and Training for the 1990s.* United Nations Educational, Scientific and Cultural Organization, Paris, and the United Nations Environment Programme, Nairobi.

Chapter 7:

Much of this chapter is based on work done by a Primary Environmental Care Workshop, convened by the Direzione Generale per la Cooperazione allo Sviluppo (DGCS) of the Italian Ministry of Foreign Affairs and the Second World Conservation Strategy Project. We are indebted to the workshop participants, to Minister A. Catalano de Melilli, who chaired the workshop, and to G. Borrini who originated the concept of PEC used here.

Hardoy, J.E., and Satterthwaite, D. 1989. *Squatter citizen: life in the urban Third World.* Earthscan Publications, London.

Holling, C.S. (Ed.). 1978. *Adaptive Environmental Assessment and Management.* IIASA, Vienna.

Malcolm, S. 1989 (2nd edition). *Local action for a better environment: helping people to get involved.* Steve Malcolm, PO Box 452 Ringwood 3034, Victoria, Australia.

McNeely, J.A. 1988. Op. cit.

Chapter 8

Preparation of this chapter was substantially assisted by two workshops convened by the Second World Conservation Strategy Project: one on economics of sustainable development

(Bedford, UK, 30 June-2 July 1989), organized by the International Institute for Environment and Development, and chaired by D.W. Pearce; the other on policy, planning and institutions (Racine, Wisconsin, USA, 2 April-1 May 1990), organized by the Johnson Foundation, and chaired by D.A. Munro. We are grateful to the organizers and participants of both workshops. Paragraphs on economics were reviewed in draft by E.B. Barbier, to whom we also express warm thanks. Statements on law were kindly supplied by N. Robinson, Center for Environmental Legal Studies, Pace University School of Law, and M. Forster, Freshfields, London.

Baines, J.T., Wright, J.C., Taylor, C.N., Leathers, K.L. and O'Fallon, C. 1988. *The sustainability of natural and physical resources — interpreting the concept.* Studies in Resource Management 5. Centre for Resource Management, Canterbury, New Zealand.

Berg, R.J. 1989. Public administration for sustainable societies. The Johnson Foundation, Racine, WI, USA.

Berkes, F., Feeny, D., McCay, B.J. and Acheson, J.M. 1989. The benefits of the commons. *Nature* 340:91-93.

Colby, M.E. 1989. Economics and environmental management: the case for environmental taxes. Draft. The World Bank, Washington, DC.

Hicks, J.R. 1948. *Value and capital.* Clarendon, Oxford.

Lund, H.G. and Preto, G. (Eds). 1989. *Global Natural Resource Monitoring and Assessment: Preparing for the 21st century.* American Society for Programmetry and Remote Sensing, Vols. 1-3. Maryland, USA.

MacNeill, J., Cox, J. and Runnalls, D. 1989. *CIDA and sustainable development.* The Institute for Research on Public Policy, Halifax, NS, Canada.

Ministry for the Environment, New Zealand. 1988. Draft guide for scoping and public review methods in environmental impact assessment. Ministry for the Environment, Wellington, New Zealand.

Pearce, D.W. 1989. Sustainable development: an economic perspective. IIED/UCL London Environmental Economics Centre, Gatekeeper Series LEEC 89-01. International Institute for Environment and Development, London.

Pearce, D.W., Markandya, A., and Barbier, E.B. 1989. Op. cit.

Repetto, R., Magrath, W., Wells, M., Beer, C. and Rossini, F. 1989. *Wasting assets: natural resources in the national income accounts.* World Resources Institute, Washington, DC.

Richardson, N. 1989. *Land use planning and sustainable development in Canada.* Canadian Environmental Advisory Council, Ottawa.

Sagasti, F.R. 1988. National development planning in turbulent times: new approaches and criteria for institutional design. *World Development* 16:431-448.

Tolba, M.K. 1990. Address to the 4th International Conference on Environmental Future: Surviving with the Biosphere. Budapest. UNEP, Nairobi.

UNEP. 1988. Environmental impact assessment. Basic procedures for developing countries. United Nations Environment Programme. Regional Office for Asia and the Pacific, Bangkok.

WCED. 1987. Op. cit.

Chapter 9

Dourojeanni, M.J. 1989. Public policy, global change and the future. *Geotimes* 34(8):17-19.

IUCN. Draft Covenant on Environmental Conservation and the Sustainable Use of Natural Resources.

IUCN. 1991. *A strategy for Antarctic Conservation.* IUCN, Gland, Switzerland.

Latin American and Caribbean Commission on Development and Environment. 1990. *Our Own Agenda*. Inter-American Development Bank, Washington and United Nations Development Programme, New York.

UNESCO. 1990. Joint Statement on the Environment. Draft final report of the feasibility study. United Nations Educational, Scientific and Cultural Organization, Paris.

WCED. 1987. Op. cit.

World Bank. 1989. *Sub-Saharan Africa: from crisis to sustainable growth*. The World Bank, Washington, DC.

World Bank. 1989. *World development report 1989*. Oxford University Press, New York.

Chapter 10

Goldenberg, J. 1991. A Carbon Tax to Prevent Climate Change. *Ecodecision* 1:1. Montreal.

Holdgate, M.W., *et al*. 1989. Op. cit.

Intergovernmental Panel on Climate Change. 1990a. Op. cit.

Intergovernmental Panel on Climate Change. 1990b. Op. cit.

Chapter 11

Preparation of this chapter has been assisted by the Industry and Environment Office (IEO) of the United Nations Environment Programme, the UNEP/IEO Technical Report 2 "Environmental auditing", and the UNEP *Industry and Environment Review* Vols. 12.1 and 12.3/4. Further contributions came from a workshop on policy, planning and institutions (Racine, Wisconsin, USA, 28 April-1 May 1990), convened by the Second World Conservation Strategy Project, organized by the Johnson Foundation, and chaired by D.A. Munro.

Elkington, J. 1990. *The environmental audit: a green filter for company policies, plants, processes and products*. SustainAbility, London, and WWF-UK, Godalming, UK.

Elkington, J. and Burke, T. 1989. *The green capitalists: how to make money and protect the environment*. Gollancz, London.

Huisingh, D. 1988. Good environmental practices — good business practices. Wissenschaftszentrum Berlin für Sozialforschung, Berlin.

UNDP. 1989. *Natural endowments: financing resource conservation for development*. Report of UNDP International Conservation Financing Project (ICFP). World Resources Institute, Washington, DC.

WCED. 1987. Op. cit.

Chapter 12

Cochrane, G. 1983. Policies for strengthening local government in developing countries. World Bank Staff Working Papers 582, Washington, DC.

Furedy, C. 1989. Appropriate technology for urban wastes in Asia. *Biocycle*, July 1989.

Hardoy, J.E. and Satterthwaite, D. 1989. Op. cit.

Holdgate, M.W., Kassas, M. and White, G.F. (Eds). 1982. *The World Environment, 1972-1982*. UNEP. Tycooly International, Dublin.

Rondinelli, D.A., Nellis, J.R. and Cheema, S.G. 1984. Decentralization in developing countries a review of recent experiences. World Bank Staff Working Paper 581, Washington, DC.

United Nations Centre for Human Settlements (Habitat). 1990. The Global Strategy for Shelter to the Year 2000, as adopted by United Nations General Assembly, Res. 43/181 (1988). UNHCS, Nairobi.

United Nations Environment Programme and United Nations Centre for Human Settlements (Habitat). 1987. *Environmental Guidelines for Settlements Planning and Management.* 3 vols, UNHCS, Nairobi.

WCED. 1987. Op. cit.

WRI. 1988. Op. cit.

Chapter 13

Alexandratos, N. (Ed.). 1988. World agriculture: toward 2000. An FAO study. Belhaven Press, London.

Andres, L.A., Oatman, E.R. and Simpson, R.G. 1979. Re-examination of pest control practices. In: Davis, D.W., Hoyt, S.C., McMurtry, J.A. and AliNiazee, M.T. (Eds). 1979. *Biological control and insect pest management.* University of California, Division of Agricultural Sciences.

Bentley, C.F. and Leskiw, L.A. 1984. *Sustainability of farmed lands: current trends and thinking.* Canadian Environmental Advisory Council, Ottawa.

Commission on Plant Genetic Resources. 1989. Assessment of the current coverage of base collections in the world, with regard to crops of interest to developing countries. CPGR/89/7. February 1989 for Third Session, Rome, April 1989. FAO, Rome.

FAO Committee on Agriculture. 1989. Preservation of animal genetic resources. Tenth Session, 26 April-5 May 1989, COAG/89/6. FAO, Rome.

Georghiou, G. 1989. *World status of insect resistance.* FAO, Rome.

Grainger, A. 1990. *The threatening desert: controlling desertification.* Earthscan Publications, London.

Hansen, S. 1988. Structural adjustment programs and sustainable development. Committee of International Development Institutions on the Environment (CIDIE), Nairobi.

Hardoy, J.E., and Satterthwaite, D. 1989. Op. cit.

Lutz, E., and Young, M. Agricultural policies in industrial countries and their environmental impacts: applicability to and comparisons with developing nations. Environment Working Paper 25. The World Bank, Washington, DC.

McNeely, J.A. 1988. Op. cit.

McNeely, J.A. Undated. Agriculture and biological diversity: international policy issues. IUCN, Gland, Switzerland.

Norse, D. 1988. *Policies for sustainable agriculture: getting the balance right.* FAO, Rome.

Pearce, D.W. 1991. Deforesting the Amazon: Toward an Economic Solution. *Ecodecision* 1.1. Montreal.

Prescott-Allen, C., and Prescott-Allen, R. 1986. *The first resource: wild species in the North American economy.* Yale University Press, New Haven and London.

Shaxson, T.F., Hudson, N.W., Sanders, D.W., Roose, E. and Moldenhauer, W.C. 1989. *Land husbandry. A framework for soil and water conservation.* Soil and Water Conservation Society, Ankeny, Iowa, USA.

Simmonds, F.J. 1970. Biological control of pests. *Tropical Science* 12:191-199.

Swift, J. 1989. Pastoral land tenure. In: *The IUCN Sahel Studies 1989.* IUCN, Gland, Switzerland and Nairobi.

UNEP/IRSK. 1990. *Global Assessment of Soil Degradation.* UNEP/ISRK, Nairobi.

van Emden, H.F. 1974. *Pest control and its ecology.* Institute of Biology, *Studies in Biology* 50. Edwin Arnold, London.

WCED. 1987. Op. cit.

WRI. 1988. Op. cit.

Chapter 14

Alexandratos, N. (Ed.). 1988. Op. cit.

Arden-Clarke, C. 1990. *Conservation and sustainable management of tropical forests: the role of ITTO and GATT.* WWF International, Gland, Switzerland.

Clark, W.C. 1989. Managing Planet Earth. *Scientific American* 261 (3):19-26.

Colchester, M. and Lohmann, L. 1990. *The Tropical Forestry Action Plan at the crossroads.* World Rain Forest Movement/The Ecologist.

FAO and UNEP. 1982. Tropical forest resources. *Forestry Paper* 30. FAO, Rome.

FAO Forestry Department. 1988. *An interim report on the state of forest resources in the developing countries.* Food and Agriculture Organization of the United Nations, Rome.

Goodland, R., Asibey, E., Post, J. and Dyson, M. 1990. Sustainability of hardwood extraction from tropical moist forests. The World Bank, Washington, DC.

Hummel, F.C., Palz, W. and Grassi, G. (Eds). 1988. *Biomass forestry in Europe: a strategy for the future.* Elsevier, London.

Janz, K. 1990. The present state of boreal forests. FAO, Rome.

Lovelock, J. 1988. *The ages of Gaia: a biography of our living earth.* Bantam Books, New York.

Molion, L.C.B. 1989. The Amazonian forests and climatic stability. *The Ecologist* 19:211-213.

Pearce. D.W. 1991. Op. cit., pp.40-49 and 95.

Poore, D. 1989. *No timber without trees. Sustainability in the tropical forest.* Earthscan Publications, London.

Poore, D. and Sayer, J.A. 1987. *The Management of Tropical Moist Forest Lands: Ecological Guidelines.* IUCN, Gland, Switzerland and Cambridge, UK. P.p 1-63.

Postel, S. and L. Heise. 1988. *Reforesting the earth.* Worldwatch Paper 83, Washington, DC.

Repetto, R. 1988. *The forest for the trees? Government policies and the misuse of forest resources.* World Resources Institute, Washington, DC.

SCA Skog AB. 1987, *Forestry and nature conservation: a policy statement.* SCA Skog AB, Sundsvall, Sweden.

Tropical Forestry Action Plan: report of the independent review 1990. Kuala Lumpur, Malaysia.

Tropical Forestry Workshop. 1990. Consensus statement on commercial forestry, sustained yield management and tropical forests. The Smithsonian Institution and International Hardwood Products Association, Alexandria, Virginia, USA.

UN/ECE and FAO. 1985. *The forest resources of the ECE region.* UN Economic Commission for Europe, Geneva.

Winterbottom, R. 1990. Taking stock: the Tropical Forestry Action Plan after five years. World Resources Institute, Washington, DC.

WRI. 1988. Op. cit.

WRI. 1990. Op. cit.

WWF International. 1989. *Tropical forest conservation.* Position Paper 3. WWF International, Gland, Switzerland.

WWF International. 1990. *Reforming the Tropical Forestry Action Plan.* WWF International, Gland, Switzerland.

Chapter 15

This chapter owes much to a workshop kindly organized by the Department of Water and Environmental Studies, Linköping University, Linköping, Sweden, 30 August-2 September 1990.

Décamps, H., Fournier, F., Naiman, R.J. and Petersen Jr., R.C. 1990. An international research effort on land/inland water ecotones in landscape management and restoration 1990-1996. *Ambio* 19(3):175-176.

Falkenmark, M., *et al.* 1987. Water-related limitations to local development. *Ambio* 16(4):191-200.

Global Environment Monitoring System (GEMS). 1988. *Assessment of freshwater quality.* UNEP, Nairobi, and WHO, Geneva.

McNeely, J.A. 1988. *Economics and Biological Diversity: Developing and Using Economic Incentives to Conserve Biological Resources.* IUCN, Gland, Switzerland; citing: MacKinnon, J.R. 1983. Irrigation and watershed protection in Indonesia. Report to the World Bank.

Reid, W.V. and Miller, K.R. 1989. *Keeping options alive: the scientific basis for conserving biodiversity.* World Resources Institute, Washington, DC.

Scudder, T. and Conelly, T. 1985. Management systems for riverine systems. *FAO Fisheries Technical Paper* 263.

Tall, R. 1990. Community-based environmental management for the promotion of water supply, health and sanitation and food production. Service International d'Appui à la Formation et aux Technologies en Afrique de l'Ouest/Sahel (AFOTEC), Dakar, Sénégal.

The Hinduja Foundation. 1988. *Drinking water for the millions.* The Hinduja Foundation, India.

WCED. 1987. Op. cit.

WRI. 1988. Op. cit.

WRI. 1990. Op. cit. Chapter 22, Freshwater, p.170.

Chapter 16

Much of this chapter was prepared during a workshop on coastal zones and oceans convened by the Second World Conservation Strategy Project and held at Dunsmuir Lodge, University of Victoria, British Columbia, Canada, 22-25 June 1990. We are greatly indebted to the participants for their contributions.

FAO Committee on Fisheries. 1989. Review of the state of world fishery resources. Committee on Fisheries, 18th Session, Rome, April 1989. COFI/89/Inf.4. Food and Agriculture Organization of the United Nations, Rome.

FAO. 1984. Report of the FAO World Conference on Fisheries Management and Development. Food and Agriculture Organization of the United Nations, Rome.

FAO. 1990. FAO yearbook. Fishery statistics. Catches and landings 66 (1988). Food and Agriculture Organization of the United Nations. Rome.

GESAMP. 1990. Protecting and managing the oceans. Report of 20th Session, May 1990.

IMO/FAO/UNESCO/WMO/WHO/IAEA/UN/UNEP Joint Group of Experts on the Scientific Aspects of Marine Pollution (GESAMP). 1990. The state of the marine environment. Reports and Studies GESAMP 39. United Nations Environment Programme, Nairobi.

Maclean, J.L. 1988. Thanks for using Naga. *Naga, ICLARM Quarterly* 11 (3):16-17.

Ray, G.C. 1989. Sustainable use of the global ocean. In: *Changing the Global Environment.* Academic Press. Pages 71-87.

Thomson, D. 1980. Conflict within the fishing industry. *ICLARM Newsletter* July: 3-4.

United Nations. 1989. Law of the Sea. Protection and preservation of the marine environment. Report of the Secretary-General. United Nations General Assembly. A/44/461, September 1989.

Chapter 17

CPL Scientific Limited. 1989. Funding mechanisms for the fund for biological diversity. WWF International, Gland, Switzerland.

UNDP. 1989. *Natural endowments: financing resource conservation for development.* World Resources Institute, Washington, DC.

World Bank. 1989. *World development report 1989.* Oxford University Press, New York.

Acknowledgements

Each of the two main drafts of this text was circulated for comment to the members of IUCN — governments, government agencies and non-governmental organizations, to many among the large number of professionals who constitute IUCN's Commissions, to the networks of correspondents associated with UNEP and WWF, and to other individuals who heard of or became associated with the preparation of the Strategy during the two years preceding its completion. The responses received and the results of specialist workshops and general consultations in various regions have contributed significantly to the shape and content of this document. The contributions of individuals who took part in workshops and of those who submitted written comments are acknowledged in the list at the end of this section. Apologies are extended to anyone who has been inadventently omitted from the list.

While all this assistance contributed immensely to the breadth and authority of this document, it does not pretend to be a universal consensus. Were it so, it would not be needed. IUCN, UNEP and WWF provided core funding and through a steering committee steered the evolution of the basic themes and structure of this document. In addition to the executive heads of the three organizations, the members of the Steering Committee were Jeffrey McNeely, Reuben Olembo and Frank Schmidt. The three partners take responsibility for the document and staff members of each organization commented extensively. Within that partnership, IUCN, through its President, Director General, Project Director, Senior Consultant and senior staff, has taken the lead in preparing the text.

Other members of the United Nations family and international organizations that collaborated in the preparation and review of the document were Asian Development Bank; FAO Food and Agriculture Organization of the United Nations; IIED International Institute for Environment and Development; ILO International Labour Office; ICHM Istituto Superiore di Santa; OAS Secretariat, Organization of American States; United Nations Centre for Human Settlements - Habitat; UNDP United Nations Development Programme; UNESCO United Nations Educational, Scientific and Cultural Organization; UNFPA United Nations Fund for Population Activities; The World Bank; WHO World Health Organization; WHO World Meterological Organization; WRI World Resources Institute. Their collaboration was both helpful and inspiring. But they bear no responsibility for any errors in the text nor should it be assumed that they fully accept all the positions that it sets out.

Financial support was generously provided by CIDA - Canadian International Development Agency; DANIDA - Danish International Development Assistance; FINNIDA - Finnish International Development Agency; International Centre for Ocean Development; Ministère de l'Environnement du Québec, Ministry of Environment of Quebec; Ministero degli Affari Esteri, Direzione Generale per la Cooperazione allo Sviluppo, Italy; Netherlands Minister for Development Cooperation; NORAD - Royal Ministery of Foreign Affairs, Norway; SIDA - Swedish International Development Authority; Canadian Wildlife Federation; The Johnson Foundation Inc.

Those who contributed comments included the following: Abrahamsen, J., (Norway); Abrougui, M.A., (Tunisia); Abuzinada, A.H., (Saudi Arabia); Adipati, E., (Indonesia);

Agarwal, A., (India); Ahmad, Y.J., (Kenya); Ahujarai, P., (India); Al-Julayand, M.A.S., (Saudi Arabia); Alam, A.A.M.N., (Bangladesh); Albrecht, S., (United Kingdom); Alcantara Valero, A.F., (Spain); Alizai, S., (Pakistan); Allo, A.A., (Cameroon); Altieri, M.A., (Chile); Anderson, N.W., (USA); Andersson, I., (Sweden); Arbella, M., (Uruguay); Arden-Clarke, C., (United Kingdem); Armstrong, H., (United Kingdom); Arturo, L., (United States of America); Arze, C., (Bolivia); Ashby, K.R., (United Kingdom); Atchia, M., (Mauritius); Aubrey, D.G., (United States of America); Ayoub, A., (Sudan);

Bagader, A.A., (Saudi Arabia); Baile, S., (France); Balazy, S., (Poland); Baldi, P., (United States of America); Baquedano, M., (Chile); Baquete, E.F., (Mozambique); Barbier, E., (United Kingdom); Barclay, W., (Zambia); Barrett, S., (United Kingdom); Barrett, M., (United Kingdom); Barrientos, C., (Costa Rica); Barstow, R., (United States of America); Batisse, M., (France); Bean, M., (United States of America); Beanlands, G., (Canada); Belli, R., (Italy); Bengtsson, B., (Sweden); Benneh, G., (Ghana); Berg, R.J., (United States of America); Bergmans, W., (Netherlands); Berkes, F., (Canada); Berry, R.J., (United Kingdom); Besong, J.B., (Cameroon); Bessarab, R., (Australia); Biswas, D.K., (India); Bjorklund, M., (Sweden); Blockhus, J., (United States of America); Boer, B.W., (Australia); Bolshova, L.I., (USSR); Borgese, E.M., (Canada); Borrell, S.M., (Spain); Borrini, G., (Italy); Bortnyk, G., (United States of America); Boskova, S., (Czech and Slovak Federative Republic); Botero, L.S., (Italy); Botnariuc, N., (Romania); Bottrall, A., (India); Brackett, D., (Canada); Branton, I., (United Kingdom); Braun, J., (Poland); Brooks, D.B., (Canada); Bruce, J.P., (Canada); Buonguti, A., (Italy); Burgers, C.J., (South Africa); Burgess, J., (United Kingdom); Burhenne-Guilmin, F., (Belgium); Burns, C.W., (New Zealand); Butylina, T.P., (USSR); Börlin, M., (Switzerland);

Caccia, C., (Canada); Cade, A., (United Kingdom); Calvo, S., (Spain); Camino, A., (Peru); Campbell, D., (United Kingdom); Cardenes, J.J., (Colombia); Carpenter, R.A., (United States of America); Castelow, R.A., (Australia); Castensson, R., (Sweden); Cecil, C., (United States of America); Cederwall, K., (Sweden); Cellarius, R.A., (United States of America); Cernea, M.M., (United States of America); Challinor, D., (United States of America); Chaniago, D., (Indonesia); Child, G., (Zimbabwe); Chitrakar, A., (Nepal); Chittleborough, D., (Australia); Christoffersen, L.E., (United States of America); Claparols, A.M., (Philippines); Clark, J., (United Kingdom); Clarke, W.J., (Fiji); Cokelberghs, J.-P., (Belgium); Connolly, M., (United States of America); Connor-Lajambe, H., (Canada); Cortez, J., (Bolivia); Coulmin, P., (France); Cox, G.W., (United States of America); Croal, P., (Canada); Cull, D.A.N., (Canada); Cutler, M.R., (United States of America);

Da Cunha, L.V., (Portugal); Dahl, A., (United States of America); Dahlberg, K.A., (United States of America); Daly, H.E., (United States of America); Dankelman, I., (Netherlands); Datschefski, E., (United Kingdom); Davidson, J., (United Kingdom); De Azcarate y Bang, T., (Spain); De Barros Filho, N., (Brazil); De Benavides, N.H., (Ecuador); De Caires Vilanova, A., (Portugal); De Groot, R., (Netherlands); De Larderel, A., (France); De Lozada, A.S., (Bolivia); De Morales, C.B., (Bolivia); De Oliveira Costa, J.P., (Brazil); De Silva, A.L.M., (United States of America); De Silva, L., (Sri Lanka); Debele, B., (Ethiopia); Delacroix, P., (France); Delahunt, A.-M., (Australia); Dennis, F., (United Kingdom); Dennis, E., (United Kingdom); Di Melilli, A.C., (Italy); Di Vecchia, A., (Italy); DiSano, J., (Australia); Doboekar, V., (India); Doronina, O.D., (USSR); Doumenge, F., (Monaco); Drake, S., (United States of America); Dribidu, E., (Uganda); Driver, P., (United Kingdom); Dugan, P., (United Kingdom); Dunster, J.A., (Canada); Duran, G.G., (Colombia); Dutt, P.S., (India); Duville, V., (Martinique);

Edinburgh, H.R.H. The Duke of, (United Kingdom); Edwards, M.H., (Canada); Edwards, S., (United States of America); Egloff, R., (Switzerland); Elder, D., (United States of America); El-Sabbagh, A.T., (Saudi Arabia); Engel, J.R., (United States of America);

Enthoven, C., (Netherlands); Erize, F., (Argentina); Escalona, A.I., (Spain); Escobar, E.M., (Colombia); Espinosa, D.A., (Ecuador); Evteev, S. (USSR);

Faizi, S., (Denmark); Falkenmark, M., (Sweden); Fauchon, J., (France); Fearnside, P.M., (Brasil); Fernandez, S., (Chile); Fernando, V. (Sri Lanka); Ferrando, E., (Peru); Fitter, R., (United Kingdom); Flint, V., (USSR); Forno, E., (Bolivia); Forster, M., (Australia); Forster, M., (United Kingdom); Freire da Silva, R., (Brazil); Friedman, Y., (France); Frisen, R., (Sweden); Fry, A.E., (Switzerland); Fuller, S., (Canada); Furtado, J.I.D.R., (United Kingdom); Futehally, Z., (India);

Gallopin, G.C., (Argentina); Gammell, A., (United Kingdom); Garratt, K., (New Zealand); Gatahi, M.M., (Kenya); Gawn, M., (Canada); Gebremeddin, N., (Ethiopia); Geesteranus, C.M., (Netherlands); Gerber, S.A., (South Africa); Geyger, E., (Bolivia); Gil Mona, E., (Peru); Gligo, N., (Chile); Godrey, S.P., (India); Golovnin, A.N., (USSR); Gomez, E.D., (Philippines); Gordina, F.Y., (USSR); Gordon, I., (United Kingdom); Gorin, D.A., (USSR); Goulet, D., (Poland); Greene, G., (Canada); Greenwalt, L., (United States of America); Greuter, W., (Germany); Gucovsky, M., (United States of America); Gudynas, E., (Uruguay); Gwynn, M., (United Kingdom); Gyulai, I., (Hungary);

Hall, D.O., (United Kingdom); Hamilton, L.S., (United States of America); Hannan-Andersson, C., (Sweden); Haq, K., (United States of America); Hardoy, J.E., (Argentina); Harrison, P., (United Kingdom); Hatley, J., (United Kingdom); Hawari, M., (Germany); Hedstrom, I., (Costa Rica); Helms, H.J., (Denmark); Herring, R.J., (Canada); Hesselink, F.J., (Netherlands); Heywood, V., (United Kingdom); Hiroshi, Y., (France); Hiraishi, T., (Japan); Hollis, G.E., (United Kingdom); Holowesko, L.P., (Bahamas); Holt, S., (United Kingdom); Hopkins, E., (United Kingdom); Howard, B., (United States of America); Htun, N., (Myanmar); Huismans, J.W., (Netherlands); Hussain, A., (Pakistan);

Iliasu, S., (Nigeria); Imbach, A., (Argentina); Illueca, J.C., (Panama); Irvin, R., (United States of America); Ishio, T., (France);

Jacobs, P., (Canada); Jagannath, E.V., (India); Jakob-Hoff, R., (New Zealand); Jakowska, S., (Dominican Republic); Jan, A.U., (Pakistan); Janssen, M.P.M., (Netherlands); Jayal, N.D., (India); Johannes, R.E., (Australia); Johnson, J., (Germany); Juchnowicz, S., (Poland); Judge, A.J., (Belgium);

Kakabadse, Y., (Ecuador); Kanygin, E., (USSR); Kapusta, M., (Czech and Slovak Federative Republic); Karmouni, A., (Morocco); Katko, T., (Finland); Keckes, S., (Yugoslavia); Kelleher, G., (Australia); Kenyon, G., (Canada); Khan, S.S., (Pakistan); Khanna, P., (India); Khosla, A., (India); Kim Ock-Kyung, (Rep. of Korea); Kismadi, M.S., (Indonesia); Knight, I., (United Kingdom); Koeyers Sr, J.E., (Australia); Kokine, M., (USSR); Korten, D.C., (United States of America); Krasilov, V.A., (USSR); Kriz-Randranarisoa, O., (Switzerland); Krueger, F.W., (United States of America);

Lamb, J., (United States of America); Lamb, R., (United Kingdom); Lampe, K., (Philippines); Lapointe, E., (Canada); de Larderel, J.-A., (France); Larson, S., (United States of America); Lausche, B.J., (United States of America); Leake, W.D., (United States of America); Leal Filho, W.D.S., (Germany); Lee, M.J., (Korea); Lee, S.W., (Taiwan); Lefeuvre, J.-C., (France); Lenton, R., (Sri Lanka); Letizia, G., (Italy); Letts, G., (Australia); Lieberherr-Gardiol, F., (Switzerland); Lightfoot, C., (Philippines); Linet, C., (Belgium); Litvinov, N.N., (USSR); Llewellyn, O.A.A.R., (Saudi Arabia); Lloyd, B., (Fiji); Long, T., (Belgium); Longobardi, F., (Italy); Lord Ross of Newport (United Kingdom); Loriaux, M., (Belgium); Lothian, A., (Australia); Lubbers, H., (Netherlands); Lucas, P.H.C., (New Zealand); Lundqvist, J., (Sweden); Luti, R., (Argentina); Lyonette, K., (United Kingdom);

Machado, A., (Spain); Maddum Bandara, C.M., (Sri Lanka); Madueno, J.M.M., (Spain); Maler, K.G., (United States of America); Maltby, E., (United Kingdom); Mancama, B.V.,

(Zimbabwe); Marconi, M., (Bolivia); Markandya, A., (United Kingdom); Markham, A., (United Kingdom); Marquez G. (Colombi); Marstrand, P., (United Kingdom); Martin-Brown, J., (United States of America); Mascarenhas, J.P., (Seychelles); Mason, L., (United States of America); Mathews, F., (Australia); Matte-Baker, A., (Chile); McAllister, D.E., (Canada); McEachern, J., (United States of America); McIntyre, A.D., (United Kingdom); McNeely, J., (United States of America); Martin, Claude, (Switzerland); Medawar, J., (United Kingdom); Medford, D., (Zimbabwe); Mercado, R., (Bolivia); Merkle, A., (Germany); Mhlanga, L., (Zimbabwe); Mileva, M., (Bulgaria); Miller, K.R., (United States of America); Misley, K., (Hungary); Missoni, E., (Italy); Moles, J.A., (United States of America); Morello, J., (Argentina); Morey, M., (Spain); Morgan, V.H., (Costa Rica); Morillo, C., (Spain); Morishima, A., (Japan); Morris, D., (United Kingdom); Mumtaz, K., (Pakistan); Munasinghe, M., (United States of America); Munro, R.D., (Canada); Myers, D., (United Kingdom);

Nachay, G., (Hungary); Nasseef, A.B.O., (Saudi Arabia); Navarro, J.C., (Panama); Nerfin, M., (Switzerland); Neronov, V.M., (USSR); Ngari, P., (Kenya); Nicholson, E.M., (United Kingdom); Nijhoff, P., (Netherlands); Nikolsky, A.A., (USSR); Nishimura, T., (Japan); Noton, C., (Chile);

O'Riordan, T., (United Kingdom); Ofosu-Amaah, W., (United States of America); Oldham, J., (United Kingdom); Olembo, R., (Kenya); Olokesusi, F., (Nigeria); Opschoor, H., (Netherlands); Ortiz, O., (Chile); Ouédraogo, D., (Mali); Ovington, J.D., (Australia); Oza, G.M., (India);

Painter, M., (United States of America); Pannocchia, M.C., (Netherlands); Panwar, H.S., (India); Paparian, M., (United States of America); Partha Sarathy, M.A., (India); Pearce, D., (United Kingdom); Pearse, P.H., (Canada); Pellew, R., (United Kingdom); Penfold, M., (United States of America); Pepper, S., (United Kingdom); Perez-Borrego, V.P., (Spain); Perrings, C., (Botswana); Petersen, R.C., (Sweden); Peterson, R.M., (United States of America); Phillips, A., (United Kingdom); Piddington, K.W., (New Zealand); Pieters, J.B., (Netherlands); Piret, E., (Belgium); Pirot, J.-Y., (France); Pitt, David, (New Zealand); Pellew, R., (United Kingdom); Pletscher, D.H., (United States of America); Polunin, N., (Switzerland); Poore, D., (United Kingdom); Potts, M., (United States of America); Potts, M., (United Kingdom); Pretes, M., (Finland); Priscoli, J.D., (United States of America); Pullin, R.S.V., (UK);

Quesada, C., (Costa Rica); Qutub, S.A., (Pakistan);

Rabb, G.B., (United States of America); Raga, M.N., (Papua New Guinea); Raghunathan, M., (India); Rajotte, F., (Switzerland); Rakosi, J., (Hungary); Rao, K., (India); Rao, S., (United States of America); Ray, C., (United States of America); Redclift, M., (United Kingdom); Robertson, J., (France); Robinson, N., (United States of America); Robinson, S., (United Kingdom); Robinson, N.A., (United Kingdom); Roch, P., (Switzerland); Rodda, J.C., (Switzerland); Rooda, F.E.E., (Netherlands); Roth, E., (Bolivia); Royston, M.G., (Switzerland); Rozanov, B., (USSR); Runnals, D., (Canada); Ryden, P., (Sweden);

Safronov, S., (Switzerland); Sadik, N., (Pakistan); Sampson, R.N., (United States of America); Samways, M., (South Africa); Sanchez-Parga, J., (Ecuador); Sandbrook, R., (United Kingdom); Sankaran, J., (India); Sarabhai, K., (India); Satterthwaite, D., (United Kingdom); Saunier, R., (United States of America); Sayer, J., (United Kingdom); Schadilov, Y.M., (USSR); Schroeder, P., (Netherlands); Schueler, E., (United States of America); Schultze, D., (Sweden); Segnestam, M., (Sweden); Segovia Espiau, C., (Spain); Seiler, H., (Switzerland); Seng, G.K., (Thailand); Sequeira, D., (Finland); Shapiro, H.A., (Japan); Sharma, I.K., (India); Sharp, T., (Thailand); Shaw, R.P., (Canada); Shenoy, B.V., (India); Shepherd, G., (United Kingdom); Sherman, K., (United States of America); Sigdyal, K.P., (Nepal); Simon, M., (Canada); Simon, A., (Colombia); Skinner, R.G., (France); Slocombe, S.D., (Canada); Slooff, R., (Switzerland); Smith, T.M., (United States of America); Smyth, J.C., (United Kingdom);

Snidvongs, K., (Thailand); Sommi, M., (Italy); Soutter, R., (South Africa); Spiridonov, G., (Bulgaria); Stahl, M., (Sweden); Stahr, E., (United States of America); Stawicki, H., (Poland); Stein, A., (Argentina); Stuart, S., (United Kingdom); Sullivan, C., (United States of America); Swaminathan, M.S., (India);

Tall, R., (Senegal); Tamrakar, K., (Nepal); Tarlo, K., (Australia); Thacher, P.S., (United States of America); Thiadens, R., (Switzerland); Thorsell, J., (Canada); Timberlake, L., (United Kingdom); Tisdell, C., (Australia); Toniuc, N., (Romania); Torell, M., (Sweden); Torres, H., (Chile); Torres, E.B., (Philippines); Trzyna, T.C., (United States of America); Turner, R.K., (United Kingdom);

Ural, E., (Turkey); Urbaez, R., (Dominican Republic); Urban, F., (Czech and Slovak Federative Republic);

Vadineanu, A., (Romania); Van den Oever, N., (Netherlands); Van Noordwijk-van Veen, J.C., (Netherlands); Van der Zwiep, K., (Netherlands); Vanicek, V.L., (Czech and Slovak Federative Republic); Variava, D., (India); Veit, P., (United States of America); Vermeer, E., (Netherlands); Vernon, G.C., (Canada); Viederman, S., (United States of America); Visscher, T., (Netherlands); Vittery, B.W., (United Kingdom); Vlachos, E., (United States of America);

Waldichuk, M., (Canada); Waller, H., (Australia); Waiyaki, B., (Kenya); Wallman, P., (Australia); Watanabe, T., (Malaysia); Wells, M.P., (United States of America); Winpenny, J., (United Kingdom); Westing, A.H., (United States of America); Wetherup, D., (Canada); Whitaker, N., (United States of America); Whitby, L., (Canada); Widstrand, C., (Sweden); Wilkes, B., (Canada); Williamson, L., (Australia); Wilson, G.R., (Australia); Woodley, S., (Australia); Woolaston, P., (New Zealand); Wooster, W., (United States of America); Wray, P., (United States of America);

Yagil, R., (Israel); Yurjevic, A., (Chile);

Zakonyi, J., (Hungary); Zeballo, H., (Mexico); Zedan, H., (Egypt); Zehni, M.S., (Italy); Zentilli, B., (Chile); Zylicz, T., (Poland).

The text paper, recycled SylvanCoat 80 gm², is 45% woodfree unprinted waste and 45% woodfree printed waste. Paper is deinked without bleach. The mill says its advanced treatment system ensures no harmful discharges result from manufacture.

The logo for *Caring for the Earth* is based on the symbol used for the first World Conservation Strategy. The circle symbolizes the biosphere — the thin covering of the planet that contains and sustains life. The three interlocking, overlapping arrows symbolize the three objectives of conservation:
— maintenance of essential ecological processes and life-support systems;
— preservation of genetic diversity;
— sustainable utilization of species and ecosystems.

For Product Safety Concerns and Information please contact our EU
representative GPSR@taylorandfrancis.com Taylor & Francis Verlag GmbH,
Kaufingerstraße 24, 80331 München, Germany

Printed and bound by CPI Group (UK) Ltd, Croydon, CR0 4YY
01/05/2025
01858395-0002